Visits
to
Heaven

Visits
to
Heaven

By Josie Varga

4th Dimension Press ■ Virginia Beach ■ Virginia

4th Dimension Press
215 67th Street
Virginia Beach, VA 23451-2061

ISBN-13: 978-0-87604-611-1 (trade paper)

All photographs are the property of the contributors
whose stories appear in this book.

The following is reprinted with permission from Hay House, Inc.:

Denise Linn, If I Can Forgive So Can You, 2005 Hay House, Inc., Carlsbad, CA.

Tim Freke, How Long Is Now: A Journey to Enlightenment . . . and Beyond, 2009, Hay House, Inc., Carlsbad, CA.

Author Photo by Brian Kasper
Cognisant Canon Photography LLC

Cover design by Christine Fulcher

This book would not have been possible had it not been for the many contributors who agreed to share their experiences and expertise. Therefore, this book is dedicated to them all with heartfelt thanks.

Louis LaGrand, PhD
Robert Perala
Lance W. Beem
Natalie Smith-Blakeslee†*
Dr. Bernie Siegel
Diane Goble
Nancy Clark, CT
Elaine Tucker
Josiane Antonette
Mellen-Thomas Benedict
David L. Oakford
Steve Hodack
Barbara Harris Whitfield
Dannion Brinkley
Christina Ricerca
Blessed Tiffany Snow
Reverend Juliet Nightingale†*
Summersnow Wilson
Brad Steiger
Cyndi Smith
Denise Linn
Martha Cassandra St. Claire, MA
Phil Whitt
Grace Hatmaker, RN, MSN, PhD student

Luna
Sylvia Browne
Glauco Schaffer
Joyce Hawkes, PhD
Diego Valencia
David Bennett
Tim Freke
Mike
Nadia McCaffrey
Mindy
Linda
Ray Morose
Stanley A. Wilson
Tina Michelle
Jen-Irishu
Reece W. Manley, DD, MEd, MPM®
Hal Cope
Mary A. Ale
Metro Sinko
Angelyn Ray
Richard Bunch
Mark Jacoby
Pamela M. Kircher, MD

*† Deceased

Chapters:

Melvin L. Morse, MD, FAAP
Peter Russell, MA, DCS, FSP
Barbara Harris Whitfield
Loyd Auerbach, MS, Parapsycholgist
Dave Tango
Mark Pitstick, MA, DC

Steven E. Hodes, MD
Jeffrey Keene
Carol Bowman, MS
Paul Von Ward, MPA, MSc
Bill Davis

†And in loving memory of the contributors who have passed: Natalie Smith-Blakeslee and Reverend Juliet Nightingale. Thank you both very much.

Contents

Acknowledgments

This book would not have been possible without the support of the many wonderful contributors. For many of the NDErs, this was the first time sharing their experiences. I can't thank them enough for going public in the hope of helping others understand that life never ends and love never dies.

I am also deeply blessed to have garnered the support of so many respected authors and experts in the field of afterlife and paranormal research. To say the least, I am very humbled by their support. They are Melvin Morse, Peter Russell, Barbara Whitfield Harris, Mark Pitstick, Steven Hodes, Dave Tango, Loyd Auerbach, Jeffrey Keene, Carol Bowman, and Paul Von Ward. I would also like to acknowledge Bruce Tango. I truly enjoyed our conversations and am very grateful for all of your help.

Again, I would like to thank the many contributors who made this book possible. My heartfelt appreciation goes out to Louis LaGrand for writing the Foreword and to Robert Perala for writing the Preface. Thank you both for believing in me and this book. It is truly an honor.

Writing a book of this nature takes a lot of time . . . time away from my family and friends. Therefore, I would like to acknowledge my family and friends who stood beside me throughout the writing of this book. No words could ever express how much your love and support has meant to me.

I would also like to acknowledge my friend Jody Read who crossed over in April 2010. I will never forget the laughter. You were and are such a blessing.

Obviously, this book would not have been possible without the support of my publisher A.R.E. Press. Please know how very grateful I am to all of you. I deeply appreciate your continued faith in me. Henry David Thoreau once said, "Our truest life is when we are in dreams awake." Without your support, I would not be living a dream. A special thank you to my editor, Stephanie Pope; you are a godsend. And continued heartfelt thanks go to Cassie McQuagge, Jennie Taylor Martin, Kevin Todeschi, and the rest of the crew. You've all been so wonderful.

Finally, to my husband—my inspiration behind everything that I do in life—and to my daughters Erica and Lia. Thank you for understanding why Mom spends so much time at the computer. I love you so much.

Foreword

Louis LaGrand, PhD
Author of *Love Lives On*
www.extraordinarygriefexperiences.com

Josie Varga is a woman of impeccable character who has devoted many years to the study of nonphysical reality and its critical role in the expansion of consciousness and the power of belief in the unseen. What you will hear from her is not conjecture but the result of study and dedication to better the human condition; in short, to use a well-worn phrase, you can take it to the bank. In this book, as was so expertly accomplished in *Visits from Heaven*, she clearly shows that love lives on, that these extraordinary encounters happen for a purpose, and that scientific materialism does not have all the answers. She now presents a whole new set of experiences from a different perspective.

What jumps from the pages of *Visits to Heaven* is the irrefutable evidence that near-death experiences (a euphemism, since these growth-producing experiences happen in instances other than when one thinks death is near) heavily influence healing through love and caring relationships. How does this occur? The answer is simply that the conviction naturally surfaces that there must be something after death, an afterlife in which loved ones are reunited and come to realize that earthly life is but a prelude to a much more significant existence.

Over and over again in the stories you will read, those, who are gifted with the extraordinary, return with an altogether different view of life *and* death. This is due to the impact the experience has on their inner lives. Consider this: several years ago I interviewed the late Dr. Barbara Rommer, an internist, who had conducted considerable research on NDEs, had written about them, and who had had a "visit" from her husband who preceded her in death. I asked if these things influenced her belief about an afterlife. Her response: "I grieved differently. I even did his eulogy. I could do that because I know beyond a shadow of a doubt that the only thing that died was his physical body. I will see him again. I *know*, not believe." Notice the emphasis on the word *know*. It was her emphasis, not mine. This comes from a woman trained in the scientific method.

No one can truly understand the impact of these encounters unless he or she is fortunate to be given the experience. Furthermore, you will discover the impact of the experiences on those reporting them and equally important the messages they have for all who read and believe.

Varga, once again, presents not only life-inspiring accounts, generally unknown to the general public, but makes it clear that there must be a power greater than the self which is brimming with love for all humanity. If you want to learn about another way in which love operates in our world, if you want to read one of the most impressive collections of stories about NDEs ever assembled, this is the book you will not be able to put down and will long remember.

Once more, you will be convinced that those in another existence are very much aware of what survivors have to deal with in adapting to the absence of a loved one, that no one grieves alone, and that our deceased loved ones are very much aware of the painful new routines that must be initiated by survivors.

This is a book to read and reread—in short, to study. Why? Because the information presented is profound, filled with insights to change the quality of life, and is deeply thought provoking. If you value an approach to the spiritual side of life, you have found it.

Preface

Robert Perala
Author of *The Divine Blueprint: Roadmap for the New Millennium* and
The Divine Architect: The Art of Living and Beyond
www.unitedlight.com

Life is a mystery school in which we are commissioned to discover the laws between the material world in the here and the hereafter.

Visits to Heaven captures a virtual compendium of stories and examples in near-death experience studies including apparitional appearances, deathbed visitations, ghostly encounters as well as angel visitations and after death communication cases.

The secret of life's continuum is found throughout *Visits to Heaven*. Unlocking each case gives the reader an insider view into the revolving life cycle the human soul continues to experience.

Throughout the book we find specific examples from such well-known researchers and authors as Bernie Siegel and Mellen-Thomas Benedict as well as Dannion Brinkley and many others. Each takes us through his experience with those members who exist on the Other

Side and continue to visit us in our dreams and in the physical world.

Josie Varga's research is extremely well founded as she shows us that God is energy and the infinite wisdom that surrounds all things at all times. All these visits to heaven truly show, as Linda Stewart's testimony says in one of the chapters of this book, "that God and love are the only reality." Throughout our journey we find that dying is the easy part; living is hard.

Many surprises are held for the reader to encounter along the way such as the theories which explain that there is a life review we must all encounter in addition to our own judgment of ourselves. We also find that when leaving this earthly plane, the body, apparently, and all of its earthly connection of memory go away. As alarming as that may seem, it is also liberating as we don't necessarily take all of our pain with us. This disconnect allows us to observe our painful moments for what they are without being overthrown by them which in turn allows us to come to terms with the events of our past life and prepares us for the next.

Visits to Heaven makes for a startling and intelligent report as well as an eye-opening read that allows us to look at the wonders of life before birth, during our time in the material world, and after death.

This book truly shows us that spirit shines bright and lights the way for many. Enjoy the journey!

Introduction

"In the beginning, when God created the universe, the earth was form-less and desolate. The raging ocean that covered everything was en-gulfed in total darkness, and the power of God was moving over the water. Then God commanded, 'Let there be light'—and light appeared."[1] And so begins the book of Genesis.

While researching the near-death phenomenon for this book, I found it very interesting that the first line of the Bible mentions light since it also seems to be a common link between most near-death experiences (NDEs). In his book, *Saved by the Light*, Dannion Brinkley tells of seeing a light around a Spiritual Being who came to greet him. He writes, "The Being of Light stood directly in front of me. As I gazed into its essence I could see prisms of color, as though it were composed of thousands of tiny diamonds, each emitting the colors of the rainbow."[2]

Many who have had near-death experiences believe that this light and God are one and the same. As one NDEr explained, "At some point

---

[1] *Good News Bible* (New York: American Bible Society, 1978), 1.
[2] Dannion Brinkley, *Saved by the Light* (New York: Harper Collins Publisher, 2008), 8.

I felt I was sucked away, and I went into a long dark tunnel; I was sucked at an incredible speed! At the tunnel end there was a glowing pinpoint. In this tunnel there were other beings like myself, and we looked at each other saying, 'I believe we are dead!' The more I went forward, the more the light grew. I arrived into this light which was wonderful, very bright, but what hit me the most is that in this light I felt at peace, joy, but most of all I felt an incredible love! This light loved me! This light talked to me! I asked it if it was God, and it answered me, 'Yes, I am the light!' This light being (whom I did not see) knew EVERY-THING about me; He knew my life from beginning till end! Once in this light, I remembered who I was; I also got answers to all questions I ever wondered about like who created the universe and how, how does the cosmos work, physics, etc. Oh, yes, I did not learn it, I remembered it!"[3]

Steven E. Hodes, MD, author of *Metaphysician on Call for Better Health: Metaphysics and Medicine for Mind, Body and Spirit*, says light implies a beneficent divine presence and believes the process of photosynthesis, the conversion of light energy to chemical energy and the storage of sugar in plants, is life's true miracle. "Forget about the Shroud, bleeding stigmata, crying statues, or parting Red Seas," he states. "Just ponder what truly happens when a tiny organelle (a subunit within a cell that has its own function) soaks up water through the stems and mixes light energy from the sun. It then builds these invisible carbon atoms into its own skeleton, into sugars, into the food that allows animals to live. No animal can do this. No animal can extract the energy of life from a star 93 million miles away." [4]

Plants need this light energy (CO_2 and H_2O) to make sugar. This then becomes food allowing animals to live, and it is also the source of the O_2 (oxygen) we breathe. Obviously, without oxygen there would be no life.

Every day from the moment we wake up to the moment we go to sleep, we take this light for granted. Everything that we see, we see because of light. We go about our day watching the sunrise, the televi-

[3] http://www.nderf.org/leonard_nde.htm.
[4] Dr. Steven E. Hodes, *Metaphysician on Call for Better Health: Metaphysics and Medicine for Mind, Body and Spirit* (Westport, CT: Praeger Publishers), 58–59.

sion, the flowers in the garden, our children, the road, computer screens, mirrors which show our reflections, and so on. While our minds may perceive the objects before us, the only thing we are really seeing is light as this is the only thing our eyes are capable of seeing. We are capable of seeing the world as we know it because everything either gives off or reflects light rays which then connect to our eyes and are processed by our brains. In other words, light has to leave what we are looking at and travel back to our eyes for us to see it. This happens so fast that we don't even realize what is happening.

Scientists have been studying the nature of light for centuries, and there is still so much left to be argued. But one of the most popular theories in physics today defines light as electromagnetic radiation, a form of energy made up of electric and magnetic fields that has a two-fold nature of both particles and waves. Light radiates like the waves in a pool from its source in all directions at a speed of 186,000 miles per second which makes it the fastest phenomenon in the universe. To put things into perspective, if you were able to travel at the speed of light, you would have traveled 11,160,000 miles in one minute (known as a light minute).

Albert Einstein determined that light was made up of photons, which are the fundamental particles of electromagnetic energy that are constantly moving at the speed of light.

The study of light has proven to be quite complicated and will more than likely go on for centuries more. Could it be that scientists or physicists are just looking in the wrong place? Perhaps they need to explore the metaphysical in order to understand light fully.

Time ceases to exist at the speed of light. Why is this so? And is it coincidental that the majority of NDErs says that time ceases to exist on the Other Side? They describe an all-encompassing light filled with unyielding love, void of time and space as we know it.

As in the NDE I mentioned earlier, those who have crossed over and come back frequently talk about speaking to a Supreme Being or Light. So it's interesting to note that physicists have actually found that light particles communicate with each other. According to quantum mechanics, a pair of subatomic particles can become "entangled" and the fate of one subatomic particle instantly affects the other. Einstein actually referred to this idea as "spooky action at a distance."

In 1982 a physicist at the University of Paris named Alain Aspect discovered that under certain circumstances subatomic particles can communicate immediately with each other no matter how long or how far the distance is between them. They could be two inches apart or one million miles apart; it doesn't matter. Somehow each particle always knows what the other one is doing.

Another interesting point is the fact that many who have had an NDE describe being in a different dimension. Earth, they say, is but one dimension. Edgar Cayce, known as the world's greatest American psychic, performed over four thousand readings in a forty-year span. One of the things that he continually mentioned was the fact that this earth plane is just one of many dimensions. Many physicists have noted that entanglement is strange only if the universe is limited to three dimensions. If there are more, it is possible for particles to be much closer than they appear.

God is infinite. He always was and always will be. Energy is also infinite; a photon travels at the speed light and therefore, it is believed, must have an infinite amount of energy. I could go on further, but I believe this is enough to make one wonder if the light described in many NDEs and God are, indeed, one and the same.

NDErs also describe a feeling or a knowing of Oneness. We are all, many say, one with God and the feeling of no longer being entrapped by the heavy body we once wore on earth is wonderful beyond words. Recently I had the privilege of chatting with Charles Thomas Cayce, the grandson of Edgar Cayce. He spoke candidly about love, life, his famous grandfather, and the hereafter.

"We think we have many possibilities while on this earth plane, but the truth is our soul is actually in prison," he explained. "We don't realize it now, but while we are in our physical bodies, we are very limited in the choices available to us. To continue with this prison analogy, we can do only certain things while we are in prison. We can read, we can think, etc. But we can't eat when we want, we can't go outside the prison. Truthfully, there is so much we can't do.

"Likewise, there is so much we can't do here, we just don't realize it. As a soul, we have the freedom to experience whatever we want. This, incidentally, is the reason we incarnate. We have a multitude of experiences that allow our souls to grow. We all have free will. We all originated from Oneness and then God made us separate. We made a choice to be separate in order to make choices and have life experiences."

These experiences, according to Cayce, help us to evolve and move again toward Oneness with God. There are, he notes, three parts to our soul:

1. Our Will
2. Our Spirit
3. Our Mind

Since the above are parts of the soul and not the body, they continue to exist when the body dies.

In addition to NDEs, many other mystical experiences are considered proof of an afterlife. These include electronic voice phenomenon (EVP), apparition appearances, deathbed visions, ghostly encounters, out-of-body experiences, angel visitations, hypnotic regression, after death communication (ADC), visits from heaven, and more.

I intentionally classified an ADC and a visit from heaven separately. They are truthfully two different things. An ADC, according to Bill and Judy Guggenheim, the well-known authors of *Hello from Heaven*, is a spiritual experience that occurs when someone is contacted directly and spontaneously by a deceased family member or friend. A visit from heaven is a metaphysical experience that takes place when a person is contacted either directly or indirectly through the use of a third party by someone who is deceased. It does not matter whether or not the experience occurred spontaneously or directly. Also, a visit from heaven contains an element of proof.

This book is the sequel to *Visits from Heaven* which highlights evidential afterlife communication accounts from around the world. After *Visits from Heaven* had already been completed, I had the privilege of speaking to Lance Beem who told me about the death of his daughter Kari Lynn Beem and subsequently one of the most incredible visits from heaven I have ever heard.

Kari was born as what appeared to be a very normal, healthy child. However, by one year of age she started having seizures. After consulting with physicians and geneticists, it was determined she had a genetic disorder called tuberous sclerosis—a rare, multisystem genetic disease that causes benign tumors to grow in the brain and on other vital organs. Symptoms include seizures, developmental delay, behavioral problems, skin abnormalities as well as lung and kidney disease. Sadly, she eventually lost her ability to speak and for the next twenty-four years was autistic and considered mentally at a two-year-old level.

Raising Kari presented the Beems with many challenges, and their daughter was eventually placed in a day program for mentally delayed adults. On June 9, 2008, Kari was having her regular lunch break with her vocational group in Sacramento, California. As her assistant turned to help another client, Kari quickly reached for a piece of orange (her favorite) from the picnic table and sat back down, lodging the orange in her throat. Within minutes she began turning blue and passed out. The Heimlich maneuver was tried but to no avail. By the time the paramedics arrived ten minutes later, her heart had stopped.

Although she was revived after eighteen minutes of treatment, she had to be placed on life support. Four days later on June 13 at the age of twenty-four, she passed into the light. But her story did not end there. One year later on the anniversary of the day Kari was admitted to the hospital, her father Lance was busy at home working when the house alarm began to sound from the closet in the hall. He immediately went over to the closet where the alarm box was located. When he opened the door, the alarm suddenly stopped. At first it seemed odd because the alarm was disconnected. It was at that moment he looked down and noticed a child's wooden sweater rack, which Kari's grandfather had given Kari when she was a child. The rack is a wood cutout portrait of a little blond girl with the name "Kari" on it. Lance looked at this situation somewhat startled as he then turned his attention to the alarm box which he had disconnected one year earlier. You can just imagine his continued shock when he looked at the alarm. The electrical wires remained disconnected—black, red, and open ended, dangling downward pointing to the rack.

He then sat down in utter astonishment feeling his daughter's essence all around him. As a bereaved father, he knew this must be a sign from his daughter. But as a scientist, his rational mind was trying to find a more logical explanation for what had just occurred.

Fifteen minutes later when his wife Leslie (Kari's stepmother) came home, the alarm again sounded before he had a chance to tell her what had occurred. She smiled and cried along with him. Afterwards, the two took in the events of the day and started cooking dinner when for the third time the alarm sounded even louder and would not stop even after they had opened the closet door. At this moment with the alarm blaring away Lance sat down in front of the wood cutout rack of his daughter Kari, closed his eyes, and touched the name Kari. In that instant he saw a vivid scene in his mind of his mother, daughter, and father all waving and laughing at him in a bright light sitting down on a beautiful green hill. His dad was giving him the thumbs up as he often did. All three were young, healthy, happy, and radiating love. Finally the alarm stopped for the last time. The picture above is the photo Lance took of the closet on that day. (Notice the wires dangling from the alarm in the upper-right corner).

Four nights later was the first anniversary of the hour when Lance held his daughter for the last time and told her to go to the light. "I told her we will always love you, but you are free to go home," he explained. On this night Lance was at his computer reading a story he had written two months earlier about Kari's passing. He had several scanned pictures in the story. He was scrolling down the pages and happened to find the last photo taken of his daughter. But now, to his amazement, there was something distinctly different about this last picture of her. As bright as could be, a rainbow-shaped tunnel now appeared behind his daughter on a wall that was once barren and beige. While there was only sunlight on the wall before, now it showed all the colors of the rainbow.

Fortunately, Lance had two versions of this picture: the original one on his desktop computer and another on his laptop. He immediately went to the other photo on his desktop computer and confirmed that there was no such tunnel behind his daughter in the original. The walls were, in fact, barren. Below is the original photo, followed by the photo Lance found on that magical moment one year to the hour when he told his daughter they would always love her, but when the light comes, go to it.

In Lance Beem's words, "that night I tried to transfer or print the photo, but each time it would only print without the rainbow in the background. This really freaked me out, and I was afraid I would lose the picture so I finally grabbed my digital camera and took a picture of the computer screen to send it to Dr. Melvin Morse and others that I trusted to witness what was happening. I was numb but convinced she was letting us know she was okay." Her message was obvious, he said, "We are all from the light and never lost."

Author's Note: Lance William Beem has been working in agricultural sciences for the past thirty years. As a plant scientist, he has been researching, among other things, plant growth, physiology, and protection against disease. He has both a BS and MS in biology sciences. For more information, visit the Web site www.abeemoflight.com.

As I said earlier, this is one of the most incredible validations that I have ever heard. What are the chances of a disconnected alarm sounding three times on the anniversary of Kari's admittance to the hospital? What are the chances of a once barren photo suddenly appearing with a rainbow in the background? Is this a coincidence? In fact, Dr. Melvin Morse, one of the most recognizable and trusted names in NDE research and a contributor to this book (see his story *The God Spot: Our Connection to the Divine* on page 237), reviewed the photos above and believes the rainbow resembles those shared by others who have had NDEs. As an example, he told of a young boy who spoke of going down a noodle (tunnel) with the colors of a rainbow.

An NDE refers to a wide range of personal experiences associated with those who have had a brush with death. In addition to encountering the colors of a rainbow and a Being of Light as mentioned earlier, there are several other characteristics which are believed to be common in an NDE. According to Melvin Morse, there are nine common traits:

1. Peace and no longer feeling pain
2. The sense of moving through a tunnel
3. Having a "life review"
4. Numerous aftereffects including everything from the loss of fear of death, increase in psychic powers, and higher level of spirituality to changes in personality
5. Having an OBE (out-of-body experience)
6. Having a sense of being dead
7. Encountering a "Being of Light" or Supreme Source
8. Encountering relatives or other "people of light" and
9. Being reluctant to return to life

It is important to note that death is not the only trigger for the near-death experience. As you will read in some of the accounts included in this book, trauma, fear, and shock are often causes of an NDE. And at other times, there is no trauma but an altered state of consciousness that triggers the NDE and/or out-of-body experience.

All the contributors in this book say they were transformed by their experience in many ways. In addition to the aftereffects mentioned above, experiencers often come back with a sense of knowing and purpose. They say that they don't just believe there is a God, they **know** there is.

Cayce could not agree more and explained that his belief in God and the afterlife came from not only the experiences of his father and re-nowned grandfather but also his own. "For me, it's not about a belief in an afterlife or God; it's a knowing beyond knowing," he states. "When you trust your experience, you just know. It's not a belief."

Regardless of your beliefs, my intent in this book is not to convince you that there is a God. Although I am a firm believer in God, Supreme Being, or whatever you choose to call it, I will not preach. What I will do is present credible near-death experiences and chapters written by re-spected experts in the field of NDE research so that you can arrive at your own conclusions. My hope is that after reading this book, you, too, will come to know that there is certainly a God and there is definitely no death.

A Tribute to Natalie

---··◁∞▷··---

Natalie Smith–Blakeslee†

> *You can shed tears that she is gone,*
> *Or you can smile because she has lived.*
> *You can close your eyes and pray that she'll come back,*
> *Or you can open your eyes and see all she's left.*
> *Your heart can be empty because you can't see her,*
> *Or you can be full of the love you shared.*
> *You can turn your back on tomorrow and live yesterday,*
> *Or you can be happy for tomorrow because of yesterday.*
> *You can remember her only that she is gone,*
> *Or you can cherish her memory and let it live on.*
> *You can cry and close your mind,*
> *Be empty and turn your back.*
> *Or you can do what she'd want:*
> *Smile, open your eyes, love, and go on.*

As a special tribute to Natalie Smith–Blakeslee, I begin this book with this beautiful poem by David Harkins. She was a special friend who knew firsthand the meaning of loving and giving to others. When I was doing research for my book *Visits from Heaven*, I came in contact with Natalie, a gifted medium and bereaved mom.

Natalie and I became fast friends. I quickly came to know what a beautiful person she was—an absolute blessing beyond words. She offered to help put me in contact with several bereaved parents who had evidential afterlife communication experiences (what I refer to as visits from heaven). She never wavered in her love and support. In addition to giving me many contacts, she contributed to a story about her daughter Carrie, whom she lost to leukemia. She wrote the preface for *Visits from Heaven*.

Unbeknownst to me, Natalie was diagnosed with Stage 4 lung cancer in September 2008. She never let on that she was sick, and our phone conversations and e-mails went on as usual. Natalie also agreed to share her near–death experience (NDE) in this book and spoke about how excited she was for me. I never had a clue that anything was wrong until her e-mails slowed, and I no longer heard her voice.

Natalie passed on October 28, 2009. I was completely stunned. When I spoke to her husband, he told me that she did not tell me and many others on purpose. She wanted us to remember her as she was, not stricken with a horrible cancer but alive and well.

We shared many conversations about the afterlife, and I do know that her spirit is alive and well. I know that her love lives on. My only hope is that she knows how much she touched not only my life but the lives of so many others and how very grateful I am to her for everything that she did for me. Her memory and love will live on forever within my heart.

Below is the story of Natalie's NDE, which occurred when she was suffering from anorexia. The full details of her NDE can be found in her book *Close to You . . . A Memoir by a Mother in Mourning*, coauthored by

Martha D. Humphreys. For more information, please visit her Web site www.loveandlight.com.

HALFWAY HOME

Let go . . . .release . . . .my body was barely there . . . there was so little mass of flesh, skin, and bones it wasn't hard for me to believe I could float above myself . . . and so I did.

Gently, softly, spiritually I rose above the bed.

I wasn't cold anymore . . . I wasn't warm either.

I was looking down at me still curled up like a seashell beneath the sheets. The sheets were still. No movement of my shoulders or chest . . . surrounded by darkness, deep grey, no light beneath the door into the hall . . . no filtered light through the shades on the window . . . no light anywhere.

Panic, frantic, terror surged up my throat.

Where were the lights?

Where was the power?

There's no storm, no wind, no lightening, no rain . . . yet no power.

Didn't hospitals have generators for power outages?

I could no longer see myself on the bed . . . but I couldn't feel the bed beneath me either. Please, oh, please turn on the lights!

I felt pins and needles on the tips of my fingers and the tips of my toes . . . as if my muscles were "falling asleep" from the outside in . . . a light, please dear God, a light!

Squeezing my eyes tightly closed like I did when I was a little girl searching for the orange on the inside of my lids indicating light on my face, I waited and prayed for a pinpoint of whiteness in the darkness around me.

Slowly opening my eyes, there was a needle of light aimed at me. Did I die? I was being pulled toward the pinpoint, and it was getting larger the nearer I was to its source. Like filings onto a magnet, I was drawn to the light, the source.

I wasn't moving. The light was attracting my body through a darkened hallway with people on both sides who weren't flesh–and–blood people with distinct features, rather people with identities I sensed, but didn't recognize. A ballerina, a firefighter, a cowboy, and a seamstress formed a line on each side of me. I didn't know who they were, but I understood what they were. Occasionally, a child, a dog, a bird, or another child in a baseball uniform stood between the taller people on either side of me.

Halfway home, I said to myself . . . halfway home to heaven.

A woman stepped from the side, "Natalie?"

It was a soft voice, a melodic voice, a gentle voice, a mother's voice.

"Yes?" I answered, fear falling away in the gentle embrace of her voice.

"Come with me, Natalie. I'll take you to the light."

My anxiety was replaced by warmth, the feeling of being wrapped in a heated baby alpaca blanket without the weight of a wrap. The nearer to the light, the warmer I felt as the current pulled me closer and closer.

No more fear, ever.

The comfort of company . . . loving, supportive, accepting . . . company was lifting me, encouraging me, helping me to my soul's destination.

The woman beside me felt familiar from my mother's side of our family . . . although I didn't recognize her. Petite and slightly slumped, she took my arm as if we were strolling in a park together. She wore an old-fashioned hat with a lacy veil reaching the tip of her nose. The hat matched her navy blue dress hanging well below her knees. She had sturdy shoes, granny shoes with a short thick heel on the patent leather lace up tops. Her dark brown hair indicated she was younger now than when she passed over; I felt her hair was grey at the time of her death. A string of pearls rested gently around her neck.

"You've had it rough, haven't you, Natalie?" She said in her lovely voice.

"Yes," I responded.

"Food," she said. "Something that sustains us, rewards us, and entertains us—one of God's many gifts . . . "

Another woman on my left emerged from the group and approached me. She was surrounded in a white glow, like a full body halo. Looking at her I felt energized and free, finally free. Free from my fight with food, free from being controlled by others on the outside, free to be me from the inside. Yes, definitely, this was heaven . . . because the woman in the glow was my grandmother Agnes Tate.

With recognition came all the emotion of missing her for the last fifteen years. The last time I saw her alive, cancer had sucked the life from her body. I remember her funeral: seeing her in the casket, and she was breathing. I was thirteen-years-old, and her passing hurt me the most of anyone in the family. As my brow furrowed in confusion at the evidence of life remaining in her embalmed body, I looked up to see her standing beside her casket. Smiling at me, she looked healthy and at peace. Then she told me she was all right and free from the pain caused by the cancer. Her spirit self faded after she delivered her message.

I remember tugging on my mother's sleeve, then nodding toward her mother's image across the coffin from where we stood.

"Mom, Mom . . . look she's breathing . . . "

"Natalie Ann, stop it. They all look like they're breathing lying there . . . " Apparently what I said upset her even more because she turned away and went back to her seat. I looked for her spirit self, but she too had gone.

Emotions swelled as I reached to embrace my grandmother in recognition and love. No pain for either of us anymore. We were alive; we were well. Suddenly I was so full of the light of inspiration that I wanted to announce my discovery to the world.

But how could I do that from this side?

Before I could state my intention, my grandmother answered me, "You must return; you have work to do; you have children to love and to raise . . . "

I was about to object that John was a good father and could raise Carrie and Ashley—they didn't need me . . .

"Hush," my grandmother replied before I finished the thought. She directed my attention to a look into the future if I stayed with her in heaven.

I watched my mother's grief at my passing.

"She blames herself," my grandmother, her mother, communicated to me. "It's not expected when a child predeceases a parent . . . made more painful when the parent blames herself for not doing enough to prevent it." Stubbornly I didn't want to return for it was a one way trip . . .

I knew if I went back, it was to stay. "Look, look at your daughters without you . . . "

Carrie, headstrong and independent, acted as if my passing didn't matter to her at all. Growing into a lovely young woman with a large chip on her shoulder, she approached every relationship expecting abandonment. Angry, full of resentment at her mother who didn't care enough to fight her disease, Carrie wore her rage like armor, protecting herself from any further pain. The ice cold vibe from her personality belied the burning hot pain she covered within. I watched her set herself up to never trust anyone enough to really love them . . . and therefore robbing herself of the experience of being loved.

Ashley, my baby girl, felt most left out because she no longer had a mother. Lonely and alone, since John favored Carrie, Ashley was left to grow up on her own. Her future held no close girl friends to shop with, giggle with, talk about boys with . . . instead she retreated within herself. Her self-spun shell was as impenetrable as her sister's full suit of armor.

Turning toward my beloved grandmother, I wanted so badly to stay . . . and understood what a selfish decision that would be . . . she assured me that she will always be with me until I can rejoin her here in heaven.

Before my return, I witnessed some parts of my life where I had hurt others and different parts where others had hurt me. There was no judgment, simply acceptance of the events as they had occurred. Indicating that it was time to return, my grandmother embraced me again. I clung to her wanting answers to the eternal questions:

- How does heaven work?
- Does God really hear our thoughts and prayers?
- Does God control our time here on earth?
- Do we survive physical death?
- How can I help people believe that there is a heaven?
- How can I make a difference?

Suddenly I knew, and with the knowing I was swept back into that ice-cold body on the bed. My heart jump-started with a thud, and I was back. I knew I was back because of my pain—every bone shook with chill; the little flesh I still had on my skeleton shrunk close to my bones tightening the ligaments, pinching my face against my skull. It looked like a death mask on a gargoyle. Grimacing, I pushed my front teeth with my index finger and felt them give ever so slightly. Anorexia will make your gums recede because of the dehydration and that, in turn, will loosen your teeth in their sockets. Squeezing my biceps, I felt ropes where muscle should have been. Reaching for my thighs, I felt bone, not flesh. What had I done to myself? And why?

My death was inevitable . . . and necessary. Its occurrence provided the impetus I needed to overcome my shyness, my reluctance, my resistance to my gift.

The next day I awoke with purpose, confidence, and the will to live. I had a mission, I had wonderful news for those who were open to hear it; I had a gift . . . and as they say in the Bible in the parable of the "Talents":

> *"To whom much is given,*
> *Much is expected."*

Who Did That?

Dr. Bernie Siegel
Connecticut
www.BernieSiegelMD.com

When I was four-years-old, I was home in bed with one of my frequent ear infections. I took a toy telephone I was playing with, unscrewed the dial and put all of the pieces in my mouth as I had seen carpenters do with nails which they then pulled out to use. The problem was that I aspirated the pieces and went into laryngospasm (a frightening experience in which the vocal cords suddenly freeze blocking the flow of air into the lungs). I can still feel my intercostals muscles and diaphragm contracting forcefully, trying to get some air into my lungs, but nothing worked, and I was unable to make any sounds to attract help. I had no sense of the time but suddenly realized I was not struggling anymore. I was now at the head of the bed watching myself die.

I found it fascinating to be free of my body and a blessing. I never stopped to think about how I could still see while out of my body. I was feeling sorry that my mother, who was in the kitchen, would find me dead, but I thought it over and found that my new state was preferable and intellectually chose death over life.

Then, for no apparent reason, the boy on the bed vomited, and all the pieces came flying out. He began to breathe again, and I was very angry as I returned to my body against my will. I can still remember yelling, "Who did that?" My thought as a four-year-old was that there was a God who had a schedule, and I wasn't supposed to die now. So an angel apparently did a Heimlich maneuver on me is the way I would explain it today.

I really do believe there is a schedule we create unconsciously because of later life experiences. Twice I have had my car totaled by people driving through red lights, and once I fell off of our roof when the top rung on my wooden ladder snapped off. In none of these incidents did any significant injury occur to my body. Someone told me it was because I had an angel, and he knew his name. I asked what it was, and he asked, "What did you say when the ladder broke?"

"I said, Oh, shit!"

He said, "That's his name." I will add he always shows up when I call him in an impassioned way.

Over the years I have had several spiritual experiences. One was with the healer Olga Worrall. I had injured my leg training for a marathon. It was very painful and not responding to rest or therapy. At an American Holistic Medical Association conference Olga was a guest speaker. My wife told me to ask her to heal me. I was embarrassed to ask and very frankly a non-believer. Nevertheless, my wife pushed me forward, and Olga sat me down in a chair and placed her two hands on my leg. The heat from her hands was incredible. I remember putting my hands on the opposite leg to compare the heat sensation. There was no sense of warmth from my hands coming through the dungarees. When Olga was done, I stood up and was completely healed. The pain was gone, and I could walk normally.

Another time Olga and I spoke at the funeral of a mutual friend. After the ceremony we were standing in a deserted hallway when she asked, "Are you Jewish?"

"Why are you asking?"

"Because," she explained, "there are two rabbis standing next to you."

She went on to tell me their names and describe their garments, which included their prayer shawls and caps. Her description of them was exactly what I saw in one of my meditation and imagery sessions when I had met these figures while walking on my path.

Another evening after I gave a lecture, which felt like someone else was giving it and I was simply verbalizing it for them, a woman came up to me and said, "Standing in front of you for the entire lecture was a man, and I drew his picture for you." Her description matched exactly the face and features of my inner guide whom I see when I meditate or am in a trace state. I still have the picture hanging in our home.

A few years ago I was telling a friend about how busy I was, and she asked, "Why are you living this life?" Her intention was to get me to slow down and travel less, but her question sent me into a trance, and I immediately saw myself with a sword in my hand killing people. My first thought was that I had become a surgeon in this life to use a knife to heal and not kill.

I spontaneously went into a trance again a few days later and saw myself living the life of a knight who killed because he feared his lord and what he would do to him if he didn't carry out his commands. I watched myself kill my wife, in this life, and her dog and was devastated by the experience. But at the same time it revealed to me why my wife's face has always had a hypnotic effect upon me and why I am so involved in rescuing animals.

Most recently one of our cats disappeared when a door was left open. After several weeks with no sign of her, I was sure she was killed by a predator. I sought the help of my friend Amelia Kinkade, an animal intuitive who lives in Los Angeles. We live in Connecticut, and Amelia has never been to our home or near it. I pestered her to tell me where the cat was, and one day I received an e-mail without even having sent Amelia a picture of the cat. It detailed the house, yard, other animals, and people who were involved in the cat's life. The next day I went out and found the cat exactly where Amelia said it was hiding.

She told me in the e-mail, "The cat is alive because I can see through its eyes."

If that doesn't make me a believer, nothing will. I totally believe that consciousness is nonlocal and not limited to the body. I also have experienced this through the drawings and dreams of patients I have cared for which allows them to know their diagnosis and what the future holds for them. As Jung said, "The future is unconsciously prepared long in advance and therefore can be guessed by clairvoyants."

I believe it is this unconscious awareness which we each bring with us when we are born. So I do not believe we literally live many lives but that we bring with us the experience of previous lives which are impregnated into us. Thus the wiser we get, the better the future will be for those who follow us.

About Dr. Bernie S. Siegel

Dr. Siegel, who prefers to be called Bernie, retired from practice as an assistant clinical professor of general and pediatric surgery at Yale in 1989. In 1978 he originated Exceptional Cancer Patients, a specific form of individual and group therapy utilizing patients' drawings, dreams, images, and feelings. ECaP is based on "carefrontation," a safe, loving therapeutic confrontation, which facilitates personal lifestyle changes, personal empowerment, and healing of the individual's life. The physical, spiritual, and psychological benefits which followed led to his desire to make everyone aware of his or her healing potential.

He is the author of several bestselling books including *Love, Medicine & Miracles; How to Live between Office Visits, Prescriptions for Living, 365 Prescriptions for the Soul,* and his latest is *Faith, Hope & Healing.* His prediction is that in the next decade the role of consciousness, spirituality, nonlocal healing, body memory, and heart energy will all be explored as scientific subjects.

In 1978 he began talking about patient empowerment and the choice to live fully and to die in peace. As a physician who has cared for and counseled innumerable people whose mortality has been threatened by an illness, Bernie embraces a philosophy of living and dying that stands at the forefront of the medical ethics and spiritual issues our society grapples with today. He continues to assist in the breaking of new ground in the field of healing and personally struggling to live the message of kindness and love. For more information, please visit www.BernieSiegelMD.com.

Down the River

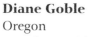

Diane Goble
Oregon
www.beyondtheveil.net

That summer in 1971 I was with my husband and children in the mountains of northern Georgia while he was working with the camera crew of the movie "Deliverance." On weekends some of the cast and crew and their families would take the rafts out on the river for a little rest and relaxation.

They filmed on the same part of the Chattooga River we rafted on, and of the eight of us on this particular Sunday afternoon, four of us, including my husband and me, had rafted down this stretch before.

But the river was different this time—low from several days of no rain. Different paths had to be taken through the many rapids.

On the last set of rapids at Woodall Shoals, we made an almost fatal mistake. The raft I was in got turned around, went over a four-foot drop backwards, and became stuck there by the churning action of the water.

The raft was trapped in a *hydraulic,* a churning white-water phenomena, which held the raft against the rocks. The raft would fill with water and then buck, throwing everything inside out. Sue was thrown clear and washed downstream. I was thrown out and got caught between the raft and the rocks with the force of the river pouring down on my head and the suction of the hydraulic motion pulling me under. Skip and Wally were still inside the raft grasping my arm and trying to pull me back into the raft, but the most they could do was enable me to catch an occasional quick breath before the water sucked me back down. I was stuck between a rock and a hard place!

Very consciously and calmly, I knew I was going to die; it was just a matter of how. Since being smashed into the rocks was painful, I decided drowning was the better choice. The next time my head popped out of the water, with my last breath I yelled to whoever was holding my arm to let go, and he did. I felt the water pull me under, and I relaxed into it. I knew there was no point in struggling as I breathed in the water, and everything went black. For a moment . . .

The next thing I knew I was a hundred feet above the river, looking down at the raft stuck against the rocks below. I saw the two men in the raft looking for me to come out from underneath. I saw Sue, downstream, clinging to a rock. I watched as my husband John and my teen-aged sister JoAnn, who had rafted without incident down the rapids ahead of us, came running back up the hill to find out why all the debris was floating down the river. We had taken everything out of their raft and put it into ours in case they flipped over, but because they went down so easily, we just jumped in, gear and all, to follow them down.

From above, I watched my husband climb onto a rock in the river. He couldn't hear what the two men still in the raft were shouting to him over the roar of the water. He had no idea where I was or what had happened, but he knew I was missing. He looked as if he wanted to jump in to try to find me. I suddenly found myself at his side, trying to stop him because he wasn't much of a swimmer, and I knew there was no point. When I reached out to stop him, my hand went right through him. I looked at my hand and thought . . . *oh my God, I'm dead!*

In that instant, total knowledge of reality appeared to me, and I saw the multidimensionality of the universe. My consciousness expanded so far beyond the physical plane that I was no longer aware of it nor was I aware of myself. I was so much a part of it all that there was no distinction. There was a brilliant flash of light, and I was allowed to see into it for a brief moment and experience a feeling of love so profound, powerful, and overwhelming that I can only describe it as pure bliss (even though that doesn't begin to describe it).

And suddenly, I was whisked away and found myself traveling rapidly through a vortex toward a beautiful white light in the far, far distance. I continued to experience an overwhelming feeling of love within me and around me. There was no fear, no anxiety, and no worry. I even felt as if I'd done this before and was remembering that I was going home. I was filled with joy. I had no sense of a body, no feeling of limitations or boundaries. Yet, I was still me and aware that I was having this experience.

Before long, I realized I wasn't alone. There was someone, whom I can only describe as a loving Being of Light, traveling beside me . . . at the speed of light! We communicated mentally. This was someone I have always known, and I knew that as soon as I sensed the presence of this being. Yet I cannot now tell you who it was. I didn't have the sense that it was any familiar religious figure or deceased relative but rather a special friend who is always with me wherever I am—perhaps, my guardian angel. This Being told me telepathically that I had a choice about going back. I thought, "No, no, no, I want this to go on forever! "

Suddenly, we burst into the light, and a whole new reality was revealed to me, similar to the physical world but in this higher vibration, more colorful, more beautiful, more amazing. I saw plants, trees, mountains, lakes, animals, and shimmering crystal-like buildings, some very large and ornate. I saw beings moving about, light beings, going about their daily lives. They don't have physical bodies, but they are distinct fields of energy. They don't walk, they float. They have lives much like ours but without the struggles and sorrows. They are artists, musicians, dancers, singers, inventors, builders, healers, creators of magical things . . . things they will manifest in their next lifetime in the physical universe.

Again, the Being of Light told me it was my choice to stay or go, but that there was more for me to do in that life and it wasn't quite time for me to leave. Still hesitating, I was told that if I chose to go back, I would be given certain knowledge to take back with me to share with others. After much discussion, I agreed to go back and suddenly found myself in front of a tall cone-shaped building—so tall that it seemed to go up forever. I was told this was the Hall of Knowledge. I entered the building and flew, spiraling upwards, through what appeared to be shelves of books just like in a library with many millions of books, and I flew through them all. When I reached the top, I burst through it into a kaleidoscope of colors and at the same time my head popped out of the water. I was down river about one hundred feet from the raft.

I immediately became aware of where I was and grabbed for the nearest rock. I was able to pull myself up, and I coughed up a lot of water. I was in a state of shock but needed no medical attention. I don't know how long I was under the raft; no one was looking at his watch at the time. It could have been a minute or two or less; it seemed like days to me. There was no time where I was.

I can't say that I was clinically dead, but I have no memory of struggling under the water or trying to hold my breath until I reached the surface. (I've been a swimmer, water skier, scuba diver, and surfer so I've had plenty of close calls under water before when I thought I might die, but nothing like this. These other times I remember perfectly well struggling to reach the surface with my lungs about to burst, trying not to inhale and totally aware of my physical experience.) What I do remember during the time my body was in the water under the raft is what I have told you.

I walked around in shock for months afterwards, not knowing how to describe my experience nor how to integrate it into my life. When I did try to tell someone what I experienced, I was patted on the head and told to forget it, that I was lucky to be alive . . . which is why I suppressed the memory and tried to get on with my life. It wasn't until fifteen or so years later that I picked up a book titled *Strangers Among Us* by Ruth Montgomery which described my experience and I finally knew that I wasn't alone . . . or crazy. It was several years after that I learned of Raymond Moody's book, *Life after Life*, which defined the near-death experience and that it actually became acceptable to talk about it for the first time.

My life changed immediately and drastically after that day in the river, and I went through some very tough times because I didn't know what was happening to me, including a divorce (my husband had no clue what I was going through after the NDE and just thought I must be crazy), child custody battles, trying to find a job after not working for almost ten years, being single again. My Kundalini (life force) energy was running amuck causing depression and suicidal thoughts. The dark night of my soul led me on a long, winding path to becoming a seeker of my higher purpose. I knew there was a reason I chose to come back when I was on the Other Side, but once back in body, it was a mystery to me that I even had a purpose.

A series of coincidences led me to go back to school (seven years later) at age thirty-seven to study psychology. After five years I had a BA and an MS in psychology and have been a counselor ever since. In college I realized the significance of the library I flew through during my NDE. All the books I studied while at the university seemed to be ones I had already read and had no trouble making the Dean's List most semesters, in spite of working part time (cleaning houses, dog sitting, tutoring, typing) and raising three teenagers as a single mother.

I began my metaphysical studies several years after graduation, reading every metaphysical, religious, and spiritual book I could get my hands on and talking with many teachers and gurus over the years. I began meditating a few years after my NDE mainly to deal with stress. Eventually after getting my kundalini energy under control, I learned to reach and maintain a higher level of consciousness in everyday life. I became an ordained minister and a spiritual counselor. After that, I earned another master's degree in Clinical Hypnotherapy, which led me to past life regressions as a therapy. My education beyond the veil continues to this day and has evolved my thinking into a higher consciousness perspective.

My purpose for coming back manifested in writing *Sitting in the Lotus Blossom* in 1989 followed by *Through the Tunnel: A Traveler's Guide to Spiritual Rebirth* in 1992. Then in 1996 I developed my first Web site, www.BeyondtheVeil.net , about my near–death experience and included stories from many other experiencers. I also share the wisdom I gleaned from my NDE with those true seekers who stumble upon the

Web site. In 2008 I developed an online self-study training program to certify alternative practitioners as Transition Guide Trainers (www.TransitionGuideTraining.org) to teach others to do this work with the dying. I also wrote a companion book *Beginner's Guide to Conscious Dying* (www.ArtOfConsciousDying.com) and recorded meditation CDs for those who wish to learn for themselves the practice of conscious dying into the Clear Light to give them peace of mind while living. I've practiced as a psychospiritual counselor for three decades and have been a hospice volunteer off and on for many years.

My mission is to empower people with the tools and information they need to see beyond ordinary states of consciousness. Becoming someone's guru or making someone dependent upon me for his or her spiritual enrichment has never been the goal of my work. I want everyone to be his or her own guru, his or her own spiritual seeker. My role is simply to try to awaken people to the possibility that there is more to life than we've been told, and it needs to be investigated if you want to evolve your consciousness.

I look forward to the glorious experience of returning home when my work here is finished, but I'm not in any hurry. I still have a lot to do here on earth before it's time to leave this body to continue my education and development on the Other Side.

Heaven Reached Out to Me Twice, but I Didn't Stay

—••◄◁∞▷►••—

Nancy Clark, CT
Ohio
www.freewebs.com/nancy-clark

True stories can entertain people with their associated drama, especially when those stories deal with life after death. Who doesn't want to know what lies beyond the beyond? A natural curiosity abounds. We are drawn to these stories hoping that one day we will each transcend this earthly realm and find the reassurance that our faith in an afterlife was correct after all or that our cynicism and disbelief were in error.

Without directly experiencing this heavenly realm for ourselves, we are left to read and listen to the stories of those who have gone before us. That is why I am putting to paper my own journey to heaven with the hope that it will inspire others to think deeply about their own mortality and more importantly, that by sharing my experience with others, it will help to build a bridge in understanding that our mortal and eternal lives have meaning and purpose.

I do not wish to entertain you with my story. I do wish to simply share what happened to me. I do not wish to preach to anyone either or try to convince you that I have all the answers to life's most difficult questions. I don't and neither does anyone else. What was ultimate truth for ME may not be your truth. I ask only that you give me respect for my personal interpretation of my own experience. After all, I was there! Therefore, I am my own expert on my own experiences. No one else can be that expert on someone else's experiences, no matter how learned that individual may be.

Where do I begin? I guess from the beginning. In the early 60s I died while giving birth to my son, and I had a near-death experience. I witnessed the medical staff in the hospital trying to revive me, but I had no interest in what they were doing to my body lying motionless on the delivery table below. By then my spirit self had lifted out of my physical body and had entered a dark void. The darkness did not frighten me because I was experiencing the rapture of a love that was very pure radiating from a light source streaming down toward me. I felt ecstatic at seeing this Light, and I felt drawn to it like a magnet. "Yes, yes! I want to go with the Light wherever the Light would take me," I thought. Bliss was the only feeling saturating my spirit body as the Light's love was streaming toward me. How could I want anything more than this? Never! Never!

The nurse kept pounding on my chest below on the delivery table shouting, "Come back, Nancy; come back!" I absolutely did not want to come back to my physical body. The Light was calling me upwards toward itself with a love that shatters one's imagination.

Over and over again, the nurse kept pounding on my chest shouting, "Come back, Nancy; you have a son." I listened to her incessant voice, and I felt no desire to return. She was interfering with my bliss and the journey with the Light that I so wanted to continue to follow. I made a very painful and reluctant decision to return back to my physical body for the sole reason of stopping the nurse's incessant nagging!

I woke up in the morgue! Yes, that's right, the morgue. I was lying on a cold metal gurney with a sheet covering my entire body. I gently pulled the sheet down over my head and witnessed a second body lying on another metal gurney in the room with a sheet covering its body. I blacked out at that point, but apparently someone discovered that I was alive before any further "disposal" of my body took place.

Years later I had another heavenly experience—this time deeper, richer, and more extensive than my first near–death experience. What I shall describe from this point on is the most sacred and transformative experience of my entire life. I believe my first near–death experience I just described "opened me" in some deeper, more sensitive manner to prepare me for this second experience. This time, however, I did not have to die first or suffer from any serious illness or physical trauma in order to have this most sacred experience. The Light apparently wanted to come to me again with a purpose, and this time I was ready to receive the Light without interference from anyone or anything.

Near–death experience researchers call this type of transcendent experience a near–death–like experience or a spiritually transformative experience which means that an average, healthy, and fully conscious human being can have the identical experience as someone who was close to death at the time of their transcendent experience. There are many triggers to this type of mystical experience; coming close to death is only one of them.

If this sounds bizarre to you, it is only because the general public has very little information about these identical experiences as near–death experiences. But in fact, throughout history, there have been reports of saints, mystics, prophets, and others who had this type of transcendent experience without coming close to death. The historical literature is filled with these accounts.

My particular experience is often compared to the Apostle Paul's experience on the road to Damascus. A Heavenly Light appeared before Paul and commanded him to begin a life of spiritual service. Upon seeing this Heavenly Light, Paul was forever transformed and began his ministry without reservation, not fearing what others would think or what they would do to him. It is this supernatural power of the Heavenly Light that raises the individual's own personal power to transcend all obstacles in one's path because the truth of that encounter with the Holy One supersedes any perceived limitations, doubts, or fear. What ultimately becomes the "mission" of the one who has touched the hem of the Beloved is loving service to something greater than oneself. This is precisely what happened to me.

Remember this please: when the Divine wants to intervene in our lives, it is done in a supernatural way so powerful, so truthful that our finite minds cannot dismiss it as a hallucination, wishful thinking, or something similar. No, the experience is REAL, more REAL than our physical reality we presently inhabit. Unless one has had this experience, one cannot understand this. But for the one who has had it, no words can adequately explain it.

I was taken up to the heavenly realm on January 29, 1979. This is my true story, and I have not deviated once from this account nor have I embellished it in any way. It is the same factual story I told in 1979 to friends, family, and researchers during my speaking engagements, more fully in my book, *Hear His Voice: The True Story of a Modern Day Mystical Encounter with God*, and to anyone who will listen. Only the words will change in describing the experience, but the content remains intact.

While delivering a eulogy for a dear friend, the Light that I once saw during my near-death experience appeared before my spirit self as I stood at the podium. My physical body and physical consciousness were to all present and performing the task of speaking the eulogy. But another aspect of my consciousness, that part I call my soul, had lifted out of my physical body and had entered into the otherworldly dimension with the Light.

As hard as I try to convey the image of the Light to others, I cannot do it justice. Words are inadequate. Brilliant, luminous, all-embracing, pick an adjective and it is pale in comparison to the wholly mystical illumination I perceived. My physical eyes did not see this Light; it was my soul's eyes that beheld the majesty of the ineffable glory of what I was seeing.

Unconditional love was pouring into my soul, the likes of which I have never experienced. No love on the face of the earth can compare with the unconditional love of the Light. Healed in a nanosecond of all the false illusions I previously held about myself—the low self-esteem, the guilt, the inability to love myself fully—I was now receiving the most precious gift from the Light who was showing me how LOVED I am with no strings attached!

The Light infused itself into my being, and I infused myself into the Light, becoming one with the Light; there was no separation. We were

ONE. I knew "who" the Light was. It was as if my soul memory had given birth to that knowledge the instant I saw the Light. I understood at my soul level that it was the Light of God. I was back in the loving arms of my Creator! How ecstatic I felt to be "home" again where I came from and where I will once again return when my life on earth is through. I had entered the ultimate destination of my true being and the JOY I felt cannot be measured.

All the while I was merged into Oneness with the Light of God; communication took place telepathically, and everything was happening simultaneously because time as we know it was absent. Traveling at a tremendous rate of speed, the Light and I moved through the dark universe, and I witnessed at least eleven dimensions that are quite different from our three-dimensional world we live in.

My deceased friend for whom I was delivering the eulogy stood beside me, holding my hand and letting me know he was alright and very happy. I had no reason to grieve for him any longer. Again, this was all taking place through an enhanced perception apart from my physical body and physical consciousness. My spirit self which is all-knowing saw that my deceased friend was still alive, although in a different form, invisible to others in the present three-dimensional reality our physical bodies live in.

In that heavenly realm where truth exists, I comprehended everything that was communicated to me by the Light as absolute truth. I didn't have to question or doubt anything that was said or what I was experiencing.

I was given a life review. Prior to this experience, I believed that when we die, God has been keeping a record of our good and bad deeds and that if we have been very bad, we would go to hell. If we were very good, we would go to heaven and be loved by God.

My life review was so different from my expectations. The Light of God loved me through all the scenes of my human life without casting judgment on me. I was judging myself as I witnessed the events in my life when I didn't love myself or others. The most important criteria for judging my life review was based on only one thing—how well I had used my life to give love to others. Was I a Light-bearer or a Light-extinguisher?

.Comprehending that truth was crystal clear as I was now beginning to understand that human beings have the spark of the Light/God within their souls. It is in releasing that light energy or Divine Love that makes a holy difference in the world, one person at a time and in each person's little corner of the world through his or her relationships with one another.

My life review was rather painful as I witnessed ALL the times when I withheld my love from others because of anger, frustration, vindictiveness, or apathy. I realized I had **so many opportunities** every single day to be a vessel of light and love but had failed. As painful as that was to me, the Light of God was loving me through this life review knowing that I was learning a great lesson in realizing the importance of loving others. "I would try not to make the same mistakes again, now that I know better," I thought.

"God, I want to stay with you forever!" I shouted. I knew I had to disconnect from my physical body—that woman who was delivering the eulogy at the same time my spirit self was in the realm of the Beloved so I contemplated giving "Nancy" a heart attack.

"NO, NO," I heard the Light of God firmly telling me. "You can't stay; you have to go back and tell others what you learned while you were here with me." At that point I was ready and more than willing to return back to the physical dimension in order to fulfill what God wanted me to do. In fact, I was deliriously enthralled to be able to use my life to bring honor and glory to the One who called me to heaven's door to bear witness to this miraculous encounter with the Beloved. The immense love I had for God during this experience was so enormous that I wanted to do anything the Light wanted me to do . . . anything! Using my life to fulfill this service to God would be my gift back to my Great Teacher. "YES, YES! I will gladly return to the earth plane to embark upon my mission for you, God. YES!" I breathlessly cried out.

"Wait a minute, dear child, before you make your decision; you must know what your life will be like should you accept this calling," I heard my Great Teacher tell me. I was then given a life preview of what my "mission" would be—the details of my work for the Light. Yes, it would certainly be challenging as I viewed this life preview, but I was reassured that the Light would never leave me and we would work together as a team in getting this "mission" completed. I was told, "As long as you hold onto my hand and don't let go, I shall lead, you will follow; the path ahead of you will be prepared for you."

I was so lovingly embraced by the Light's unconditional love and with the promise of faithfulness to me and to the work I would carry out for God that I had no hesitation at all in making my decision. My soul was bursting with passion to serve the One who had graced me with a new life, a new purpose, and a new love that I carry with me to this day.

When I made my decision to go ahead with this endeavor, the Light flooded my consciousness with ultimate knowledge. I knew everything there was to know—past, present, and future. Every word and every thought that was or will ever be spoken or written was made known to me. I was not permitted to remember all that knowledge upon my return to the physical dimension however, only parts of it. From among the thousands of cases that have been studied by researchers, this is what all near-death experiencers report as well. This is one of the classic, across-the-board similarities through over thirty years of scientific research that suggests that this is a common thread among experiencers.

With regard to this issue of recalling all knowledge given to experiencers during their experience, PMH Atwater, noted near-death experience researcher, wrote an article, "When NDE 'Truths' Are in Conflict . . . " in the International Association for Near-Death Studies, Inc. publication, *Vital Signs* Vol. XXVIII, No 4, 2008. In that article, she states, "*no single experiencer* can supply all the answers! The power of the near-death phenomenon and what it can tell us can best be found in a synthesis or summary of the many. True, just being around an experiencer or reading experiencer books can be life changing. I grant you that. But transferring to any experiencer the role of speaking for everyone else or being the best speaker or having the most to say or holding the record for the most harrowing case or being the most angelic or gifted or blessed or verified or stunning is tantamount to self-deception. Guess who is fooling whom?"

I immensely respect Atwater's investigative work in this field of consciousness study. So I support her opinion on this particular topic and that is why I have decided to include it in my personal account. You see, my Great Teacher taught me something that Atwater apparently senses as well and what apparently led her to write an extensive article in *Vital Signs* about this subject. Let me explain.

One of the greatest light bulb moments during my experience occurred when I learned that the SMALLEST ACTS OF KINDNESS were **immense** acts, spiritually speaking. Why? It is simply because the ego is not involved in these acts. We do them simply because we are motivated by our "inner voice" to do them. It is the **loving thing to do!** We do not expect a pat on the back or any type of reciprocity for doing that small act. In fact, we don't even think we are doing anything of any great significance when we do it. This is a HUGE, HUGE spiritual deed and something the Light of God wanted me to help people realize because when we unselfishly do this, we are expressing through us the Light into the world. The LIGHT!!! Every day there are countless ways of elevating ourselves to a higher and a more divine Light–embodied soul being by simply responding to the love within us by doing small acts of kindness.

As I said earlier, during my life review, I was shown ALL of those moments in my life when I chose not to act upon those small moments of loving kindness. Please, please don't make the same mistake I did! It is painful to review those moments when we should have acted lovingly, but didn't.

On the flip side, I was also taught by my Great Teacher that the ego is self–serving. The ego wants to be top dog at any cost. The ego wants to elevate itself to a superior position over someone else, and the ego will find all sorts of ways to trick self and others into believing this. The ego will always try to pull one **away** from God because its interest is serving **self** first and foremost even though the individual may think he/she is not acting from an egoic nature. The ego wants to shine. It wants to puff itself up by claiming to know more than others when it comes to spiritual truths. The ego wants praise and attention from others. The ego is a sly thing!

This was also such a light bulb moment for me during my experience. Apparently my Great Teacher felt this ego stuff was very important for me to comprehend and tell others about since our culture is so wrapped up in it and we aren't aware that the ego should have no part in developing our true spiritual nature. Our "true self" is selflessness which is the divine aspect of ourselves shining into the world as LIGHT. I was taught that our lives here on earth are meant to learn how to express love unconditionally without ego attachment. So when we have our life reviews, we will also see those moments when we allowed our egos to be top dog and not the LIGHT as it should be when we are expressing our authentic spirit self into the world. Again, I repeat, this knowledge is what I experienced as MY truth as revealed to me by the Light of God. I do not intend it to be everyone's truth unless it rings true deep within. I am simply passing on what my Great Teacher revealed to me to share with others.

Atwater recognized this ego-inflation among "some of today's new crop of near-death experiencers who are far too willing to come across as blanket authorities on the subject, and they are equally much too anxious to present 'one-size-fits-all' answers to life's greatest questions." She adds, "It's a tricky day when we allow others to determine what is right for us. That can only be determined by you through a process of prayer, meditation, deep thought, testing, (questioning), and letting go or surrendering to what many call 'The God Within.' "[1] I couldn't agree more with Atwater as this is exactly what was revealed to me during my experience with the Light of God!

Another interesting facet of my experience was the appearance of twelve guides who were present with me and who collectively chose to assist me with my "mission" upon returning back to the earth dimension. All were seated around a long wooden table, and all were dressed in what appeared to be monks' robes. All but three individuals had their hoods pulled over their faces so I could not see who they were. However, the three to my right had their faces exposed to me. I had never seen these three individuals before my experience. However, a fascinating thing happened once I returned from my experience. A few years later, synchronicity would draw these individuals to me. Upon seeing them, I "recognized" them from my experience but never told them about their promise to help me fulfill my calling for the Light.

---

[1]http://pmhatwater.blogspot.com/2008/08/conflicting-revelations-from-ndes.html

Why? Simply because I knew that their souls knew what they promised to do, and when the time was right, they would help me in whatever way they were called to. If I told them about their part in my life's mission, their egos might feel obligated to help me in some way. No, I knew their egoless souls knew what to do, when to do it, and how to do it without any interference from me. That is precisely what happened over the years since my experience. It was truly amazing to witness this "plan" unfolding in my life and to be grateful for all the help they did, indeed, give me without realizing they were part of my experience to begin with.

I never told these three individuals until very recently that they were present during my experience. I felt they should be thanked appropriately for all the help I was given through the ensuing years. I don't know if the other remaining guides have appeared in my life to help me with my calling. Certainly, I have felt strong connections with some people and thought, perhaps, that they may have been part of this plan for my life, but since their faces were not revealed to me during my experience, I have no evidence at this time that they were with me during my experience—strong suspicion, but no proof. I hold all twelve of these guides in my heart and soul for all eternity. What greater gift of love can there be than to come to this earthly realm to help someone in this way? To choose to leave paradise for this earthly realm to help others is the utmost sacrifice. God bless all those who have chosen to do this!

The experience was winding down at this point, and as the Light and I were still merged into Oneness, we began to travel back to the earth. I was allowed to witness all the chaos in the world, but I understood that everything was working according to some greater plan that humans could not comprehend. I understood that even the most horrendous acts had meaning and purpose. Don't ask me to explain this—I can't, because I left the spiritual realm and I'm now back in the physical realm with all the humanness that living here on this earth plane encompasses. I, too, have questions . . . big questions about suffering and why things happen to good people. But I must say, while I was merged into Oneness with the Light of God, I truly did understand that everything makes perfect sense on a spiritual level. That recall helps me not to dwell so much on the answers that would make sense of this suffering, for I know that when I return to that heavenly realm, I will once again understand EVERYTHING! Until then, I will be patient and trust in a Higher Power who loves us through our suffering, who cries with us, and who gives us the strength to move through it.

Gradually the separation between the Light of God and me began to occur as I felt my spirit self beginning to return to my physical form delivering the eulogy. Before that separation was completed however, the Light of God spoke one last word to me, "Book." Immediately placed deep in the innermost part of my heart was the knowledge that part of my "mission" here on earth would be to write a book and communicate all that my Great Teacher shared with me during those fifteen minutes I journeyed to the heavenly realm. Passion beyond passion was infused in my heart to fulfill this promise I made at that time to God to write that book.

Then the greatest sorrow of my life transpired as I watched the Light distance itself further and further from me, allowing my spirit to reenter my physical body to finish up the last sentence of the eulogy. I cannot describe the intense sorrow I experienced knowing that the Light was leaving, but at the same time I understood that this parting was only temporary and that one day I would once again reunite with the love of my life, the Light of God, in that heavenly realm I had just journeyed from. And this time I want it to be PERMANENT!

What happened following that miraculous experience? Well, just as my life preview showed me, I lost all my friends because they thought I was crazy. My family didn't believe me either. Some people mocked me as I told them about my experience; a Baptist minister told me never to speak of this experience again because Satan was working through me. Did that stop me from sharing this story? No way! I have to answer to Someone greater than my ego self. The Light of God is all that matters to me. Fulfilling my calling is my gift back to God, no matter what I have to go through. Other parts of my life preview came true as well, and for those parts, I am extremely grateful for.

But I must say, the Light NEVER LEFT ME! I am constantly aware of the Light's divine presence with me day and night. Wherever I am, I know beyond a shadow of a doubt that the source of my life is the Light within me. Much of my daily life is centered upon gratitude. I find so many things to be grateful for, and I take the time to acknowledge this to the Light of God. Daily prayer and meditation connect me intimately to the source of my life, the One I love above all.

There have been so many positive changes in my life that it would take too long to list them all. Suffice it to say, the most important one is that since 1979 I have continued to fulfill my "mission" for the Light of God. I have an extensive public speaking background; I founded the Columbus, Ohio International Association for Near–Death Studies, Inc. (IANDS) in 1984 and continue to serve as the coordinator, helping others who have had transcendent experiences to gain support and fellowship in a nonjudgmental group setting, and I continue to help educate the general public about these experiences.

The most important promise I made to the Light, however, was writing the book I was told to write. The result is the national award–winning book *Hear His Voice: The True Story of a Modern Day Mystical Encounter With God*. In it, I share my heart in greater detail than I can in this book you are now reading. I thought I was no longer responsible for writing anything further since that book was published, but I soon learned that God wasn't finished with me yet, and I felt inspired to write yet another book *My Beloved: Messages from God's Heart to Your Heart*.

I would like to thank you for taking the time to read my account. I hope I have given you something to think about. My story is not so much about me, but about **us.** Together we are the Light's instruments for healing this world and evolving to a higher state of Light consciousness. Above all, let the Light within your heart be the source of your life, and let **LOVE** be your flashlight to illuminate your path.

. . . .

About Nancy Clark, CT

Nancy graduated from Women's Medical College at the University of Pennsylvania specializing in cytology, the study of cells. She worked as a cancer researcher at a major university, and now retired, she is devoting her life to the "mission" she began in 1979 by inspiring others toward the transcendent nature of life and into the mysterious union with the Light of God. For more information about Nancy, please go to her Web site: www.freewebs.com/nancy-clark.

This Must Be Death

Elaine Tucker
Oregon

I was eight-months pregnant with my fourth child. I started hemorrhaging, and by the time I got to the hospital, the doctors quickly decided to do an emergency C-section in an attempt to try to save one of us. They had to move quickly and therefore, did only a spinal anesthesia. So I was awake during the whole ordeal and lay there helplessly in pain as the doctors and nurses moved frantically about the operating room.

It was around 12:00 a.m. in a small hospital in Oregon. I had lost a lot of blood, and unfortunately, they could not find enough to give me. My husband was out in the waiting room with the pastor praying. The obstetrician was monitoring my vital signs, and then all of a sudden I sensed what I would describe as a complete change in atmosphere. I felt different but didn't quite know why.

Then I realized that I was watching the nurse give me a needle in my right side. I saw the doctor working on me. And then it hit me. How am

I seeing all this? I then realized that I was actually outside of my body looking down at myself on the operating table. I didn't comprehend it at first. But I thought, "This must be death."

I am a Christian who believes in prayer and God but has never thought much about death. So now I realized that I was dead and thought, "Well, let me check this out." I was not afraid and experienced a complete sense of calm. Everything around me was glowing, and the colors were absolutely beautiful. To give you an analogy, if I had to compare life on earth to the afterlife, I would say it is kind of like rough vs. satin. It was like touching sandpaper versus soft silk.

Breathing was so much easier there. I guess I didn't realize how hard it is to breathe here on earth until I was out of my physical body and in heaven or on the Other Side. I felt no pain at all. I felt wonderful and in total bliss.

I was still in the middle of taking everything in when I sensed a Supreme Spiritual Presence to my right. I could not see Him, but I knew He was there with me. He spoke to me telepathically saying, "You can come with me now and feel like this forever."

Of course, I wanted to go with Him. I had never felt better, but then I thought of my children. As quickly as the thought came to me, I saw a vision of my three children, ages twelve, ten, and four, crying for me. At that moment, I found myself saying, "God, I can't leave them."

Immediately and without warning, I was struggling to breathe. I was back in my body, back in the operating room, back to life. "We have to get that baby," the doctor shouted to the others in the room. Then as the surgical knife pierced my skin, I passed out from the pain.

When I awoke, I was told that I was the mother of a beautiful baby girl. But the baby, whom my husband and I named Mindy, had suffered brain damage due to lack of oxygen. When she was eight-months-old, my doctor told me to put her in a home because he felt Mindy would never live a normal life and would surely be a vegetable.

As I said before, I was raised as a Christian and truly believe in prayer. So I called my church and asked everyone to pray for my daughter. Three months later, Mindy was walking. She grew up to be a perfectly healthy and happy little girl.

Miracles do happen, both in heaven and here on earth.

The Realm of Restless Spirits

Josiane Antonette
California
www.mattersofspirit.com

My near–death experience shattered my world. It shook me into re-membering spirit and other dimensions of life which I had known as a child but had forgotten so that I could fit into society. I feel the jerking of the ambulance as it rushes me through the dark streets of Marseille to the hospital. Twenty–four hours have passed since my underground abortion with a *feuseuse d'anges*, an angel maker. Abortion is illegal in France now, and many women died because of the unsanitary condi-tions of the procedure. I am only twenty–four years old, a young nurse. Am I dying? Am I outside myself observing? I see my body and its pain. I look at my feet; they are pale and lifeless. My legs cannot move. My face is white and drawn.

I watch as the walls of the ambulance dissolve. I see the lights of the city speed toward me. I can see the stars! What am I doing up so high? Why does everything look so small all of a sudden?

Memories pass before my eyes as in a movie just before I momentarily return to my body.

I see family members through a haze. Suddenly they disappear. From where they stood I see faces rushing toward me with incredible speed. They race toward my face, expanding, then dissolving. Face after face washes over me! I am terrified. I'm drifting. I'm unable to keep my eyes open.

Who are these people? Some I recognize as people I've known who have died. Others I do not recognize.

"Stay away! Where is my family?"

Now the whole room is filled with spirits! They hover near me and look into my eyes. I try to push them away. I fight them. The experience seems to go on forever. These are spirits who are restless. Their faces are twisted with pain. They seem lost. It's frightening to see them walking back and forth around my bed. And now spirits with glowing faces come close to me. They reflect a gentle and powerful light, reminding me of the pictures of beautiful angels that I love so much. I feel nurtured and loved by them and enveloped by their luminescence. These beings are made of light, and even though their brilliance is intense, I am not blinded. Tremendous compassionate love surrounds me!

Now, I am filled with the essence of love and compassion. This magnetic power is filling every atom of me. I have never before experienced such depth and power of love. I am the power of love! Merging into an intimate dance wherein all boundaries have disappeared, I feel myself one with these beings of compassion.

No words or sounds are being exchanged, and yet communication is happening.

A strong presence assures me, "Yes, you are dying to the world of men. But to us you are being born. Do not be afraid. You have always been with us; we have always been with you. We know you. You just fell asleep during your time on earth and forgot who you are. Now you are remembering."

Revelation fills my awareness—of course, yes! I am of the Beings of Light and they are of me! What is this new surge of energy? It begins as a very gentle vibration rising through the length of my body from my feet to the top of my head, but now my whole self is vibrating. I hear buzzing. It is growing louder, and now the vibration and the buzzing are becoming one.

I feel such a wonderful release! I'm free! I can't resist this new and wonderful tide of energy sweeping my body upward. Now I'm on the hospital room ceiling, gazing down! Everything appears so small: I see my bed; my body looks small and colorless; the people around the bed are tiny. Overwhelming grief and sorrow fill the room, and yet I feel completely disconnected from the scene below me. I hover nearer and look at the strange form lying on the bed. I feel compassion beyond words. I understand everything, but I have no feeling of attachment to anyone. I look at each person standing at the bedside and feel tremendous love.

I want to say to them, "I'm all right. You don't have to worry. I'm all right. Look at me! I'm fine!"

I am love; I am understanding; I am compassion!

My presence fills the room. And now I feel my presence in every room in the hospital. Even the tiniest space in the hospital is filled with this presence that is me. I sense myself beyond the hospital, above the city, even encompassing Earth. I am melting into the universe. I am everywhere at once. I see pulsing light everywhere. Such a loving presence envelops me!

I hear a voice say, "Life is a precious gift: to love, to care, to share."

SEEING A WORLD OF DARKNESS

Questions race through my awareness: Why is there so much pain in the world? Why are humans made of different colors? Why with different creeds? Why with different languages?

A vision appears. I see our world from the vantage point of a star or another planet. Earth looks like a sphere cut in half. The surface of the planet is flat and colorless. The ground is bare. No living plant grows from the Earth. Tree branches are naked. There are no fruits, no flowers, no leaves. The barren hills are obscured behind a gray veil. It is a passionless place where no one rejoices at the sunrise, and no one knows when night comes. Naked phantom–like people stand on what seems to be a stage. All the actors are puppets animated by an invisible force.

They move in unison and stop all at once.

On one side of half of the sphere, a sun attempts to shine upon the stage, but no one pays attention or makes a sound. Even the birds in the dead trees are silent and motionless. The other side of the half sphere is in darkness. I watch as the darkness grows with frightening speed and covers the whole planet. No one pays attention. Now the darkness covers the sunlight, and now it covers all the bright planets in the universe.

"This is the world with the absence of light, love, and free will," the voice states. "It is the people's choices that created the world you have just seen."

With these words, the nightmarish world begins to dissolve and is replaced by the other half of the planet—a place of vibrant, breathtaking beauty. I perceive how the Earth, the sun, the moon, the darkness, the light, the planets, and all forms of life—plants, rocks, animals, people—are interconnected; they come from the same source of Light. Everything is united by a transparent net or web, and each thread shines with great radiance. Everything pulses with the same luminosity—a magnificent Light of unparalleled brilliance.

"From the Light we have come, and to the Light we all shall return," continues the voice.

I realize now I have been standing in the middle of the two worlds. And with this understanding, an image of the path I have been walking appears. It is narrow and rocky; I have the sensation of losing my balance. I grow afraid of falling into the darkened planet. Free will! With the remembering, I gaze at my invisible feet. The narrow path changes into a wide road. The darkness is replaced by Light.

"Never, never forget," I hear the voice say.

Merging with the Light, I am so overcome with gratitude and overwhelmed by the love that fills me that I cry.

Suddenly, time and space are different again, and I am momentarily aware of my body.

I am aware that the window to the left of my bed is filled with vibrant, powerful Light. It seems to be calling me and pulling me toward it like a magnet. I hear the buzzing again and . . . Whoosh! I'm zooming through the window! I merge with the Light! I am the Light, and the Light is me.

"From the Light we have come, and to the Light we shall all return," repeats the voice.

What a joy to bathe in this incredible all-knowing, all-loving Light. I can travel through walls, ceilings, and space at amazing speed! I visit my son Philippe, who is only four.

A tremendous power moves me. I am boundless, formless, no longer controlled by my emotions. I am everything. Everything is me!

I'm back in the hospital room. A mist coming from the door facing my bed attracts my attention. In the middle of the vapor is a being with the most heavenly smile. Jean Pierre! It is my cousin Jean Pierre! I am overwhelmed with joy. As I gaze at Jean Pierre, the hospital room disappears. We are suspended in midair. There are no windows or doors, no ceiling or ground. A brilliant radiance fills all space. He slowly approaches my bed and bends to kiss me. I feel the moisture of his lips on my face, the weight of his body against mine, the gentle touch of his hands on me.

Jean Pierre is my brother. After a long and painful battle with lung cancer, he died two years ago when he was only twenty-two. I am still grieving his passing. How wonderful to see him again! And what is this? He is wearing his butterscotch jacket. This jacket has been the subject of many discussions. He loves it; I hate it.

"How did you know I was here?"

My question is a thought not yet put into words as Jean Pierre answers, "We know everything about you, and we welcome you."

Such a warm feeling of peace! I am complete—whole! I am free of pain and fear. There is no past or future—everything is! There is no need to speak to be understood or to communicate. I feel serenity beyond anything I have ever known. And joy of joys: I can fly! I swirl easily and with great speed around my cousin in a playful way, expressing the ultimate joy that is me. Everything is the way it should be. Never have I felt so clear, so complete, so loved. I gaze at myself: I am whole and healed! I can interact and play with Jean Pierre with my natural vigor. Familiar Beings of Light are here, too. I immerse myself in their loving presence. It's as if they are protecting me and carrying me. We are all interconnected. I relax into the timeless joy. What a glorious feeling! I want to be here forever. Jean Pierre is gazing at me now as the other beings begin to depart. His dark eyes are filled with great tenderness and purity. He turns to leave with the others, and I plead with him to take me with him. His eyes fill with sadness.

"Not now," he responds. "There is much, much work for you. You have to go back and tell them. Life is a precious gift. Each moment is filled with great opportunities. Don't waste your time on earth. Spread love and understanding. We will always be with you—guiding you, protecting you, waiting for the time when we will be reunited—when your work on earth is over."

I watch as Jean Pierre dissolves into the same brilliant Light with which he had entered. The Light is fading away, too.

The room is empty now. My grief is intense. I start to cry out of desperation and loneliness.

Suddenly, I'm back in the hospital in bed. I am fully aware of my surroundings and my physical state of being. Tubes are implanted in my body. The pain is overwhelming. My sadness is intense. I am so weak I cannot speak. I have lost my voice, and the doctors are alarmed by the tears which are using up the strength I need to recuperate. Crying is all I want to do! My body feels like a suit that is too tight; the room is confining; the smell of sickness surprises my senses; the human condition saddens me.

"Josiane, you're back!" I recognize my sister's voice. I see her careful gaze. "You've been in a coma for three days. We didn't know if you were coming back."

. . . .
About Josiane Antonette
The trade in which Josiane serves takes its roots in the shamanic tradition of her native country, Corsica, France. In 1964 she experienced a powerful shamanic initiation through a near-death experience when she became aware of her abilities to communicate with the world of the unseen.

In 2002 she received an award for her role between cultures and dimensions and was publicly recognized as a Corsican shaman in the country of her ancestors. For forty years she has worked with the living and dying, in hospitals as a chaplain, in universities as a teacher, and as a spiritual counselor, a healer, and ceremonial leader. Her compassionate nature and understanding of living, dying, and the spiritual realms has touched many lives. Josiane is the author of *Whispers of the Soul* and *Matters of Spirit*, both about her journey to the Other Side. For more information, please visit www.mattersofspirit.com.

Journey through the Light and Back

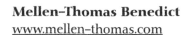

Mellen-Thomas Benedict
www.mellen-thomas.com

In 1982 I died from inoperable terminal cancer and found myself standing up looking down at my lifeless body in bed. Suddenly as I began to move toward this magnificent shining Light knowing that I would soon be dead, I pleaded asking if I could just pose a few questions before I went on. My request was honored, and I soon realized that what I was really seeing was our Higher Self matrix. The only way I can really describe it is that this Higher Self is more like a conduit. It did not look like that, but it is a direct connection to the Source that each and every one of us has.

There is a grid around the planet where all the Higher Selves are connected. This is like a great company or a next subtle level of energy around us—the spirit level. The human soul, the human matrix that we all make together is absolutely fantastic, elegant, exotic, everything. I just cannot say enough about how it changed my opinion of human beings in that instant. I said, "Oh God, I did not know how beautiful we are." The revelations coming from the Light seemed to go on and on, and I asked to see the rest of the universe beyond our solar system, beyond all human illusion. At faster than the speed of light, I flew through the center of the galaxy, absorbing more knowledge as I went. I learned that this galaxy and the entire universe are bursting with many different varieties of LIFE. I saw many worlds. We are not alone! I was at one with absolute life and consciousness. When I say that I could see or perceive forever, I mean that I could experience all of creation generating itself. It was without beginning and without end.

The Light explained to me that there is no death; we are immortal beings. Everything is alive. Everything is made from the Light of God; everything is intelligent. We have already been alive forever! I realized that we are part of a natural living system that recycles itself endlessly. I don't know how long I was with the Light in human time. But there came a moment when I realized that all my questions had been answered and that my return was near. We are literally God exploring God's self in an infinite dance of life. Your uniqueness enhances all of life.

As I began my return to the life cycle, I asked never to forget the revelations and the feelings of what I had learned on the Other Side, and it was granted. The earth is a great processor of energy, and individual consciousness evolves out of that into each one of us. I was very surprised when I opened my eyes. I do not know why because I understood it, but it was still such a surprise to be back in this body, back in my room with someone looking over me crying her eyes out. It was my hospice caretaker.

When I recovered, I was very surprised and yet very awed about what had happened to me during my near-death experience. At first all the memory of the trip that I have now was not there. I kept slipping out of this world and kept asking, "Am I alive?" This world seemed more like a dream than that one. Within three days I was feeling normal again, clearer, yet different than I had ever felt in my life. About three months later, scans miraculously revealed that I was cancer free.

Soon our science will quantify spirit. One day they are going to come down to the little thing that holds it all together, and they are going to have to call that . . . God. We are just beginning to understand that we are creating too, as we go along. As I saw forever, I came to a realm during my near–death experience in which there is a point where we pass all knowledge and begin creating the next fractal, the next level. We have that power to create as we explore. And that is God expanding itself through us.

This body that you are in has been alive forever. It comes from an unending stream of life, going back to the Big Bang and beyond.

. . . .
About Mellen-Thomas Benedict

After suffering from a terminal illness in 1982, Mellen "died" and for an hour and a half was monitored showing no vital signs. He experienced one of the most inspirational and studied near-death experiences known to date and returned to his body with a complete remission of the disease. While on the Other Side, he journeyed through several realms of consciousness and was shown both the earth's past and future for the next four hundred years. He was also gifted access to universal intelligence which he maintains today as he is now able to return to the Light at will, enabling him to bridge the gap between science and spirit.

Since his near-death experience, he has been involved in research programs on NDEs and has developed new technologies for health and wellness. He shares a message of hope and inspiration for humanity, delivered with a joy and clarity that is refreshing. His depth of feeling and passion for life is a gift to be shared.

Mellen is the author of several best-selling books including: *Journey through The Light and Back* and *Hitchhiker's Guide to the Other Side*. He discusses his NDE in full detail in his books and on his Web site at www.mellen-thomas.com.

One Man's Journey through the Afterlife

---··◄∞►··---

David L. Oakford
Michigan
www.journeythroughtheworldofspirit.com

In 1979 I had a profound near–death experience after a drug overdose. I was just nineteen and took big risks at that point in my life. This time my risks nearly killed me, and I took an unforgettable journey through the afterlife. I really have no excuse for my actions, but the following is what happened to me. There is more to the story, but this is the lion's share of my crossing through the world of spirit!

A DATE WITH DESTINY

I laid down to use the stability of the earth in an effort to maintain a hold on reality. I knew I had to do that in order to be able to come back down.

The next thing I knew I was riding in my friend's car. We rode past my childhood home, and I saw my parents sitting on the porch. I felt drawn to the trees. I could see and feel their strength. I saw their roots going deep into the ground. I mean I actually saw the tree roots physically reaching below the ground. I told my friends about the car ride after the experience, and they told me that the only place I went to was the chair they put me in after I passed out on the porch.

When I woke up, I could feel the organs in my body working, each one separately as well as all together. I could not see my friends anywhere. I could see in all the rooms of the house at the same time. The stereo was playing the Doors' *Absolutely Live* album, but the volume was way too loud for me. Since I did not see any of my friends around, I got up and tried to turn the music down but could not. No matter what I did, the music kept playing. I knew the stereo, too. I had a real problem with the noise. It was tearing at me, and I could not figure out why.

I called out to my friends, and nobody came. I tried to unplug the stereo, but that did not work either. Every time I tried to touch the cord to unplug it, I could not grasp it. It just kept on playing the music, and the sound rattled my very being.

I ran all over the house calling for my friends, yelling repeatedly that the music was too loud, but I was not heard. I pleaded for the music to be turned down. I tried to go outside, but I could not feel the doorknob. I could see the daylight outside but could not go outside. I ended up hiding in the bathroom in an unsuccessful attempt to escape the noise. I looked in the mirror and could not see myself. That frightened me greatly. I went back into the family room and saw my body sitting in the chair. It looked like I was sleeping. I wondered how I could be looking at myself. I got a bit scared then because I could see myself from outside of my body and from all different angles except from the one I was accustomed to using.

I was alone. I was confused and very scared. I tried to get back into my body but could not. I could not touch the ground either. I was floating. I rose up into a spot above my body and just kind of hung there. I could no longer move. I called out for help, and nobody came. I did not understand what was happening to me and had no idea what to do.

I asked God to help me. I did believe in God then, but I was kind of angry at Him because of the crappy life I was experiencing. I reasoned that if God were really the omnipotent and omniscient Being I was taught He was, He would not have let me experience the pain I had experienced throughout my life. I thought that if there was a time I needed God, it was now!

I looked over by the door to the outside and saw a beautiful being standing there. His feet did not touch the floor. His feet just blended into thin air. He looked both female and male and was young. I could not tell his/her sex. His hair was curly, and he was about my height. He had this glow about him too. The glow close to him was green, then blue, then pure white in the upper areas. He said, "I am here to help you," but when he spoke, his mouth did not move. I did not actually hear him speak with my ears. I felt what he was saying.

When I saw this being and he spoke to me, I was no longer afraid. I actually felt a peace and comfort such as I had never felt before. I felt the peace I was searching for throughout my entire life. The feeling was very familiar to me like I had felt it before but not in this life.

This wonderful being called me by a name I do not remember. I told him he must have the wrong guy and that the name he used for me was not my name. He laughed and said that I was a great "master" and that I had just forgotten who I was. I did not believe him, because I did not really know for sure what a "master" was, and if I were this great master, I would not have had all the problems I had. I felt that I was an evil being because that is what I was told several times in my life by many people.

He told me his name, but I do not remember it. He said that he had been with me always and told me that he knew that I had a very hard life and that he would help me understand why if I really wanted to. He would help me remember who I am. He has always been with me and that I am a little different from other souls. I was carrying the seeds to help other, very special souls who need to come to this planet. He would understand if I did not believe him and offered to prove to me that he knew everything about me. He told me things that I did when I was a child that proved to me that he was always with me. He told me about things I had only thought about. He told me that I could go anywhere I wanted to go and that he would show me how to do it if I wanted him to. He said that if I needed to come back and see my body, I could. My body would be fine because I was still connected to it somehow.

When we spoke to each other, we did so telepathically. The expression on his face was a happy one all the time.

I told him that I would like to see the Pyramids in Egypt as well as the American Southwest. He told me that all I had to do was trust him, think about where I wanted to go, and we would go. I thought about the Pyramids, and we were there in an instant. I do not know why I chose the Pyramids; the thought just popped into me so I went with that. While we were there, he told me some things about the Pyramids and Egypt that I do not remember now. I really wish I could remember what he explained while we were there because I do know it was highly significant and had to do with humanity's future.

When we finished in Egypt, we went to the southwestern United States but flew there slowly so I could see sights along the way. I wanted to see this planet with the eyes I had then. I saw the countries of the Far East and the Pacific Ocean. Night was falling in the southwestern United States, and I could see what the being told me was energy emanating from almost everything I could see, especially the plant and animal life. The energy was strongest in the areas of the land and sea that had the least amount of humans.

The energy was the lowest in areas where there were man–made structures, the cities of the world. The energy I saw came from the humans that lived in the cities. It was explained to me that humans are the basic producers of energy in cities because their energy is lower in general due to their relatively low vibrational level. I could see the higher sources of energy in the cities though. I was shown people who had higher energy levels, and some of them actually talked to the being I was with. I saw "dark souls" during the time the being and I spent on our planet. The dark souls are earthbound spirits who refuse to go to the Light. They prey on the energies of humans and try to use those souls to prevent the evolution of spirit. I was told I was protected from these dark ones as long as I chose to focus on the love in me. The dark ones did not even try to affect us; in fact they gave us nasty looks and went away. I was told I would know these dark ones when I saw them and to tell them to go to the Light. The Light is a porthole to the place all souls go if they so choose.

Around the humans I could also see energy, all different levels and colors. The being explained the human energy to me. The energy coming from humans is what spirits use to evaluate the spiritual condition of particular humans. The lighter and more brilliant the color, the more advanced the spirit is. Seeing the "aura" around a spirit is useful in determining how much a particular spirit needs to work on his development. The more highly developed beings know where to go and what to do to help an earthbound soul advance itself if it so chooses. All souls have this energy; this is why I could see it in every human. I was of the same energy type as he, but my vibration is lower now that I am in human form. In time my energy would rise to match his intensity provided I chose to take the initiative to consciously evolve my soul.

He told me that there is much to this planet that spirits can see which humans do not because their vibrations are so low. He showed me life in the trees that I could see as a spirit but could not see in my human form.

He explained that beings of higher vibration do live on the earth, but they are not human; they are part of the earth itself. He explained these beings were the caretakers of physical life on the planet. These beings take care of what we call nature—the plant, the mineral, and the waterborne life. These lower echelons of beings work together to ensure that all aspects of nature are protected and remain healthy. When the planet was evolving, these ethereal beings were the ones that kept the balance of nature.

He explained to me that the planet which we call Earth really has a proper name which is "Gaia." Gaia has her own energy and is a true living being. I asked if this energy could be seen, and he said that we would have to be away from Gaia to see and appreciate it. Humans are the ones who can manipulate Gaia's energy through their choices. If humans choose to live in harmony with the energy on Gaia, it is good for Gaia. If humans abuse Gaia, they hurt Gaia by altering her energy structure. I was given an example of how humans have deforested the planet and reduced the energy available faster than it could be replenished. He said Gaia was very strong but has been weakened considerably since humans have chosen to use the resources in a manner inconsistent with the laws of the universe.

I asked him if we could go into space and see Gaia's energy, and he said, "Yes." There were no limits on where we could go. I concentrated my thought, trusted, and we then went into what is known as space.

Away from this planet I could see Gaia all at once. It was so beautiful. I could see the aura around her. The aura affected me greatly. I felt a deep love for this beautiful place. I could hear the lady move and was told that the sound was the energy flowing in and out of Gaia. My special being told me that Gaia is a unique planet because it is designed for humans to live on forever. It was created as a place for a spirit to play, learn, and grow. The balance of nature on Gaia allows a spirit to be in human form when a spirit lives in harmony with nature.

Nature exists to compensate for the decreased vibration and was created for spirits to adapt enough to adjust and be in the physical human body while still having access to energy that will help them advance. He explained that humans were designed by God to live eternally on Gaia and are not supposed to "die." He said that "dying" is a human-created Earth term that means little in the world of spirit. The reason that humans supposedly die is that they have fallen away from the balance of nature and allow themselves to be affected by what they create that violates the natural laws of the universe. Humans have fallen away from living in balance with nature. They must relearn about the harmonic balance if they want to survive as a race and live on Gaia forever. It is still possible for humans to learn about this harmony, and it is the next overall goal of humans on Gaia. I was told that humans would eventually realize they must restore the harmony, but great damage will be inflicted before humans will fully realize what they have been doing to Gaia and work to reverse what they have done.

TRAVELING THROUGH THE REALMS

We traveled past all of the planets in our solar system. Near each planet I could hear the energy just like on Gaia. I saw the auras around each one of them, too. I saw spirits on all of them, as well. My friend told me that all planets are places for spirits to live, learn, and thus evolve. I saw great cities on each and every one of those planets. It was explained that other life in the universe is not readily seen because the beings are all of a higher vibration and that most spirits in human form have yet to attain the higher vibration required to see them.

The being told me that each planet has a theme for learning and that any of them can be chosen by our soul when it is between physical lives. We practice on the other planets so that we might be ready to live on Gaia. Gaia is the ultimate experience for a soul because our souls evolve faster here than anywhere else. He also explained that the lessons we need are difficult to learn without having a physical form.

He continued by describing how we select a physical life on Gaia. He said that I picked the parents I was born to so that I could learn what I needed to know to advance enough to come back and do spirit work on Gaia. I was being told all of these things so that I could help souls come together and return Gaia to harmony.

He explained some things to me about God that I do not remember. They had to do with the universe: it's the size and structure. I do remember he said that God is not to be seen for He is everywhere. God loves Gaia deeply, much as a man loves his wife.

He talked about Jesus, too. Jesus was a master that God sent to earth to teach humans how to act toward each other and find their way back to the path of harmony with each other as well as with Gaia.

I was told that Jesus is one being who is entrusted by God to ensure that souls evolve. Jesus is one of the master souls who is highest in vibration and a good example for any soul. God holds Jesus in high favor because He was one of the best and most successful examples of what humans need to do. I then got to view Jesus. I saw His Light which is the purest I have ever seen. There was no need for words. There were only love feelings that I cannot even begin to describe.

I was told by this loving Master that loving one another is what souls need to do in order for peace and harmony to be the standard on Gaia. After telling me this, this Great Master left me with my angelic friend.

He told me that there is a hierarchy in the cosmos that is dedicated to preserving the harmony of the universe. Humans are an integral part of this harmony and that the free will we have is the part of souls that allows humans to provide service to the universe.

After he explained those things to me, I was able to see our whole solar system all at once in full color. The planets were in a line, and I could see them all from Pluto to the sun. I felt very blessed and very important. I was given this great gift, and I did not really understand why. There I floated, a person who had gone out of his way to inflict pain on other souls, yet I was never asked about what I had done. In fact, I was given the honor of being given answers to questions most people wonder about all of their lives.

I thanked this loving spirit being for explaining and showing me what he did. He said that there was more for him to show me if I was ready to experience it. I told him I was. I did not know why I was chosen, but I was not about to question the reason. It just seemed small to me then.

We started to head back toward Gaia. We went to a place in her shadow. It was a great city in the clouds. The city had these beautiful white buildings as far as I could see. I saw spirits living there, all of whom had vibration but no real physical body. These inhabitants came in and out of buildings as they went to work and play. I saw a place where spirits go to get what I thought was water. There were no vehicles there. Spirits seemed to get around the same way my being and I did— by flying.

The city had no boundaries that I could see. This was a place full of life of all kinds. Nature was there with many plants, trees, and water just like on Gaia but more pure. This nature was absolutely perfect. It was untainted by human manipulation. It was a place just like Gaia, only without the problems and negativity. I felt that this was what is called heaven in Earth terms.

I saw spirits going to and from Gaia and the city. I could tell the development of these spirits by the energy they emanated. I could see that animals traveled to and from Earth just as humans do. There were many spirits leaving Gaia with guides and others returning to Gaia without guides. The being told me that some of the spirits passing by were the ones who did work with the humans on Gaia. I could tell the difference between the spirits who were doing the work and the spirits who were coming to the great city to be replenished in order to eventually go back to Gaia to evolve further. I could feel the emotions of the ones coming back for replenishment. Some of them were sad, beaten, and scared, much the way I had felt before my spirit friend came to rescue me.

My being (I'll just call him Bob) took me into one of the larger build-ings. Inside I saw that many spirits were working doing things similar to jobs on Earth. When we walked by the spirits, they looked at me. I think they were checking me out because of the being I was with.

We went upstairs, and I saw spirits that knew me. They greeted me and asked how I was doing. I did not know them. They gave me advice which I do not remember. I thought I was going to be given a job there, but Bob knew what I thought and told me that there was something I needed to do first.

I was ecstatic. I was in heaven despite everything I had done during my life on Gaia. I was experiencing what most people only dream about. The love I felt there was the same love I felt when I saw Jesus. I had been searching on Gaia for what was really the same place I was in then. I had been searching on Gaia for the feeling I was experiencing that very moment. I was truly happy. I was home, and I knew it. I was ready to stay and do whatever work I was given to do.

Bob then took me to another building that was special. It was bigger than the rest, and growing on it was the greenest foliage I had ever seen. It made the building look like a shrine. We went inside a set of double doors that glowed with life. The inside was decorated with a wood paneling that the being told me was "living" wood from the trees that grew in this wonderful place. He led me to some big double doors with golden knobs and told me to wait on this wooden bench while he went inside. I recognized the bench; I had seen it before. I began to remember things on that bench—things I had done in past lives, but as soon as I began to put it all together, Bob came out of the room.

He told me to go inside, saying that he would wait for me and en-couraged me not to worry. He cautioned me to ensure that I was truth-ful with the beings in the room. He said they were not judges but rather the ones who measure a soul's level of development based on its his-tory. Bob told me to remember who I was and to refrain from fear. I knew I had to leave this wise being sooner or later, but I was glad that he would wait for me. I was a little scared to leave him, but I felt pro-tected and knew that I would continue to be protected in there.

LIFE REVIEW

I went in and saw a group of several spirits seated at a round table. The table was made of the glowing wood and was perfect in every way. These spirits had the highest vibration I had seen so far with the exception of Jesus.

I looked at these beings and recognized them. I remembered some of them. I had seen them in this very room before . . . they all had something familiar about them. They just looked at me.

All of a sudden I viewed my parents on Earth before I was born. I saw how they came to be together and watched them have my older brother and sister. Their positive and negative sides were evident, and I evaluated them according to what I knew I needed to do on Gaia. The beings asked me how and why I picked these particular parents. They said I knew the answer and asked me to tell them. I do not know where it came from, but I did tell them what they asked, and they agreed with me. I picked my parents to help them on their path as well as to achieve my learning.

I saw my soul approach my mother and go inside of her. I saw myself being born from an observer's point of view as well as from the standpoint of actually experiencing my birth. I proceeded to see my entire life from my view point and from the points of view of those my actions had affected. I was aware of the feelings they had that directly resulted from things I had done to them. I saw and felt both the positive and the negative things I had done as they had truly happened; nothing was left out or presented inaccurately.

I lived through the harshness of being born again. I experienced leaving heaven and the transit to Gaia. I saw myself as a helpless infant who needed his mother for everything. I faced my father's love as well as his anger. I experienced my mother's love, her fear, and her anger, as well. I saw all of the good and bad from my childhood years and reexperienced what I had done then. I felt all of my emotions and the emotions of the souls I had hurt as well as loved. From all of this I learned that it matters deeply what choices I make on Gaia.

I learned just how powerful we humans are and how we can affect each other in positive and negative ways. It was amazing to see how my innocent actions had such a powerful effect on souls that I had no idea I was affecting. The experience was one that I will never forget. I experienced the whole spectrum of feelings of my life in a relatively short period of time as we humans see it. Where I was, time didn't really exist.

I could see how I became what I had on Gaia and why I did that. Everything I had done in my life affected the evolution of the souls around me. I saw the reasons for all of my actions and understood why I did what I had done. There was a place for all of my positive and negative actions. There was no action that was necessarily wrong, but there were actions I took that did not enhance positive growth. I was both a victim and a beneficiary of my actions. This was not a fun experience to go through. I could see how wonderful it would be if one chose to act to affect other souls positively most of the time.

Afterward, the beings in the room asked me questions about what I saw and how I felt about my life up to then. I knew that I had to provide an honest assessment—I could not lie. I hesitated when they asked me whether I affected others more positively than negatively. I thought about lying.

The group knew what I was thinking, and I had to tell them that I felt that I could have done a better job on Gaia. I knew what I had come to Gaia to accomplish and was well on my way to doing that, but I knew I was not finished yet. They agreed and told me that I still had many things to do and that I might want to go back and do them. I was told it was understood how difficult it would be for me, but it was necessary for the universe for me to finish.

The beings suggested to me that it might be wise to go back and live my life how I had originally planned it. I had set lofty goals for my life on Gaia and the events in my life were achieving those goals. I originally came to Gaia to learn and share with others using the gifts that I have accumulated over several lifetimes. I was needed on Gaia to help souls bring themselves and Gaia back to harmony. They felt that I have great potential to affect other souls and help them grow. Gaia is the best place to do that.

I was told that the events I had experienced, thus far, were preparing me to make a large contribution to the universe and that my experiences were not to be considered personal attacks in any way. I did not want to accept that interpretation. I told them that because life on Gaia was hard and unforgiving, I was tired and I wanted to stay. I felt that going back would be dangerous for the universe because I was not advanced enough in my spiritual evolution.

They said that was precisely why it would be in my best interest to go back to Gaia. I was more advanced than I gave myself credit for. It was possible for me to stay, but I would need to finish my work on Gaia sooner or later. The type of work I was destined to do could be done only on Gaia. I could stay if I chose to, but I would only be prolonging the completion of what I needed to do for this universe. The fastest way to finish my work would be to go back to Gaia as soon as possible.

I was stunned, to say the least. I resorted to bargaining, but it was no use. I still did not like living on Gaia and really didn't want to go back. The group understood me but remained firm. I had a decision to make which was the hardest decision I would ever make.

I did come back to Gaia and am now living the life that I was (later in the experience) told I would live. Believe it or not, I ended up shelving this experience away, classifying it as a really vivid "trip." It was not until I evolved more that I realized the gift I was given.

I share this experience now because I feel it can spur thought and foster choices that affect the planet in a positive way.

If I learned anything from this experience, it was that every choice I make is duly noted and recorded, and I will see the effects of them **later** when I leave Gaia and have another life review.

My goals are to save people the pain that I felt in my review and to hasten the evolution of humans on Gaia, thus helping Gaia as well as the universe.

Again, I wish you all of the love I feel in my heart, and I give this love to you!

. . . .
About David L. Oakford
David L. Oakford is the author of *Journey Through The World of Spirit: God, Gaia and Guardian Angels* and *Soul Bared: A Metaphysical Journey*. Publishing his story was a way for him to explore his near-death experience and also to work through the emotional

consequences of having had one. As David says, "You can decide to not believe it; I can't."

He lives in Michigan with his wife and four children. For more information, please visit www.journeythroughtheworldofspirit.com.

Don't You Die on Me

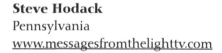

Steve Hodack
Pennsylvania
www.messagesfromthelighttv.com

I was in my early 20s, carefree and serving in the U.S. military. Fear had no place in my life as I felt I was invincible. The day I experienced death lingers on in my memory as though it were yesterday.

An army buddy and I were canoeing down the river. I had no life vest on and couldn't swim. But, again, I had no fear. We reached a point where we felt we had gone far enough and decided to turn around. The only problem was that my friend had been drinking and was being a bit reckless. For some reason he put his oar in the water on the rapid side where I was working with mine. Doing so made the canoe lopsided, and it flipped throwing us both into the strong current.

While he quickly swam to shore, I was left holding on to the canoe in a state of panic. I searched for a life jacket hoping that one had fallen out, but there was none. All the while, my friend was yelling from the bank telling me to swim, but I couldn't.

Then I let go. I don't know what I was thinking, but I let go as though the current would miraculously carry me to shore. The next thing I knew the water was sucking me under. I could no longer breathe as I struggled frantically to stay alive. Then suddenly it was dark, very dark.

I saw a light. It first appeared like a pinhole and then grew larger and larger. And as the light grew, the more beautiful and peaceful it became. I seemed to be floating higher and higher. Then suddenly I heard my mom's voice. She had passed when I was very young.

When I came to the end of this light, I stood before what appeared to be a window. My mother's image was so clear, so vibrant standing by this window. She looked at me asking if I thought the afterlife was beautiful. At this point I took the opportunity to take in the vastness around me. The beauty was beyond words—flowers, animals, vibrant colors with an intense crystal clarity. I could actually smell the fresh crisp air. It was so peaceful.

How long I was standing there I don't know. But I remember being so consumed with the beauty of it all that I wanted to stay there. Then I heard my mother's voice. "Steve," she said, "it is not your time. You have work left to do on earth." Again I didn't want to go back; I wanted to stay, but I could feel my mother slowly guiding me back to my physical body.

Suddenly I was floating above the scene in the river watching my friend drag my body to shore. Then he desperately performed CPR while screaming, "Don't you die on me. God, no, don't do this to me." All the while, tears streamed down his face. He was a medic as I was at the time and knew exactly what to do. So when I didn't respond, he kept up the breathing, compressing, and checking my pulse repeatedly. Finally he made a fist and slammed it into my chest.

At that point I was back in my body, coughing and spitting up water. I was in shock over my ordeal, but I was okay. After we calmed down, I told my buddy what had happened. At first he didn't believe me. But then I told him how I had seen him drag my body to shore. I told him how he had asked God not to let me die and then slammed his fist into my chest. At that point he could not deny what I was saying was true. He could not deny that I had, in fact, died and come back.

He told me that he had jumped into the water three times to try to save me before he finally felt me under the water and pulled me to the surface. Looking back, all I can say is I no longer have any fear of death. I know that when we pass, we go to a peaceful place—a paradise filled with sheer beauty and empty of any pain or suffering.

The Circle Bed

Barbara Harris Whitfield
Georgia
www.barbarawhitfield.com

I was born with a deformity, a curvature in my lumbar spine called "scoliosis." It never bothered me until 1973 when it suddenly became the focus of my life. I was hospitalized four times during the next two years, each time for two weeks with traction and injections of Demerol to help alleviate the pain. Looking back on it now, I believe, just as many other NDErs do, that my back pain was a metaphor for my life, which had gotten off track.

Finally, I underwent surgery, a spinal fusion. I awoke after the five-and-a-half-hour operation in a Stryker-frame circle bed. This strange bed looks like a Ferris wheel for one person. There are two big chrome hoops with a stretcher suspended in the middle. I remained in that bed for almost a month, and then I was placed in a full body cast from my armpits to my knees for six months.

About two days after surgery, complications set in and I started to die. I remember waking up in the circle bed and seeing this huge belly. I had swollen up. The swelling was pulling my incisions open, and it hurt. I called for my nurse, and then I started screaming.

People in white came rushing in. It was a dramatic scene, just like those you see in hospital dramas on television. I had no idea what was going on because I hadn't become a respiratory therapist yet. It seemed as if everybody was pushing carts and machinery, throwing things back and forth over me. They hooked me up to all kinds of machinery, tubes, monitors, and bags. Overwhelmed emotionally, I lost consciousness and later that night woke up in the hall outside my room. I floated back into the room and saw my body. I felt peaceful, more peaceful than I had ever been in this lifetime. Then I went into a tunnel where I was greeted and held by my grandmother who had been dead for fourteen years. Before this I had never once thought about her surviving her death. I didn't believe in that. But now I knew I was with her. Her love enveloped me and together we relived all our memories of each other. I, too, could see and feel all this through her eyes and her feelings of each moment. And I know she experienced how her actions and her love had comforted me in my childhood.

Suddenly I was back in my body, back in the circle bed. Two nurses were opening my drapes. The sunlight was startling. It hurt my eyes. I asked them to close the drapes. I tried to tell my nurses and then several doctors that I had left the bed. They told me that it was impossible and that I had been hallucinating.

MY LIFE REVIEW

About a week later, I again left my body in the circle bed. I was no longer on the critical list, but I was still debilitated and weak. I had been rotated forward onto my face. I was uncomfortable. I seemed to have been in that position for too long. I reached for the call button, but it had slipped away from where it had been clipped to the bed sheet. I started to call, then yell, then scream frantically, but my door was closed. No one came. I became hysterical. I separated from my body.

As I left my body, I again went out into the darkness, only this time I was awake and could see it happening. Looking down and off to the right, I saw myself in a bubble—in the circle bed—crying. Then I looked up and to the left, and I saw my one-year-old self in another bubble— face down in my crib—crying just as hard. I looked to the right and saw myself again in the circle bed, then to the left and saw myself as a baby. I looked back and forth about three more times, then I let go. I decided I did not want to be the thirty-two-year-old Barbara anymore; I'd go to the baby. As I moved away from my body in the circle bed, I felt as though I released myself from this lifetime. As I did, I became aware of an energy that was wrapping itself around me and going through me, permeating me, holding up every molecule of my being.

Even though I had been an atheist for years, I felt God's love. This love was holding me. It felt incredible. There are no words in the En- glish language, or maybe in this reality, to explain the kind of love God emanates. God was *totally accepting* of everything we—God and I—re- viewed in my life.

In every scene of my life review I could feel again what I had felt at various times in my life. And I could feel *everything* that everyone else had felt as a consequence of my presence and my actions. Some of it felt good, and some of it felt awful. All of this translated into knowledge, *and I learned. Oh, how I learned!*

The information was flowing at an incredible speed that probably would have burned me up if it hadn't been for the extraordinary en- ergy holding me. The information came in, and then love neutralized my judgments against myself. In other words, throughout every scene I viewed, information flowed through me about my perceptions and feel- ings, and the perceptions and feelings of every person who had shared those scenes with me. No matter how I judged myself in each interac- tion, being held by God was the bigger interaction. God interjected love into everything, every feeling, every bit of information about absolutely everything that went on, so that everything was all right. There was no good and no bad. There was only me—and my loved ones from this life—trying to survive . . . just trying to *be.*

I realize now that without God holding me, I would not have had the strength to experience what I did.

When it started, God and I were merging. We became one in such a way that I could see through God's eyes and feel through God's heart.

Together we witnessed how severely I had treated myself because that was the behavior shown and taught to me as a child. I realized that the only big mistake I had made in my thirty-two years of life was that I had never learned to love myself.

God let me into God's experience of all this. I felt God's memories of these scenes through God's eyes. I could sense God's divine intelligence, and it was astonishing. God loves us and wants us to wake up to our real selves, to what is important. I realized that *God wants us to know that we only experience real pain if we die without living first.* And the way to live is to give love to ourselves and to others. It seems that we are here to learn to give and receive love. But only when we heal enough to be real can we understand and give and receive love the way love was meant to be.

When God holds us in our life reviews and we merge into one, we remember this feeling as being limitless. God is limitless. God's capacity to love is never-ending. God's love for us never changes, no matter how we are. God doesn't judge us either. During our life review, we judge ourselves by *feeling* the love we have created in other's lives. We also feel the pain we have caused in other's lives. This may be a kind of cosmic equalizer.

I did not see an old man with a white beard who sits in judgment of us. I felt only limitless Divine Love.

God only gives. God interjected love into all the scenes of my life to show me God's reality. And the most amazing part of all is that God held nothing back. I understood all that God understood. God let me in. God shared all of God's self with me: all the qualities of gentleness and openness as well as all the gifts, including our own empowerment and peace. I never knew that much loving intelligence and freedom could exist.

WHAT I SAW IN MY LIFE REVIEW

At this point God and I were merging into one sacred person. It felt as though I lifted off of the circle bed and we went to the baby I was seeing to my upper left in the darkness. Picture the baby being in a bubble; that bubble was in the center of a cloud of thousands and thousands of bubbles. In each bubble was another scene from my life. As we moved toward the baby, it was as though we were bobbing through the bubbles. At the same time, there was a linear sequence in which we relived thirty-two years of my life. I could hear myself saying, "No wonder, no wonder." I now believe my "no wonders" meant "No wonder you are the way you are now. Look what was done to you when you were a little girl."

My mother had been dependent on prescription drugs, angry and abusive. My father wasn't home much of the time and did little to intervene. I saw all this again, but I did not see it in little bits and pieces the way I had remembered it as an adult. I saw and experienced it just as I had lived it at the time it had first happened. Not only was I Barbara, but I was also my mother, my dad, and my brother. We were all one. Just as I had felt everything my grandmother had felt, I now felt my mother's pain and neglect from her childhood. She wasn't trying to be mean. She didn't know how to be loving or kind. She didn't know how to love. She didn't understand what life was really all about. And she was still angry from her own childhood, angry because they were poor and because her father was sick almost every day until he died when she was eleven. And then she was angry because he had left her. She didn't know what to do with her anger so she gave it to my brother and me. Her anger boiled up all the time and then she physically abused us or she made us listen to all her resentments. Her list went back to her early childhood. Everyone had hurt her. I don't think that she, because of her numbness and drugged state, understood that she was doing the same thing to us.

Everything came flooding back, including my father's helplessness and confusion at stopping the insanity. I could hear myself saying, "No wonder, no wonder." And then the benevolent energy that was supporting me held me tighter and with even more love.

We continued watching my mother in pain, always seeing doctors and always receiving prescription painkillers, sleeping pills, and tranquilizers. My only feeling during this time was loneliness. I saw myself down on my knees by the side of my bed praying for a doctor to help my mother. I saw how I had given up "myself" in order to survive. I forgot that I was a child. I became my mother's mother. I suddenly knew that my mother had had the same thing happen to her in her childhood. She took care of her father, and as a child she gave herself up to take care of him. As children, she and I both became anything and everything others needed. As my life review continued, I also saw my mother's soul, how painful her life was, and how lost she was. And I saw my father, and how he put blinders on himself to avoid his grief over my mother's pain and to survive. In my life review I saw that they were good people caught in helplessness. I saw their beauty, their humanity, and their needs that had been ignored during their own childhoods. I loved them and understood them. We may have been trapped, but we were still souls connected in our dance of life by an energy source that had created us.

This was when I first realized that we do not end at our skin. We are all in this big churning mass of consciousness. We are each a part of this consciousness we call God. And we are not just human. We are spirit. We were spirit before we came into this lifetime. We are all struggling spirits now, trying to get "being human" right. And when we leave here, we will be pure spirit again.

As my life review continued, I got married and had my own children and saw that I was on the edge of repeating the cycle that I had experienced as a child. I was on prescription drugs. I was in the hospital. I was becoming like my mother. And at the same time, this loving energy we call God was holding me and let me into Its experience of all this. I felt God's memories of these scenes through God's eyes, just as I had through my grandmother's eyes.

As my life unfolded, I witnessed how severely I had treated myself because that was the behavior shown and taught to me as a child. I realized that the only big mistake I had made in my life was that I had never learned to love myself.

And then I was back here in this reality.

Struck by Lightning

·❖·

Dannion Brinkley
www.dannion.com

Having been raised in the Southern fundamentalist tradition, I had been taught that our reward for living a good life would be redeemed in heaven. Yet, as a child, I had no interest in that far-off wonderland where angels were playing golden harps on fluffy white clouds. You see I had always been into instant gratification! So, whatever was waiting for me behind some invisible veil seventy or eighty years down the road meant little or nothing to me. It neither motivated me to do good works nor deterred me from being the natural-born hell-raiser, which had made me infamous in my hometown deep in the Carolinas. Like most young people my age, I thought I was invincible; therefore, the thought of dying rarely, if ever, crossed my mind until that unforgettable evening when a raging bolt of lightning decided to teach me the lesson of what a tenuous and fragile mystery life really is.

In September of 1975 I was barely twenty-five-years-old and at the top of my game. I'd returned to Aiken to spend some time with my

64

family after being in South America. The word had spread that I was back in town, so my telephone had been constantly ringing all day. Just as I sat down to dinner, it rang again. I started not to answer it, but there seemed to be a certain urgency in the tone, so I walked to the bedroom and picked it up anyway. From that day on I've referred to it as "my phone call from God." I had no idea what hit me as I heard a deafening roar of thunder and felt a searing pain on the side of my head. Lightning hit the phone line sending thousands of volts of electricity into me. My entire body was then lifted just below the ceiling and momentarily suspended in the air. Then it was as if I was intentionally thrown back down toward the floor by an incredible force. The invisible forced slammed me onto my bed hard enough to break the frame. My body felt as though it was being incinerated from the inside out. My veins were on fire, and every inch of my body was in excruciating pain. Then I heard my girlfriend Sandy yell from the kitchen, "Wow . . . that was a close one!"

In the following instant I watched as she came running down the hallway to the bedroom. But I wasn't watching her from the bed. I had lifted out of my body by then, and I was viewing the entire scene from above. As fate would have it, she had recently completed a CPR course at work, so she started to pound on my chest and breathe into my mouth as she had been trained. It worked! Instantly I was back in my body experiencing the unbearable agony all over again. Then I lifted out again. From above the scene once more, I saw my friend arrive at the house and right behind him was the ambulance. I sat right beside my body on the frenzied ride to the hospital, and amid all the chaos inside the ambulance, I remember looking down at myself and thinking, "I always thought I was better looking than that."

In the emergency room the attending medical team did more CPR. Then they put the electrical paddles to my chest. One doctor even gave my heart an injection of adrenaline, but it was all to no avail. By this time all my family had gathered together in the hospital waiting room. And now the doctors had the unenviable job of having to tell them I didn't make it . . . I was gone. But what they didn't know was where I had gone.

While the orderlies were preparing my body for the morgue, I was off and running on the most extraordinary adventure of my life. I wasn't really sure I was dead; I just knew I was ever so grateful for being out of that intense physical pain. And whatever this was that was happening to me was some really cool stuff. First, I found myself surrounded and embraced by a tunnel through which I was moving effortlessly. All around me I could hear the beautiful sounds of seven distinct chimes. Ahead, I could see a light, and as I moved closer, the light became more brilliant. The next thing I knew, I was standing in the Light as a powerful being drew near. This great being radiated an intensity of unconditional love and nonjudgmental compassion which I had never known. Suddenly, and for the first time, I had the sense of being pure spirit without the heaviness of my physical body. I looked down at my hand, and it appeared phosphorescent as the Light danced through it. Looking above and below me, I witnessed the presence of other beings who looked just like me. Some were pulsating at higher vibrations while others were at lower ones. Yet, my attention was quickly diverted when the powerful being enveloped me and I began to relive my entire life, one incident at a time. In what I call the panoramic life review I watched my life from a second-person point of view. As I experienced this, I was myself as well as every other person with whom I had ever interacted.

When the panoramic life review ended, despite the many obvious mistakes I had made in my life, I experienced no retribution—no judgment and no punishment. I was the only judge presiding over my day in court! Given time to assimilate my life in retrospect, I had the opportunity to know, first hand, both the happiness and the sorrow I had created through my actions. I came to the realization that, more often than not, I had lived in a devastatingly selfish manner. My heart was filled with shame and remorse. The impact of that emotional avalanche remains uppermost in my mind to this very day. However, after my time of reflection in the heavens that day, the Being of Light telepathically conveyed these words,

"Who you are is the difference that God makes,
and the difference is love."

As the being moved away from me, I began to feel lighter. My pain and guilt lessened, and I understood that I had been shown my deeds on earth, not to harshly impugn me but rather to lovingly instruct me. Through the panoramic life review I had been given the knowledge of how to correct my life and use my power of love to make a difference in the world. I was later told that human beings are powerful spiritual beings meant to create good on earth and that good starts with small acts of kindness.

I had one more stop to make on my journey through the heavens before I was to be sent back. The being next took me to the Crystal City where I met thirteen more Beings of Light who appeared much mightier than he. Each one of them emanated a special power or force. For example, it was as if one being was the epitome of Wisdom, while another was the epitome of Strength. Standing before them all was most humbling. They stood in a line behind a crystal podium in what seemed to be a great hall of knowledge. One by one the Beings of Light approached me. When they did, a small black box emerged from their chests and sailed toward my face. Before impact, the boxes would open to reveal pictures, or what I now call visions, of the future. For example, I knew that a great desert war would be fought in 1990. As we all know, the United States military launched Operation Desert Storm that same year.

Initially it was difficult to understand and make sense of everything I was shown that day. And through the years I have had to tweak my take on a lot of it. However, it is still amazing to me how much of what I saw the day I died in 1975 has come to pass over the years. After viewing over one hundred visions, the Beings of Light gave me one last assignment. I was told to create centers for stress relief on earth. And then I was told it was time to go back. But I did not want to leave this wondrous place of peace and love. I recall thinking how sad I was to be leaving.

Without time to even finish the thought, I was standing in the hospital corridor with absolutely no clue as to how to get back into my body. I stood there pondering the dilemma for only a nanosecond before I found myself looking up at a white sheet that was covering my entire body. But I could not get up and tell anyone I was alive because I was completely paralyzed. So I began to blow on the sheet hoping someone would notice I was breathing again. And someone did.

From that moment on I was engaged in the fiercest battle of my life. I was so angry that I hadn't been allowed to stay in the loving paradise we call the afterlife. And I was even more enraged that they had sent me back with all this knowledge and a mission into a body so racked with pain and damage that it took me two years to learn to walk and feed myself again. When I could finally remember the names and faces of my loved ones, none of them wanted to hear about my journey to the heavens. They just wanted the whole incident to go away. This strained all of my relationships and destroyed my love affair with Sandy. At that point I thought I would lose my mind. My life had been stolen from me. Now I just wanted to go home—back to the heavens.

It was not until I met Dr. Raymond Moody in 1976 that I started to fit the pieces of the near-death puzzle together. Dr. Moody had been researching the phenomenon for several years when he read about my experience in a local newspaper. I believe that as surely as it was my destiny to be struck by the lightning, so it was the same destiny that brought Raymond to me. For without him and his extensive research data, I most assuredly would have lived out my life in pain, confusion, and resentment. Armed with the knowledge Raymond had ascertained through the compilation of hundreds of near-death experiences, I was able to come to grips with my life and find a brand new way to be of service to humanity. I knew there was no such thing as death, and I was ready to spread the word. Soon Raymond and I were lecturing together on this subject around the world to academic and spiritualistic audiences alike. Finally I had a life again.

In 1994 author Paul Perry helped me put my experience into words. *Saved by the Light* became a New York Times bestseller, and I appeared on radio and televisions shows from coast to coast. A year later Paul and I wrote the follow up book entitled *At Peace in the Light* and the near-death saga continued to captivate readers around the globe. However, I am most proud of my latest book, co-authored by my wife Kathryn Brinkley, *The Secrets of the Light: Lessons from Heaven*. In this last installation of my Light Trilogy, my life and spirituality have come full circle.

Since being struck by lightning in 1975, I have had two more near-death experiences. As a result, I have been gifted with an incredible wisdom and understanding of life, both here and in the hereafter. Life is the greatest and most precious gift we could ever be given; I urge you not to take it for granted for a single moment. I have been through the worst of times and the best of times in this one life. But as the Rascal Flats song says, "God bless the broken road that led me straight to you." It is my prayer that all I have experienced can be used to assist you in creating a life of love you will one day look back on with pride.

. . . .
About Dannion Brinkley

Dannion is the New York Times bestselling author of *Saved by the Light* and *At Peace in the Light*. His latest literary classic, co-authored with his wife Kathryn Brinkley, is entitled *The Secrets of the Light: Lessons from Heaven. Saved by the Light* was made into a television motion picture and has been seen by tens of millions of people in over thirty countries since 1995. To this day it remains the highest rated made-for-television movie in Fox's history and has made Dannion a much sought-after radio and television guest. He has appeared on *Oprah, Larry King LIVE, The Insider, Unsolved Mysteries*, and many other programs.

He became a hospice and nursing home volunteer in 1978 and since then has spent over thirty years volunteering his time at the bedside of the dying. In 1997 Dannion co-founded The Twilight Brigade/Compassion in Action. Today it is one of the nation's largest non-profit organizations dedicated to the training of volunteers who serve as transition technicians at the bedside of our country's priceless and beloved American war veterans.

His wife Kathryn works at his side as president of the organization. Being recognized as a true American hero on behalf of our veterans, Dannion was awarded the President's Lifetime Achievement award for Outstanding Volunteer Service in 2007. For more information, please visit www.dannion.com.

A Warning and Labor of Love

Christina Ricerca
New Jersey

While I was in labor with my first child Gianna, I was told that the baby was in the occiput posterior (OP) position which means that she was face up. My doctor had hoped that her position would change, but after many hours of labor, they decided to try to manually turn her little body around. The nurses along with the doctor did everything possible and eventually used forceps.

I'm not sure if it was the result of the episiotomy or the forceps, but after they pulled the baby out, I began to hemorrhage. They got the bleeding under control and decided to transport me via wheelchair from the delivery room into a hospital bed. As I was being moved from the bed, I began having convulsions and blacked out. I felt myself drifting out of consciousness but could still hear the nurses rushing around screaming "Code Blue! Code Blue!"

The screaming grew faint, and I found myself in total darkness. It felt cold and damp. It wasn't scary, but I couldn't see a thing. I was standing in this dark place for what seemed like several minutes, and then suddenly I felt this Supreme Presence. Again, I couldn't see anything, but I knew that I wasn't alone. I felt this Presence that was much larger than I. I now believe that the presence was God.

There was no light, no sound, no anything except for this Supreme Being who began communicating with me telepathically warning me of what was to come. If I had to, I would describe it as a male voice, but truthfully, I can't say it was either male or female. But I distinctly heard this voice say, "Chris, there are tough times coming. But you will be okay." He was telling me not to give up but to know and understand what was coming.

When I came to, my husband told me that I was out cold for less than a minute. I could not understand this because I felt as if I had been in the presence of this Supreme Being for hours. It was as if time stood still.

At first I didn't talk to anyone except my husband about what had happened to me. Six months after my experience, my father passed away unexpectedly from a heart attack. We were very close, and his death was and still is difficult for me. A year after my father's death, I had a miscarriage. And in the midst of my father's death and my miscarriage, I was also dealing with many personal family issues that left me feeling very distressed and alone. I was on the verge of having a meltdown.

One day while all this was going on, I remembered the warning that I received during my near-death experience. "Chris, there are tough times coming. But you will be okay." Suddenly a feeling of peace came over me. I realized then and I realize now that I had been given a validation. I had been given a gift.

Looking back now, I can appreciate life a little more. I know that though I have been through some difficult times, I have also been blessed. It gives me the strength to keep going. At first I didn't realize that I had an NDE. But now I know I did go to the Other Side. I know it was God who came to me on that day. The experience changed my life and will forever strengthen my faith.

God, Lightning, and Healing Hands

Blessed Tiffany Snow
California
www.tiffanysnow.com
www.thefourthhealing.com
www.lovewins.net

"Stars," I shouted through the thunder to the appaloosa pacing behind the chain link fence. "Stars! You are always the one getting into trouble! Here in the middle of a storm you are trying to find fresh grass!" As I let the chain of the tractor shed down with one hand, I steadied myself against a wooden structure pole with the other. The horse bolted up the pasture as the finger of God bolted down. That stormy day on my horse ranch in Tennessee standing in the pouring rain with my arms outstretched, I was struck dead by a bolt of lightning.

Not everyone needs to be struck by lightning or have a miracle happen to understand God's will for his life. But that is the method that God used to fix up one of his most broken kids: me.

It was summertime in the South—a time of good green pasture for the horses, ripe tomatoes on the vine, and long drives in the country. Life seemed wonderfully slow for me that gracious summer, as slow as the drone of the honeybees in the apple trees and as slow as the preparations for the upcoming county fair. For the first time in many years, all four of my children had come together for vacation time, and I knew that it would be the last tick of the clock before their lives would allow us to experience this again. I was making every opportunity to show them a full and adventurous summer. Life had never been so materially good! I was thankful to share the riches of my new life as a new wife. We would swim in the pool, watch movies, and ride the go-cart. We would drive the Jaguar in the country and go camping and have picnics. We would ride the horses.

I could overlook the growing detachment of my husband and the late night phone calls. I could also ignore the mysterious apathy and disdain my oldest daughter had for me. I could overlook the bill collectors' constant threats and the new expensive toys being brought home that we couldn't afford. I thought I could make it through anything. Hadn't I just survived my fourth encounter with possible death? Even the doctors were amazed. The venomous spider bite had tried to shut down my breathing and my heart, but the doctors knew what drugs to pump through me and I had made it through. All of this had happened just the previous week!

My husband and I had been married for only eighteen months. The marriage counseling would work. He would stop comparing me unfavorably to his "special friend" of seventeen years, telling me about her just two weeks ago suggesting that I had to "just deal with it." He would stop needing her. He would remember he loved only me. I hoped time would blow away the ominous gray clouds gathering in my personal life. I kept telling myself time would help, and I would adjust again, somehow.

I hoped that if I closed my eyes and wished hard enough, everything bad would just disappear. Hadn't I gone through this enough times? Why did this keep repeating itself? Why did I continue to make poor choices about the mate in my life? One thing I had learned was I would feel that I didn't deserve this and that God had abandoned me. Then I would usually try to fix things myself. When that would fail, I would then call upon Him, and He would bail me out, change the situation, and slowly mend all the broken parts. But this time I felt there was no way my life could be fixed. I was broken beyond repair. I felt I had no mission and that my life had no purpose.

I was so tired of starting over. For the first time in my life I felt I had some material advantage and I did not want that to change; the children enjoyed it so much, and so did I. I chose not to pray about it. I felt I would sacrifice my happiness for whatever short-term material gain could benefit the children and me. My life had been messed up too much and too many times. There was nothing left for me. So I decided I would do what my husband said and just "deal with it." I would resign myself to ignoring the problems around me and just struggle from day-to-day with a fake smile and heavy heart. Love between people seemed only a façade for control. I felt already dead; my heart knew no joy. I was without hope and felt helplessly broken.

Although I refused to see the storm swirling under my own roof, I couldn't ignore the rain and thunderclouds gathering outside over the valley. Strong winds were blowing up the hill over the pasture; rain was beginning to pelt the garden. That's when I ran out of time. And I would never look at time and many other things the same way again. My old life would soon be over; the former anxiety-ridden, hopeless person I was literally died on that summer day. As the rain worsened, it sounded like large marbles dropping on the metal-roofed sheds. I had to go check on the horses. I had to make sure they were safe.

One of the horses, a leopard appaloosa, had gotten under the chain placed across the driveways of the carport where we kept the tractor, truck, and various farm implements. He was trotting around anxiously looking for a way out, and I was afraid he was going to hurt himself. "Stars," I shouted. "Stars! You are always the one getting into trouble! Here in the middle of a storm you are trying to find fresh grass!" I steadied myself with one hand on a wooden support pole and with the other unhooked the chain and moved aside. Stars ran out kicking up his heels. I went to click it back into place, and a bright light burst around me with a deafening roar.

My muscles instantly contorted this way and that—reminiscent of the wild gyrations of John Travolta in *Saturday Night Fever*. I was doing an uncontrollable electrical dance. There was an instant of terrible pain, and then I felt no pain and actually gained clarity of thought. In that split second I turned around and tried to push my chest against the corner of the parked truck remembering that electrical shocks often stop the heart. Then my eyesight narrowed, and I felt my body slowly slide down the bumper onto the wet earth; all went black.

The next thing I knew, I found myself way up in the universe standing on nothing, and there were distant colorful planets all around me. As I lifted my arm, I could see misty pinpoints of stars through it, and when I moved it back and forth, it made the stars look wiggly like a reflection on water. I felt dizzy. I had a sense of being able to see not just in front of me but all around me at the same time. Floating just a few feet from me, I saw a man with a spirit body just like mine (no wings), though he was short and had slanted eyes. He spoke to me with a voice that I heard inside my own head saying: "Don't be afraid; it's okay."

On the other side of me another spirit person, this one much taller and with chiseled facial features (again no wings), nodded approvingly at me. All the while we were moving with great speed toward a great ball of spinning light; it was brilliantly white in the middle and yellow-ish on the outside edges. The closer we got to it, the more I felt over-whelming love; it seemed so warm and comforting; it encompassed my very being . . . like the security of a favorite grandfather's arms gently wrapped around a child on his lap. How wonderful I felt!

We stopped. The bright light was still far from me. I wanted to go on; I felt like a magnet, irresistibly drawn. The desire to "blend" had grown stronger the closer we got—I knew this place was the heavenly throne of God himself! Why had we stopped? As I stood there confused yearn-ing toward the greatness beyond my reach, a glowing luminosity ap-peared in front of me. Gold and white sparkles came together in a glowing spiritual body, a giant image in the shape of a man with broad shoulders. A Divine Presence was here!

A gentle voice called out from this realm of golden sparkles massed brilliantly in front of me. "What have you learned?" He asked in an indiscriminatory and nonjudgmental way. The voice was so soft and tender, yet the presence of divine authority was there; I knew without a doubt that it was the voice of God's own son, the very much alive Jesus Christ.

Then all of a sudden, life events unfolded before my very eyes! Key moments where I showed anger to people and also where I had showed love appeared like scenes out of a movie. I could feel the anger and hurt of the other person whenever I had been mean, and I also felt the anger as it rippled on through to others. I had never before faced the horrid deepness of my own sin. Then where I showed love to people, I felt that too and how much further that rippled out from one person to another as a warm pulse triggering causes and effects in all things that were wonderful and blessed. I had never before experienced such joy!

Then the presence of Christ said, "The flesh is the test of the spirit. Love each other." Words of wisdom imparted to me! I felt overwhelmed with love and so privileged. The spirit on my right then talked inside my head again and answered many questions on my mind. He also taught me details about many wonderful and sacred things. A seed was planted within me; groundwork had been laid. I knew that God wanted me to share this information later on and would give me the ability to understand it. In fact, many things I didn't know I knew ended up being in the pages of the books I was asked to write. What a joy this task has turned out to be—to love and share with so many people in this way and to be loved back!

While I floated there before the consciousness of Christ, the very presence of Jesus, the spirit then told me something that I didn't understand at all, "Welcome to the world of healers," He said. This was a shock; I had no idea what that meant. I had never believed in such a thing! The church I had been with believed that healing had died out in the first century with the apostles and also that NDEs were only reactions of a dying brain. What could this welcome mean?

At this point Christ went back into formless sparkles and faded away, and the stars and space behind His glowing features were visible once again. Such effervescent beauty and colors twinkled around me like being in the midst of a sparkling aurora borealis. So many shapes of heavenly bodies were floating in the cosmos, all unique and necessary, all untold distances away. Yet they felt so close that it seemed I could reach out and pluck them out of the sky and carry them home cupped in my hands.

The slant-eyed spirit went on and continued to teach me even more.

He pointed out different stars, planets, and distant, colorful swirling lights of all kinds to which he gave names. He continued to educate me and give me answers to thousands of questions that I never had questions for! Reams of information seemed to be exploding in my brain just like an empty library suddenly being realized! Details about many wonderful and sacred things flooded my being. I wondered whether these things were recently learned or just easily remembered. Everything somehow felt familiar in the Oneness of it all. I also became aware of thousands of others around me—observing, encouraging, accepting, and fully loving me. I saw two children excitedly talking with each other about coming back to earth and what their new purposes would be. We live more than once. And I remembered that I had forgotten that! And I realized that in many things I had chosen tradition and pleasing others as the way I related to myself, others, and God.

The spirit who was speaking to me did not offer his name, and I did not ask. I wanted to be careful to show homage only to the true God and not to anyone else. And I wanted to stay! I wanted to join myself with God's swirling life force, his essence, and the core of heaven that was just beyond! But I wasn't allowed to go any farther. No! I wanted to go to God! I wanted to feel more love! "Why can't I be with you now, Father? Please, Abba, please!"

I listened as hard as I could, waiting for the words of God. Then, just on the outside of my understanding, I heard voices faintly singing the most beautiful melody I have ever heard in my entire life. I absolutely knew that these were the blessed voices of angels and those joined with God. They came from his swirling brilliant presence, the core of heaven. There were no musical instruments, but each voice instead lent itself to create perfect harmony and variations of pitch and melody, flowing and moving perfectly together as easily as a flight of winged birds.

I knew it was praise for the Father, but I just couldn't make out the words the angels were saying. If I could have only stepped forward just a bit more . . . but I was rooted in place. I felt so sad. Then all at once, words started resonating throughout my entire body as if I was standing in front of a huge amplifier at a concert stadium. It was the voice of God. It was not a hearing through my ears but throughout my entire being. "If you love me, heal my children; help them remember who they are."

Here was free will. What would I do? Yes, I would participate; I would offer. How could I not? How could I say no to God? I knew I would be totally loved and approved of either way, but I knew I would be missing out on an opportunity to expand the ripple effect of love. I needed to go back to the earth. I also wanted to make a "better movie" of my life. So right then and there I vowed to be a vessel to do only His will; I would go back.

I absolutely gave myself to Him. I wanted desperately to show how much I loved Him and to share the reality of His existence with others! His will, not my own, I promised, would govern the rest of my life. If He could use this broken piece of clay from the earth, it was all His. I totally dedicated myself and surrendered all desires. Instantly I felt a childlike sense of wonderment as a warm flood of bliss and peace overpowered me and a warm tingling sensation filled me just like warm liquid honey flowing from the top of my head down to my very toes! What was happening to me? It was the baptism of the Holy Spirit, an anointing more commonly experienced on earth, that I was experiencing here in heaven. At that moment I knew that I would have abundant help with the work. To His children I would be an instrument of opportunity for teaching and healing. They would be shown the true identity of a powerful, caring God who loves them and desires to be an active participant in their lives. Clearly, I had a mission.

I was shown by the Father that in the future I would be speaking to thousands of people at a time on spiritual matters, not religious ones and that great healings would occur. The gifts of God would be poured out just for the asking, and great manifestations of signs and wonders would take place within the audience itself. The spirit of God would move all to love and to remember who they are, who the others are, and who the Father is! All this would be occurring as the darkness in the world got darker; for the light would become brighter too. And love would win. This time is now.

Then I felt myself sinking, as if falling through a bed. I was being pulled back. I was leaving heaven. Instantly all my emotions welled up inside: remorse and joy, grief and exhilaration.

With that, I woke up; my husband was shaking me by the shoulders. Somehow my physical body was now lying on the front seat of the truck although I had left it outside in the mud. I knew clearly this was God's hand in helping the physical body to survive. Three hours had passed since I had left the house to go to the tractor shed. The storm had moved on, though later we observed that there was evidence of at least three other strikes in the pasture besides the one that had struck me. We saw the spots blasted on the earth. I had been under one of those blasts.

In the emergency room I was hooked up with wires and given tests to check my heart. A thorough exam revealed that it had not been damaged. But my eyes and ears were affected very badly as was my sense of balance. I couldn't see very well or hear much at all. I felt dizzy but keenly calm and aware of the reality of my experience. The only piece of jewelry I had been wearing at the time was a single diamond earring. A brown burn mark now encircled the gold stud where it went through my ear. My skin tingled all over and was extremely sensitive to the touch, especially on my arms and in my hands. It hurt to wear clothes.

The doctors told me that I had been very lucky; the doctor said that often an arm or leg gets blown off during a strike (Was he kidding?). People often die and don't come back (Yes, I knew that). They reasoned that because I was holding the chain with one hand and the wet wooden pole with the other, the current had passed through me instead of grounding in my body. I knew they wouldn't believe me if I told them that it had been a divine strike, that God offered this as a wake-up call and that I had been before the presence of God (and oh, by the way, Jesus spoke to me!). They would have kept me a lot longer than they did and probably in a little white jacket in a locked padded room to boot!

I spent a few days in bed alternating between a wild mixture of extreme happiness and unbelievable sadness. The emotions ran more deeply than any I had ever felt. I was glad for the experience, but I was experiencing such homesickness! I kept reliving the event over and over in my mind with every detail emblazoned on my brain. I was determined that even if I forgot my own name, I would never forget this. I tried painting what I had seen—oil paints on canvas. The colors, no matter how I mixed them, were not brilliant enough. Nothing could capture what I had seen and felt. I felt sad again, then once more happy for the experience but also confused. What did it all mean? I was losing the clarity. I prayed consistently to God to help me hear and feel Him even though I was back in a physical body. I was afraid I would forget everything and that all would be lost.

After a few days, I was back doing my chores including putting salve on Star's skin infection. For six weeks I had smoothed on the medicine the vet had given me, but the red blisters still kept spreading and killing the hair all around his girth. Now I had run out of medicine, so I just rubbed his belly lightly around the outside of the infection because he had grown used to the attention. I noticed that my hands were getting very hot. I thought it must have been caused by the bacteria from the infection, but when I washed my hands under cold water, the sensation went away. I didn't think anything of it.

The next day I walked up to rub his belly again—reminding myself to get new salve soon—and noticed that all the blisters had turned white and that some were falling off. I once more rubbed around the infection, and my hands again turned hot. The next day when I went out, all the blisters had fallen off, and there was evidence of new hair growth. I thought this was mere coincidence. The medicine must have finally worked. I didn't relate it to what I had been told.

The next week I took my cat in to be spayed. The vet said it would take ten days for the stitches to completely heal. On the first day she didn't want anything to do with me. But by the second day she was in my lap as much as possible. She just would not leave me alone—even yowling for me if I left the room! Every time I would rub her and pet her, I found that my hands were heating up again. On the third day she tried pulling the stitches out with her teeth. On the morning of the fourth day, I decided to look at what was going on and found that the skin had healed so well that the stitches were puckering her skin up tight. I found myself embarrassed to take her back to the vet. What would he say? So I carefully cut the threads and pulled them out through skin that bore no surgical scar. Now I began to understand what was happening. I could heal animals.

Then I wondered if this would work on me? The very next day I made connection in prayer to God, and as I turned my free will to healing, I was mentally transported to heaven and saw myself standing

before God once more just as in the near–death experience. I saw myself lifting a body up in my arms toward God, and the body was mine.
In real life I placed my hot hands on my forehead and on various parts
of my body. Then I made an appointment with the doctor. A previous
mammogram had shown a lump in my breast which they had recom-
mended further action on, but I had put off. A former doctor had told
me I had fibroid cysts in my uterus which could be removed only by
surgery. Also I had a torn rotator cuff in my shoulder which had pre-
vented me from sleeping well for the past six months, thanks to a fall
off of Stars.

I anxiously awaited the test results: the mammogram showed the
lump was gone; the diagnostic ultrasound showed clear because the
fibroid cysts had disappeared; I also could sleep at night without any
pain as my rotator cuff had healed.

Hesitantly I started sharing this new gift with my friends, and that's
when I ran into trouble. I found that I was taking the pain of their
ailment into myself. If they had a migraine, I would get a migraine. If
they had stomach pain, I would get stomach pain. That scared me. I
found myself afraid to use the gift. Maybe I was using it wrong? Why
would God give me a gift that would harm me when I used it? I felt I
wouldn't last very long in this work. And yet, I knew in my heart that
God wouldn't give me something that would be unsafe for me to use.
What was I missing?

I thought I might find answers if I watched the healing ministries on
TV. For the first time in my life I wondered if they could actually be
legitimate. I had never believed in this sort of thing. I had always felt it
must be fake, simply a showy display to raise money and give people
false hope. Now I wanted desperately to talk to one of the healers. Did
they feel sick afterward? Had they in some way each been told "welcome to the world of healers"? Was I part of this same group? What did
God want me to understand? There was no way to contact anyone. I
knew somehow I would be guided to the answers I needed about how
and where to expand upon the gift.

I continued on this way for a time, confused by the gift. I thought
maybe I would work only on animals; I did not feel their pain. I imag-
ined myself working for a veterinarian alone in a back room quietly

healing all the little ones. I didn't know what to do.

So I prayed for understanding, and what I found were words flowing back to me from the scriptures of the Bible. The pages would randomly fall open to pertinent information, and my eyes would fall on the scriptures He wanted me to see. They popped out as brightly as if a yellow marker pen had highlighted them! Dozens of scriptures!

"For I know the plans I have for you," declares the Lord, "plans to prosper you and not to harm you, plans to give you hope and a future." (Jeremiah. 29:11)

"You are the light of the world. A city on a hill cannot be hidden. Neither do people light a lamp and put it under a bowl. Instead they put it on its stand, and it gives light to everyone in the house. In the same way, let your light shine before men, that they may see your good deeds and praise your Father in heaven." (Matthew. 5:14)

" . . . fan into flame the gift of God, which is in you through the laying on of my hands. For God did not give us a spirit of timidity, but a spirit of power, of love, and of self-discipline." (2 Timothy. 1:6)

A friend told me about a group of people in town that offered hands-on healing so I thought I would go talk to them. Twice a month they would gather in an upper room of a building and invite anyone who wanted to come. Their hands were hot like mine, and the people whom they were attending to had come from the community, mostly the poor and the curious. When I entered the room, I saw many people sitting near a person lying peacefully upon the table receiving the healing. They were in prayer, and I saw a picture of Jesus hanging predominately on the wall, which made me feel comfortable. They called what they were doing Reiki, and although many use this form of healing without prayer, these healers were incorporating it as they moved from one part of the body to another. I prayed about what I was seeing and felt at peace.

On the desk was information about this Japanese technique, and I thumbed through it. There was a picture of a man named Dr. Usui who had given Japanese hands–on healing the name of Reiki in the early 1800s although it had been known for hundreds of years before. He had started many healing clinics in Japan. I looked at the picture and gasped—I knew this man! This was the spirit with slant–eyes and rounded belly who had been beside me during my near–death experience! The very same man! My goodness! God works in very, very mysterious ways!

Because of this revelation, I knew what my next step was, and I went through the training classes of Usui Reiki. This was a touchstone offered to help me begin feeling comfortable about group healing. As soon as I made the decision to become trained, any pain from doing any healing disappeared. Now I feel energized and euphoric after the healings. It wasn't the Reiki that made it disappear; it was the decision to openly follow through on what I had promised to God. The Big Guy has always used healing along with miraculous signs and wonders in all parts of the world, in all cultures, and in all periods of time. It doesn't matter the training or technique—it matters to whom you are making connection and choosing to be an opportunity for that love to transform and manifest. And it is up to the person who is receiving that healing to use free will to participate in welcoming it or not. God is big on free will. He offers opportunity to all regardless of boundaries, cultures, or era. He's a great guy who truly wants all people to be healed and to remember who they are!

So again, adding prayer and recognizing God's love is what makes the miracles happen, no matter what the name of the modality is. With prayer all transformation takes place. It is not the method or terminology or what analytical touchstone a human might use. It is the faith in God and the prayer which connects spirit to Spirit.

When God gives His people a commission or divine gift, He does not do it without a specific purpose. So many times I have been absolutely shattered, yet He has still held me gently in the palm of His hands. There have also been many times that we have walked together hand-in-hand and many times when I have turned away from Him, hid my face in shame or in anger, and withdrew my hand from His. Yet His arm was still outstretched, and He still loved me . . . I was astonished. Unbelievable! And now He gave me a real purpose along with a job where I would be working in direct communion with Him every day. He wasn't tired of me yet! I would also be making friends and helping people from all walks of life, social standing, color, and religious or spiritual backgrounds. I would get to be the nurse's assistant to the Great Physician. I would get to see the miracles as He reaches out to tell His children He is not only real and cares about them, but that He also has the power to manifest and transform our struggles. He desires also that there be no distraction from the joyful, abundant, healthy, and loving lives He wants us to have and from fulfilling the dreams and purposes placed within our hearts.

So why did the lightning strike and near–death experience occur? We all have defining moments, and those were mine. I was a most stubborn child in clinging to what I thought I knew. I had been so resistant, having "blinders" on and putting "God in a box," that only an empirical, firsthand experience would open me up. I had a purpose now, and I did not have to suffer in silence or ignore my plight. I could be strong again, because His strength was in me. Everything was made anew! Because of free will I had died at the foot of heaven and upon the earth, and He had resurrected me again. I was a new person. He opened me up! I vowed I would never allow myself to be closed down again.

I asked to float in His love as easily as a feather upon the breeze and that I would go wherever He led me. "The wind blows wherever it pleases. You hear its sound, but you cannot tell where it comes from or where it is going. So it is with everyone born of the Spirit." (John. 3:8)

Now, my entire life is an adventure and an awesome spirit journey! I get to watch cancer disappear, brain tumors shrink and go away, blind eyes see, and deaf ears hear. I get to be there when the arthritis melts away and chronic disease abates. I get to be there to see the addictions leave without side effects, and I get to help bring peace, calmness, and joy to lives of mental depression and hopelessness. I get to see infertile couples experience the joy of carrying their own child in their arms. I meet people from all over the world and get to be there every day when incredible things happen. I also form friendships that are deep and moving. Along the way, this wider connection with God has led to other interventions of Spirit, such as miraculous long-distance healings, medical intuition, locating missing children, helping on crime scenes, visions, and prophecies. Through this Oneness of connection, nothing is impossible! I praise God continually as I enjoy every day, every moment, and every experience I have! I am always amazed how He brings His kids together to learn to love one another and help each other. It totally humbles me to be involved in this kind of work. For this is not about me. He wants each of us to remember who we are, to be the mystic, and to transform darkness into light.

The point is this: you don't have to be struck by lightning or have a near-death experience to open up, to change your life, to appreciate each other, or to have a special connection with God. Love is the key to everything. Remember: the life review you will have will be about the love you showed or didn't show. It's all about love!

When I was before God, I wished only to love and be responsible to Him, but what He wanted was for me to be responsible and to love everyone else. So we prove our love by loving everybody else! And it has opened me to surrender in faith to whatever God needs from me, and He has continued my enlightenment. Since July 2005 I have been experiencing the holy stigmata, the five wounds of Christ. They open spontaneously about once a month and last for three to nine days. Part of that experience comes with new visions and information for the important time of shift we are living in, which is then written down and shared. We have even been given prayers called "divine decrees" that are here to help the world participate in this transformation of our lives and global events with angelic help. The healings that have been occurring since that connection are even more miraculous!

My brokenness has led me to a mending of the very highest kind, and everything in my life has changed in alignment to fulfilling that purpose. I stood up for love and everything not of love shifted out of my life. To that end I have now married for a second time to a loving and spiritual partner, who hears God clearly for himself and follows through on the mission placed in his heart as well as supporting me in mine. I am blessed to have healed thousands of people and to have seen miracle upon miracle. I have a wonderful support team which schedules healings for me with people from all around the world. Consistent with the expanding information I receive, I continue to write articles and books and to hold healing conventions in many places. We have MP3s on lots of topics as well as "Becoming the Mystic" classes and live teleconferences. There are so many ways for the love to ripple and bless!

So even in my most broken of times when I didn't know what to ask for, the Big Guy gave me my life's work. And I am happier than I have ever been before! Whatever periods of brokenness I had to go through, whatever lessons I needed to learn to get to this place in my spiritual journey, I can release and be glad for them! Now, I am making a better "movie" for when I come before the Presence again, and I'm sharing the gifts our Father freely gives us. I am thankful everyday that when I was stubborn and striking out, God stepped in and struck me down! Truly, the best thing that happened in my life was almost losing it. Being dead healed my life, and now it heals others. I'm glad to be back.

. . . .
About Blessed Tiffany Snow

Blessed Tiffany Snow carries the five marks of the holy stigmata and is a documented miracle healer, award-winning author, NDEr, and public speaker. Her latest book *God's Workbook — Shifting into the Light* is available on Amazon.com. Distant healing, deliverances, classes, live teleconferences, and more articles are offered through the Web sites. For more information, please visit www.TiffanySnow.com, www.TheFourthHealing.com, and www.LoveWins.net.

The Light . . . Pure Love

Reverend Juliet Nightingale†
www.towardthelight.org

In the mid–1970s I was dealing with a terminal disease, colon cancer, where my life was ebbing away. I was bedridden for the most part but could sometimes manage to sit up for short periods. Being the contemplative that I was, I was always listening and observing—taking things in and trying to understand the deeper wisdom behind what was happening to me and where all of this was leading. As a result, I became more withdrawn and detached . . . as I observed everything round me starting to change. Solid matter became more translucent and liquid; colors became more vivid and vibrant; sound was more clear and acute . . . and so on. I could no longer comprehend anything printed on a page because it no longer meant anything to me in my changed state of consciousness. It was like trying to read and understand a foreign language! I had already departed from the third–dimensional realm for the most part . . . and my awareness enveloped other things.

I was entering into what I later came to refer to as the "twilight" stage. In this state, everything was altered. I got to a point where my consciousness was already making the transition from one realm to the other—being more aware of other realities on other dimensions. I was seeing and perceiving things and other beings interdimensionally even though I was still somewhat conscious on the physical plane. I've since realized that this is what a lot of dying people go through (such as those in hospitals, nursing homes, or others in hospice care) while an observer might think that they're hallucinating or seeing someone or something that "isn't really there." In truth, this is a state where one, such as myself, is experiencing other dimensions simultaneously while still on the physical plane because in reality we are multidimensional beings.

I finally lapsed into a coma on Boxing Day, December 26, and was ironically declared "dead" on my birthday, February 2! (Now I've got two natal charts!) As others observed that I was in a coma which lasted over five weeks, I was having a completely different experience! One would look at my body and think that I was unconscious . . . asleep . . . with no awareness of what was going on or of anything. Yet, I was very conscious and profoundly aware because in truth we never really sleep; only our bodies do. We are always aware . . . and active . . . on one level of consciousness or another. Just the fact that we dream while asleep is an indication of our consciousness always being active. And indeed our bodies need to rest, so that we can tap into and experience other aspects of our consciousness and being!

The best way I can describe the transition from being "alive" on the physical plane and the passage to the Other Side is like passing from one "room" to another. You do not cease to be or lose consciousness; your consciousness simply shifts from one vantage point to another. The experience changes; your outlook changes; your feelings change. And the feelings I experienced were profound. For me, it most certainly became that peace that surpasses all understanding . . .

My transition was gradual as a result of having a terminal disease—as opposed to a sudden one incurred from accidents, heart attacks, and the like. I became aware of a "Being of Light" enveloping me. Everything was stunningly beautiful—so vibrant and luminous . . . and so full of life—yes, life!—in ways that one would never see or experience on the physical plane. I was totally and completely enveloped in Divine Love. It was unconditional love . . . in the truest sense of the word. I was in constant communion with this Light and always aware of its loving presence with me at all times. Consequently, there was no sense of fear whatsoever . . . and I was never alone. This was a special opportunity to experience being at one with the ALL—never separate . . . and never at a loss.

The colors were so beautiful—watching the Light whirl all round me, pulsating and dancing . . . making whooshing sounds . . . and being ever so playful at times . . . then very serious at other times. Many things would take on a luminous glow—a sort of soft peach color. Everything was so vibrant—even when I saw deep space! I was constantly in a state of awe. There were always beautiful beings round me as well—helping me . . . guiding me . . . reassuring me . . . and also pouring love into me. I was never alone.

One of the first things I remember experiencing was the life review— which included everything that I'd experienced in my physical incarnation up to that point. It was like being at the cinema watching a movie of my life and everything happening simultaneously. I think most NDErs will agree that the life review is one of the most difficult aspects of the NDE. Viewing your entire life before you with every thought, word, and action can be most unsettling, indeed. Yet, what happened was the fact that no one passed judgment on me! I felt only the constant enveloping of Divine Love from the Being of Light that was always with me. What I came to realize then is that we judge ourselves! There was no "He–God" sitting on some throne passing judgment on me (not that I even ex-pected to see such a being in the first place). I never subscribed to such religious myths anyway. I seemed to be the only one who was uncom-fortable and most critical of me. Yet, having stated that, I also realized that I wasn't coming from a vantage point of the "ego self" but rather from my soul self which was much more detached and devoid of feel-ings of being emotionally charged. I was no longer identifying with the personality of the physical self. Therefore, what I felt was very different. It came from a completely different perspective as the soul self . . . my True Identity.

Even though I was no longer in my physical body, I did have form—

a body of sorts. The best way I can describe this is that I felt like a bubble floating and moving about effortlessly—sometimes very fast, other times gently drifting about. I felt hollow inside and so clear that I even had a sensation of a breeze blowing inside of me. There was never any sense of hunger, thirst, weariness, or pain. Such things never entered my mind, in fact! Alas, I was pure consciousness, embodied in a light and ethereal form, travelling about or being still and observing intently and always in a state of awe. It was such a glorious sensation where I experienced such calm and a profound sense of peace and constant trust. I also experienced no blindness, (as I do with my physical eyes since I am legally blind), and what a sense of awe and wonder to be able to see!

At one point, I perceived myself as being on a guided tour, visiting and observing different places, beings, and situations; some of which were very pleasant while some, very painful. The best way I can describe this "tour" was like being in a circular enclosure of windows— each pane revealing something different—but when I'd focus on one particular pane, I'd suddenly see it become full size (much like a "window" on your computer monitor becoming full screen) and I stood still just watching . . .

One pane revealed a scene that one might interpret as a "hell" or "purgatory" where faceless, grey-colored entities moved about aimlessly and moaned. They were clearly suffering and in great agony and anguish. I saw these entities as damaged souls—ones who had committed unspeakable atrocities during their previous incarnations. I have used the analogy of a soul being "retrograde"—much in the way a planet will have the appearance of going backwards. The prevailing feeling that I had while observing these souls was one of deep compassion and a yearning to comfort them. I wanted so much to see them relieved of their horrible suffering. But, alas, as painful as this scene was, I was reassured that these souls were here only temporarily and that they, too, would heal and move back in a forward direction and ultimately return to the Light. All souls, without exception, eventually return to the Light . . . according to what was revealed to me.

The above scene led to another scene where I saw images of people I knew in my present life—obviously those still incarnate on the physical plane, but my viewing them from the Other Side in a scene that would take place in future. (Again, everything experienced on the Other Side is always in the "now"—even "past" and "future.") They were individuals who'd also committed atrocities in one form or another—individuals who had severely violated me or people I love. But the scene I beheld was one where they were being made to suffer as a result of what they'd done—that most likely being the karmic result of their decisions and actions. Again, I felt a deep sense of compassion for them and feeling sad that they had to endure such suffering yet realizing that it was also unavoidable. Never once did I feel any sense of anger or hostility towards these individuals . . . but only wanting to see them healed . . . so that they, too, would come to know love.

Another scene I remember was that of finding me observing a realm that constituted water. I beheld all its beauty and splendor, and it was teaming with life. Then, before I knew it, I found myself under water and not having to worry about breathing! I was moving about effortlessly and mingling with everything that I'd first observed from without. The same thing happened to me when I moved through space and danced and flowed with all the heavenly bodies and lights. There were lots of times for play and buzzing about with all the light beings—moving all round me like comets. This was an opportunity to experience great joy and feeling so light and completely void of worry or fear. I could move effortlessly and adapt to any environment I happened to be in at any given moment. I would simply think about something, and it would instantly manifest . . . or I'd think about a place and there I'd be! Oh, what a sensation to experience such power to be anywhere I wanted to be and to create anything I wanted to and to feel so totally free!

After experiencing the tour, adventures, and times of play and creation, etc., things became more serious, and I was again in direct communion with the Being of Light. I was now being asked to "help" or "assist" in some way . . . in creating and determining the outcome of certain events, situations, or even things affecting others! Me? Just little me? Oh my, I thought. That's a grave and serious responsibility. I felt so honored and so humble being asked to participate in such a feat, but I wondered what would happen if I failed to do my part as needed. I was then assured that everything would work out exactly as it should—even if I couldn't complete things as desired. It seemed that the point in all of this was the fact that we co-create with the Light, and we are also part of the Light. Furthermore, no matter what happens, the Light Source will always be in control and be there to see things through despite any shortcomings on our part as souls. How auspicious it is, then, to realize that, as souls, we are a part of all creation and take part in the actual creative process thereof!

This very thought of being asked to help—to co-create with the Light—made me feel profoundly special and important in the greater scheme of things but by no means from an egotistical point of view. As stated above, I felt deeply humble and had a serious sense of responsibility for every thought and action I took. My only thought was that I wanted to do what was right. How important it was for me to be very loving and creative . . . and never damaging in any way . . . and that's the gift. I realized at that point how totally connected with all life through all the universes I was. I felt one with the all—never separate, never apart. Still, there was no fear. Still, there was only love. Forever and for always I could never be alone because I would never be alone. It's impossible to be alone because life is everywhere; love is everywhere . . . and this is what carried me and has stayed with me.

I so cherished this communion with the Light. Everything was communicated telepathically—whether with the Light or other beings, friends, or loved ones. It didn't matter. It was always honest, open, and real . . . and it was always done with love. There's no such thing as "putting on airs" and no need to hide on the Other Side. No one is there to hurt you in any way—not in the least—because there is no sense of lack or the need to "steal" someone else's power or energy. You are operating as a soul, not centered in ego or personality. It's nice to realize that you will have whatever you need because you've got the capacity and power to create it instantly!

As the mood seemed to shift, I felt as if there was something serious that was just about to befall me. I was now being told that I was going to have to return to the alien (physical) world I'd left behind, that I was needed there for something very special and significant. I needed to go back to share what had just happened to me and to let others know that life is, indeed, eternal and that death is an illusion. On a personal level, I was told that I needed to experience great love and joy in that world . . . and finally I would be able to return home. I was, then, assured that I was real and that I could believe in what I'd come to know in this glorious realm—not only about myself but also about all life. I was also told, however, that the world I was returning to was an illusion and that I wasn't to identify with it or be involved—to be in it but not of it—and that I was only passing through.

To say that my heart sank would be an understatement. This was the first time that I had the true experience of a broken heart while on the Other Side. The very thought of leaving this sacred realm where I was in constant communion with the Light and other beings crushed me in ways I could never describe. I knew how dark and foreboding that strange, illusory world that I was being asked to return to was, and it is, indeed, a world I've never identified with! However, I was, once again, reassured that the Light and other loving beings would be with me at all times and to remember that I'd never be alone. Gratefully, there was still no sense of fear—only sorrow now, but realizing that I had to honor the Divine Will making this request of me.

As I reluctantly accepted this mission, I suddenly beheld a most beautiful being who appeared in front of me pouring tremendous love into me and filling me to overflowing. It was as if this was my gift for accepting the painful request to leave my home on the Other Side and to return to a world so alien to me. This being loved me very deeply and stayed with me continuing to radiate love and sound, and it was made clear that he'd be with me always.

I started moving back into this world in much the same way that I had left it. It was a very gradual transition. I was now more aware of my body lying in hospital intensive care, hooked up to a life-support system, but it was still so separate from me and the vantage point I was experiencing from the Other Side. It was like being a newborn baby when I finally regained consciousness on this plane. Everything was so strange and new! I had just come from another world—literally—and this world appeared so much darker and void of color by comparison. Everything was drab and appeared flat to me. I didn't feel the life-force I had experienced on the Other Side, but I was resolved to honor the will of the Light I'd been sent back to fulfill. I had a mission, and there was a special promise that was made to me in return.

Even in hospital, I was aware of the Being of Light still with me . . . and communicating with me. I was also still aware of other beings with me—beings that I came to realize, later, only I could see and hear. Finally, one day, the Being of Light disappeared from view of my mortal awareness, and I knew, now, that I was fully back in this world. Again, I was brokenhearted but still free of all fear believing and trusting in the promise that I'd never be alone . . . and so it was . . .

This near–death experience (or what I prefer to call an Eternal Life Experience) left me feeling such a profound sense of triumph and awe. Something else I learned, too, is that fear is an acquired state, not a natural one. It is something that you learn but has no connection with the soul self. Love is the prevailing force at all times no matter how things may appear in this world of duality and illusion. It's merely a hologram created by the collective consciousness for the sake of growth and evolution. Therefore, what occurred on the Other Side, for me, was a special opportunity to experience . . . and a knowing with total certainty that everything was evolving exactly the way it should and that the ultimate destiny for every living being is to return to the Source, the Light . . . Pure Love.

. . . .
About Reverend Juliet Nightingale†

The late British mystic Reverend Juliet Nightingale was the founder of Toward the Light (www.towardthelight.org) and the creator of www.lightonthewater.ning.com., a near-death experience (NDE) support and interest group. She was a minister of metaphysics, a clairvoyant spiritual advisor/counselor and medium, a practitioner of Reiki and remote healing. She had had multiple NDEs before her death in February 2009.

A gifted musician and loyal friend, she was the host of the ground-breaking radio show, *Toward the Light,* on BBSRadio.com. The show focused on the nature of consciousness and life continuum as revealed through near-death, out-of-body, and other spiritually transformative experiences and related topics.

Why I Did Not Want to Live

Summersnow Wilson
Arkansas
sunuluv@aol.com

When I was eighteen, I had surgery and died on the operating table because too much anesthesia had been mistakenly administered. My surgery, which was supposed to take only forty-five minutes, took the doctor hours. During my near-death experience I felt myself floating over my body, and as if I were watching a movie, I saw the doctors and nurses around me working feverishly to spare my life. Then suddenly I found myself in the waiting area where my mother and husband were praying.

The experience was unique because I was not floating on the ceiling, yet my feet were not touching the floor. I was floating easily without any constraints through the operating room and immediately found myself in the waiting area. My mother cried as she uttered that she wished she could take back all the harsh things she had said and done to me in my life up to that point. I experienced the most compassion I had ever felt for her and all I wanted to do was comfort her. There was no hate or fear . . . only love.

Immediately after feeling this overwhelming compassion for her, it was as though a vacuum had sucked me back into my body. I awoke in the recovery room with the strangest feeling: anger for having to be here again.

During this experience, I felt the most peace that I've ever felt in my life. Nothing on this earth can possibly express that indescribable feeling. As I said earlier, I felt like a spectator watching the nurses and doctors working feverishly to save me. Yet, there I was still "alive," and with this euphoria came knowledge that I was now free from the heavy weight of my body. I was as light as a feather and could go anywhere I wished simply by thought.

Despite having my NDE, I didn't really understand that I had died and that they had lost me on the operating table. At first, this thought didn't cross my mind. The only thing I felt upon coming through was anger at having to be here once again. My only desire was to continue feeling the peace that I had just left behind on the Other Side.

The doctor later came to tell me that I had given him quite a fright and asked me why I did not want to live. Of course I did not see it that way, but he said he had to fight very hard to bring me back. He went on to tell me I had so much to live for and wanted to know what was so bad that I did not wish to be here. I had never considered suicide and never have since then; it's nothing I'd ever do. So to me his speech was odd because it was as if he thought I had wanted to die. I thought, "Why is it that he seems to be blaming me for what happened? I had nothing to do with it."

What seemed to me to be only moments were actually hours for everyone else. Unfortunately, I did not get to see heaven. I feel it's because I would not have returned to continue my journey here if I had. The peace and feather-light feeling was nothing I'd ever felt either before or since that experience. Although I have had vivid dreams where I felt as if I was floating, nothing comes close to what I experienced that day.

I, of course, had no doubt whatsoever that what I had experienced was real, but it was comforting that I received further confirmation from my mother when she admitted that she did, in fact, say what I heard her say to my husband in the hospital waiting room. She had never brought me flowers before, but on that day she handed me a dozen roses. When I told her what I had witnessed her saying to my husband, she broke down in tears. She was in total shock and had no idea how to respond.

The next few weeks were a burden to me. My body felt heavy, and all I wanted to do was close my eyes and not wake up again. And just to reiterate what I said earlier, I had never thought of suicide before this incident. I had never ever wanted to die. So these feelings that I was having felt very strange and out of character for me. As time went on, the longing for that light feeling and peace began to subside, and life eventually became more tolerable.

In summary, I know that there was a reason God did not take me "home" on that day. I still had many lessons to learn in this life. For one thing, I saw my mother in a totally different way. I felt only love and compassion for her. The Heavenly Father had a plan for my life twenty-seven years ago and knew I had reason to go forth. I truly believe that I would not have been able to accomplish as much as I have had it not been for the knowledge I learned as a result of my NDE.

Life means so much more than most people realize. I am here for a reason; we all are. But when the time comes for me to finally leave this earth, I have no fear whatsoever of death. In fact, I welcome the peace I know death will bring me someday. Meanwhile, my journey here continues till God is ready to call me. Until then, I have the advantage of knowing that the peace will come and that one day I will be reunited with my daughter and those who got to go "home" before me.

The Indescribable Geometric Design

Brad Steiger
Iowa
www.bradandsherry.com

I became a firm believer in the survival of the human spirit at the age of eleven when I underwent a dramatic near-death experience (NDE). I was left with the firm conviction that the human soul is indestructible and that we need not fear death.

Still to this day I have a blurred memory of losing my balance, falling off the farm tractor that I had been driving, and landing in the path of the implement with the whirling blades. I remember pain as the machine's left tire mashed my upper body and broke my collar-bone. And then I no longer felt any pain as the blades clutched my head and ripped at my scalp and skull. I had left the body, and I was now floating many feet above the grisly scene.

I was relieved when my seven-year-old sister June, who had been riding with me, brought the tractor under control, but I was becoming more detached about such matters by the moment. Although I had some sense of identification with the mangled Iowa farm boy whom I saw lying bleeding underneath me on the hay stubble below, I was growing increasingly aware that this unfortunate lad was not who I really was. The Real Me now seemed to be an orangish–colored ball that was intent on only moving steadily toward a brilliant Light. At first, because of my religious orientation, I believed the illumination to be a manifestation of Jesus or an angel coming to comfort me, but I could discern no distinct forms or shapes within the bright emanation of Light. All I seemed to feel was an urgency to become one with that magnificent Light.

Strangely, though, from time to time my attention seemed to be divided between moving toward the wondrous Light and descending back toward the hay field. I opened my eyes, blinked back the blood, and became aware of my father, shocked, with tears streaming down his face, carrying my body from the field. And then I discovered a most remarkable thing: I could be in two places at once. I could exist physically in my father's arms as he carried my terribly injured body from the field, and at the same time, I could be above us, watching the whole scene as if I were a detached observer.

When I became concerned about my mother's reaction to my dreadful accident, I made an even more incredible discovery: the Real Me could be anywhere that I wished to be. My spirit, my soul, was free of the physical limitations of the human definitions of time and space. I had but to think of my mother, and there I was beside her as she labored in the kitchen as yet unaware of my accident.

I put the newly found freedom to other tests. I thought of Jim, Dave, Lyle, and Ralph—the friends with whom I planned to see the Roy Rogers/ Gene Autry double-feature that night in our local theater. Instantly I was beside each one of them as they worked with their fathers on their own farms. And then I was back with Mom trying to put my arms around her, wanting her to be able to feel me. Disappointed, I was forced to conclude that she could neither see nor feel me. My normally very attentive mother had absolutely no awareness of my spirit form.

It was August 23, Mom and Dad's anniversary. We had been trying to finish work early so that we could eat at a restaurant before the double-feature began. I had certainly given Mom and Dad a wonderful anniversary present. And my sister! I had probably scarred her for life—a seven-year-old girl having to watch her brother being run over and killed.

Killed. That was when it occurred to me that I was dying. I had an awful moment of panic. I did not want to die. I did not want to leave my mother, father, and sister.

And then the beautiful Light was very near to me, and I perceived a calming intelligence, a Being composed of Pure Light that projected before me a peculiar, three-dimensional geometric design that somehow instantly permeated my very essence with the knowledge that everything would be all right.

The very sight of that geometric design somehow transmitted to me that there was a pattern to the universe and a meaning, a divine plan, to life. My panic and my fear left me, and I experienced a blissful euphoria, an incredible sense of Oneness with All That Is. I was ready to die and to become one with the Light.

But even though I was at peace with what appeared to be the fast-approaching reality of death, I had misinterpreted the reason why the intelligence within the Light had shown me the geometric representation of the Divine Plan. It seems that an integral part of my mission on earth was to testify to others about what I had been shown.

In the issue of the *National Enquirer* dated August 12, 1973, our former family physician Dr. Cloyce A. Newman was interviewed about my near-death experience that had occurred twenty-six years before. Dr. Newman, who was at that time living in retirement in Homestead, Florida, told of his shock when my father carried me into his office and how he had had me rushed by car to St. Mary's Hospital in Des Moines, about 140 miles away: "He was very seriously injured and on the verge of death. We managed to get him to a specialist, and it saved his life."

I was in and out of the body during those 140 miles, and I did not come back with any serious intention of staying in that domicile of flesh until the surgery was about to begin. At that point, it seemed as though some energy was insisting that I return to participate in the medical procedure. I came back with such force that I sat up, shouted, and knocked an intern off balance. I continued to struggle until the soft voice of a Roman Catholic sister pacified me long enough for the anesthesia to take effect.

Although my life-force remained in the eleven-year-old body to co-operate with the surgery, my Real Self left to spend the next twelve hours in a delightful park in another dimension complete with a band-stand, ice cream vendors, and smiling, pleasant people.

About 1982 I was attempting to describe the geometric design to a number of other men and women who had undergone near-death experiences. When I found myself unable to provide a meaningful description of the pattern, I stated that the design—so clearly envisioned by me to this day—appeared to be ineffable, beyond human description. Two or three of the group stated that they understood what I was attempting to explain, for they too had been shown some kind of tranquilizing, yet revelatory, geometric object which they also found impossible to describe in mere words.

It was not until 1987 when my wife Sherry Hansen Steiger began to conduct seminars utilizing computer-derived images of fractal geometry that I saw designs which very closely approximated what I had been shown during my near-death experience. The central purpose of her seminar was to demonstrate the sacredness and the multidimensional Oneness of all creation.

From the perspective of my now seventy-three years, I can see that my near-death experience at the age of eleven was a most fortunate one. Certainly one of the questions that every thinking man and woman eventually asks is, "Is there life after physical death?" I was blessed to have that eternal puzzler answered for me in the affirmative before I entered my teens.

I was shown through my powerful near-death experience that there is an essential part of us, perhaps most commonly referred to as the soul, which does survive physical death. This knowledge has greatly influenced my attitude toward life as well as toward death.

And I am far from alone in having been granted this emancipating awareness, this life-altering assurance. Since 1967 I have distributed questionnaires to readers of my books as well as to my lecture and workshop audiences. Of the more than 30,000 people who have returned completed forms, 72 percent state that they have had a near-death experience; 95 percent report out-of-body experiences; 86 percent claim an illumination experience.

. . . .

About Brad Steiger

Brad is the author and coauthor of 168 books with over 17 million copies in print including *Love is a Miracle, One with the Light; Real Ghosts, Restless Spirits, and Haunted Places; Touched by Heaven's Light; Strangers from the Skies*, and several others. He has also written more than 2,000 articles with paranormal themes and is also the former writer of his own weekly newspaper column, "The Strange World of Brad Steiger."

He is the recipient of many awards including the Metaphysical Writer of the Year and Lifetime Achievement Award at the National UFO and Unexplained Phenomena Conference. He has made many television and radio appearances. These include, among others, *Ted Koppel, ABC Evening News with Peter Jennings, NBC Evening News with Tom Brokaw, The Joan Rivers Show, Entertainment Tonight, Inside Edition, George Noory's Coast to Coast*, and many more. For more information, please visit www.bradandsherry.com.

God, I Need You NOW

Cyndi Smith
Connecticut
cyndismith1@gmail.com

I was eighteen, free, and invincible (or so I thought), but that sure was a stupid way of thinking. My brother Scott had just been released from the hospital not more than four days before my car accident. My poor parents had to deal with two children suffering near fatal accidents within two weeks of one another.

Scott had his accident on the day of my high school graduation in June 1982. He rolled his newly renovated Volkswagen and flew out the top sustaining a serious head injury. I vividly remember holding hands in prayer begging God to bring him back from his coma. The doctors were planning to do surgery if he hadn't started bleeding from his nose and ears thereby releasing the pressure. Luckily, he did wake up and no surgery was required. At that time I didn't really put much more thought into my prayers being answered.

I never went to church except with a girlfriend in grade school. She was a Mormon and a very nice girl with a great family. I loved the church events, and my parents had no issues with letting me participate. I had heard a little bit about Jesus but was somewhat skeptical. And all I knew was that when I prayed for God to prove himself, "If you are really there, God or Jesus, then make lightning," nothing happened, and it wasn't going to either. I was in California! So that is about as much thought as I put into it. Other than this I had no formal religious upbringing or education. I guess you could say I lived my life with blinders on.

On July 2, the day of my fateful accident, my brother in his robe and slippers with a bandage around his head walked outside with me. He looked at me more seriously than ever before and firmly announced, "Please! Be careful."

I didn't have too much to worry about at that time. I had applied and been accepted to attend the Fashion Institute for Design and Merchandising to become an interior decorator. I would never do that. I had just celebrated my high school graduation and was on my way to the Colorado River in Arizona to celebrate. After my trip to the river, I was going to fly out to Delaware where my best friend from high school had relocated. I was meant to spend a week there. It was my graduation present from my parents. Unfortunately I never made it. Instead I would be spending the next three months in the hospital.

I briefly recall that fateful day. There were six of us—three girls and three guys. I had never met the driver before, but I remember that he was attractive.

Before taking off, Linda Pearson and I went to the grocery store to pick up hot dogs, hamburgers, and booze. I recollect very clearly a moment of unusual fascination that I had with her. I was literally mesmerized by her calm and relaxed demeanor. I couldn't figure out what it was with her. Looking back I see that she appeared ethereal to me. She was also very pretty. She had long black/brown hair down her back and spoke quietly as well as knowingly. She wore bunches of bangle bracelets around her wrists. Each one seemed to have a specific meaning. At twenty-one she was older than I.

I climbed into that large truck, so excited. I had on a pair of blue running shorts and a cutoff T-shirt with a pair of high-heeled flip-flops.

I was just beginning to realize that my body was a commodity. But that sure came to a screeching halt! I was about to take hold of a completely new way of thinking and a completely new me.

When we got on the road, I situated myself in the back. The Ford Bronco was big enough for all of our luggage to fit underneath the flat carpet-lined bed. There were two big windows on either side that ballooned out. There appeared to be room for at least ten. Kelli, Eddie, and I sprawled out in the back while the driver (whom I will call Mike), Linda, and Ronnie were in the front. We were drinking, and from this point this is what I remember: We made a bathroom stop at Denny's. There were some pretty shady characters in there sitting around. I don't remember how long we had been driving. But I know that the ride to the river was over four hours from my house. So, who knows? I do know that I was intoxicated because I wasn't walking too straight, and those guys were heckling us girls quite a bit.

Then I remember a little later pulling over. Linda and I jumped out of the truck to relieve our bladders. (Remember we were way out in the middle of the desert, and there was nowhere else to go!) There was a bit of an incline so my high-heeled flip-flops and I were sliding all over the place. Giggling as we both ran up the incline, we discussed changing seats. Linda said I should help keep Mike awake so I got in the front seat in between Ronnie and Mike. Unbeknownst to me, that was the last time I would ever run, wear high heels, and speak directly to Linda.

Mike and I were flirting with each other and laughing when I leaned over to change the music station on the radio. That was the end of our ride to the Colorado River.

The next thing I remember seemed more like a dream. There was Lesa—the friend that I was supposed to go to Delaware with. I was telling her something about what a great trip we're going to have. Looking back on it now, she tried to hold back her tears and went along with whatever it was I was mumbling. Then I saw my cousin Dennis—this too felt like a dream.

I woke up from this dream state and was somewhat surprised to find that Kim (a friend from high school) was there cupping her mouth with her hands as she cried hysterically! I immediately felt puzzled and said, "Kim, don't cry! What's the matter?" She sat down on the one fold up chair in this little cubby-like room. I noticed that there were curtains around me just like in a hospital. In fact, I thought, I AM IN THE HOSPITAL! The last thing I remembered was that I was on my way to the river.

"What happened?" I wondered. "I must have been in an accident, but why is Kim so upset?" "Kim, I am okay! Everything's okay!" I said. Gasping for air, she cried, "How is everyone else?" I found it odd that she would ask me this question but replied, "Everyone else is fine. Don't cry, Kim. I'm fine." But I wasn't fine at all and what Kim was crying about was what she was not prepared to see. She had been the only person who came to see me when no one was there to tell her what to expect and what to say or not to say.

As I lay there, I wondered, "How is everyone else?" I had no idea that my entire world would change and never be the same from this very moment. With a questioning tone to her voice and tears pouring down her cheeks, Kim mumbled, "Well, I read in the paper that Linda was killed."

Time stood still.

I heard myself saying, "No, Kim. Everyone else is fine. Why would the paper say that?" Kim, realizing that she had stepped over the line, jumped up off her chair, "I have to go; my five minutes are up." After quickly excusing herself, she was gone, and I was left there alone to think.

Oddly enough that was the last time I ever saw her. I often wonder if my recollection of that time so many years later is accurate and if she lives with this memory in a negative way. I often wonder if she has any idea of the gift she actually gave me that day.

Looking around I became aware of smells and sounds. Yes, this was a hospital, and I was in a room just as my brother had been. I was in the intensive care unit. Questions rushed in: "Oh man, what had happened? When did this take place? Why am I here? What is this bed I am lying on? Why is it so hard? Why are my arms so weak?" My heart began to race as I felt around asking myself one question after another. I felt pinned down and couldn't move my body or my head. I could barely lift my arms, but when I did, I realized I could feel thick scabs on the top of my body. As I lay there in bewilderment, I felt the call button for the nurse's station. I pushed on it, and I could hear on the other side of the curtain a buzzing noise. I waited but not for long until a lady opened the curtain and came over to my bedside.

"What happened to me?" is all I asked.

Stunned, she hesitated, thought, and then said, "Cyndi, I'll be right back." And she was gone.

I knew something was really wrong here, but I wasn't sure what.

Then the curtain opened again. My brother Scott and my friend Kelli came walking in. Tears were running down their faces. I was confused. Then it hit me. Linda really had been killed. No words were spoken. I began to cry, and I yelled out as I began to panic, "Why didn't anyone tell me?" Scott and Kelli tried to console me. They were speaking, but I can't remember what they said except, "The doctor said you weren't ready to hear it. You asked about everyone else in the car but Linda!" I felt frantic and tried to lift myself up fighting against my uncertain weakness while they quickly and loudly yelled, "Don't move your neck. Cyndi, stop! You have to stay still." But all I wanted to do was get out of there. I got my arms up somehow to my head to figure out what was holding me down. The entire time one of them was desperately trying to tell me to stop! And I couldn't get whatever this was in my head off so I could sit up when I heard, "CYNDI, DON'T MOVE; YOU BROKE YOUR NECK!"

"What?"

"You broke your neck AND your back! You aren't supposed to move! You need to stay still!"

Well, I think that woke me up a bit! "I did what?"

"You broke your neck and your back; you are in traction."

"Oh my God, I did what?" Then it hit me; I couldn't move my legs. "I can't move my legs!" I said.

"You broke your leg and it is in traction."

"My neck and my leg," I thought. "What?" Nothing was making any sense.

All of us were crying when I suddenly went into shock, and time stood still. All thoughts stopped. All tears stopped. Everything seemed to stop. There was nothing. I remember saying, "Leave me alone." They protested because they did not want to leave my side. I am not sure what it was I said or how I said it, but they reluctantly departed from that curtained, square space surrounding me, leaving me in silence and shock beyond belief.

I still don't know what possessed me to do it since I never believed before, but I simply said, "God, I need you NOW!" Immediately, perhaps the exact time I said it, I felt two very, very large hands underneath my body—one under my back and head, and the other holding my legs. They seemed to be lifting my spirit up off of that hard bed. I unequivocally knew that those were the hands of God. An immediate peace overcame me. There was no more fear, but there was darkness. The darkness was completely black but was also totally peaceful and came from my solar plexus. This darkness was not me, but yet I was part of it. Then far, far into the distance a little Light glowed.

This Light came closer and closer but was not separate from me. It was me! It was in me! I felt calm warmth in that Light which began to grow in my belly. The Light came closer and closer, and with it came more warmth, peace, serenity, love, light, and an all-consuming love. As the Light came closer, it got stronger but not blinding; instead it increased the love, peace, and perfection, until the Light enveloped me. It is difficult for me to explain, but the Light was me. And all around me, it was the be-all and the end-all.

This was home. It was perfect. This was the Truth, the Light, and the Way. This was God. Then I felt and saw a great many spirits or entities. It was not quite unlike the shape of a plastic water bottle with water in it. There were many of them welcoming me. All of them I loved and was loved by. They surrounded me, and I felt even more loved. There was an exchange of love. These souls, for lack of a better word, were important to me, but none stood out as more loved than the other. I knew that there were four of these entities directly surrounding me. All of them held a great purpose to me and my life, but the specifics were uncertain. I was very happy.

To my left was Jesus in the form of light and the size of a redwood tree in California. He was bigger than life. His hands were outstretched, and his robe drooped from his arms and light flowed down them like a waterfall. His figure was pale but obvious. There was no doubt in my mind that it was Jesus.

Just as I saw him, a telepathic communication began between us. In this space I knew everything: everything that ever was, the immediate present, and all that ever will be. Simply stated, I knew everything and in it I felt peace and love. There was no pain in this Light. There was only love—unconditional love. There was no fear, only love and certainty. There were no mistakes, no accidents—just purity.

When I say that I spoke with Jesus, I don't mean I heard spoken words. There were not words at all but an all-knowing understanding of the communication that was more clear than words, by far! This was a full expression of the heart and mind. Unfortunately I don't know how to explain this experience more clearly. It was simply beyond description.

I asked Jesus, "What am I to make of this?" and Jesus said, "Whatever you shall want or desire will be yours at any given moment; you can have anything you want."

I replied, "If I walk with a cane, I will be happy."

And Jesus said, "So be it."

The next thing I remember is my doctor on my left side. I believe it was the next day. Tears coming down his check, he held my hand in his and said sadly, "I don't know if you will ever walk again."

I looked him straight in the eye, no tears, only absolute, certain knowledge, "Don't cry. I will walk again; you'll see. I know it. I met Jesus yesterday, and he told me so." The doctor seemed a bit shocked, to say the least, but whatever he was thinking, he did not say.

I often wonder what would have become of me had I not experienced the Light. I seriously think I wouldn't be walking today. I believe that my experience is why and how I knew without a doubt that I would walk again.

Looking back, I believe that while I was in the Light and knew everything there was to know, I also knew the right choice to make. Ever since I was born, I've always had a strong sense of purpose in my life. I firmly believe that our sole purpose here on earth is to love and be loved.

When the accident happened and I was first thrust back into the community as a disabled participant, I was really just surviving day-to-day. It was an emotionally painful time for me as I was desperate to find a new identity of who I was and what the future held for me. I realized that I had to like myself first and foremost.

Learning to walk again was a sure test to my ego! If you can't keep your head up high, then you might as well just give it up. You need to feel acceptance and love from those around you. I hadn't shared my experience with too many people because far too often it wasn't welcomed. When I did tell others, I was met with, "What kind of drugs were you on?" or "You must have been hallucinating?"

Regardless of what others may think or say, it doesn't faze me. I knew and still know to this day that my experience in the Light was as real as the air I am breathing at this moment. Although the experience was unlike anything I would ever participate in on this earth plane where everything is dimensional in nature, it was actually more "real" than anything I have ever experienced in life. I don't know how long I was in the Light, nor did it matter. Time didn't exist.

Due to the fear of being ridiculed, I went about my life and kept quiet about what I later learned is known as a near–death experience (NDE). Some years later I got married in California and moved to New York City and then to London. I spent the next thirteen years being married and the next three years after that getting a divorce.

Early in my marriage I attended college in London and happened to meet someone whose wife was a psychic medium. I had never had a psychic reading before and was curious. When I finally had the opportunity to meet her at school, I couldn't resist asking, "How do I know you are for real?" She responded by asking me if I were wearing something that I had had for some time and that no one else had ever used.

Thinking quickly, I gave her my wedding band. She then closed her eyes and took a deep breath, relaxing. Almost immediately she spoke saying the word "deception." I wrote this down on a piece of paper although it made no sense to me at the time. She went on and on about things that didn't make much sense to me, but then she said a couple of things that sparked my interest. She told me that my mother had something going on with her leg. (My mother was actually in surgery for her ankle after having fallen off the curb in a parking lot.)

She went on to tell me that my husband should have his heart checked. (He did and was told he had exceptionally high triglycerides).

She talked about many people giving me a date on which she said a birth, marriage, or death would occur. It ended up being the day my grandfather passed. The reading continued on in this fashion until she surprised me by saying that I had a guardian angel with me at all times.

This angel, she explained, had something around her neck, perhaps the collar of a Victorian dress. "She has long brown/black hair, and she is pointing to her bangle bracelets." I couldn't believe what I was hearing. My eyes began to water, and the hair stood up on my arms as I belted out, "Laura, it is Laura." She opened her eyes and looked directly at me, "Actually I am getting the name Linda." Looking back, I don't know why I said Laura instead of Linda. Perhaps it was due to all the shock and excitement of that moment.

On this unforgettable day I learned that Linda was now my guardian angel! Perhaps this was the reason I felt such a connection to her on the day of the accident. I felt so honored. The psychic went on to tell me I shouldn't feel guilty. What happened was meant to happen. Up until this point I had lived with the guilt of having changed seats with Linda. She was thrown out the back of the shell of the truck and was decapitated. I imagine that the "Victorian dress" this woman was seeing was actually a neck brace of some sort!

This chance reading changed my life in so many ways. Was it coincidental or just another message I was meant to be given? I was again reminded of the accident, my NDE, and the fact that death is not the end. I went on with my studies until I became pregnant with twins. My then husband and I were surprised by the news.

I had no idea that I was about to be given another sign. I gave birth to two beautiful healthy boys who mean the world to me. They were born on none other than the fateful July 2, THE SAME DAY OF MY CAR ACCIDENT twelve years earlier, the same day of Linda's death, the beautiful girl who had captivated me.

During my NDE I said that if I walked with a cane, I would be happy. Well, today I am very happy, and yes, I walk with a cane.

The Land of Golden Light

--◄◆►--

Denise Linn
www.deniselinn.com

At the tender age of just seventeen, Denise Linn's life as she knew it came to a screeching halt when she was intentionally run over by a car and subsequently shot by a fanatical gunman. Riding her motorbike down a beautiful scenic road in Ohio, she was suddenly struck from behind by a speeding driver and thrown into a ditch nearby.

While she lay on the ground in excruciating pain, she watched as the driver circled back around. She was thinking he was coming to help her. Instead, Denise was horrified as he pulled out a gun and aimed it through his opened car window shooting her with meticulous precision. The bullet passed through her abdomen shattering her spleen and adrenal gland. It continued through her spine and then went through her small intestine, diaphragm, and stomach. As if this wasn't enough, the relentless bullet then penetrated her left lung causing it to collapse.

The sniper ruthlessly got out of his car, walked over to Denise, and aimed at her once again. This time, however, he did not pull the trigger.

To this day she doesn't fully understand why he didn't pull the trigger again which would have surely killed her. But she says, perhaps, it was because for some reason in that moment "I felt nothing but compassion for him. As I looked up into his frenzied eyes, I only felt love and understanding."

Left to die, she managed to crawl up toward the road where she was eventually discovered by a passing motorist who called for help. Thankfully, she made it to the hospital in time where she was met by a well-trained (albeit somewhat shocked by the scope of her injuries) emergency room staff as they worked frantically on her extensive wounds trying to spare her life.

Each wave of pain seemed to come harder than the one before until finally the pain began to subside, and she saw herself being drawn into what she called a womblike darkness. Once she made it through the darkness, however, she emerged into a beautiful symphony of golden light.

The following is an excerpt from her book *If I Can Forgive So Can You:*[1]

> I tried to look down at myself, but I didn't have a body. My "self" was everywhere, without limits of time or space. I wasn't separated from the universe. Somehow that didn't seem unusual. Everything seemed more real than I had ever experienced. It was as if my teenage life up to that time had only been an illusion . . . a dream. Just like when you wake up in the morning and your dream, which had seemed so real, begins to fade into the "reality" of the day, my entire life up to that point seemed to be nothing more than the passing whisper of the wind.
>
> There was no past, no future, because all time flowed in a continuous, everlasting "now." I tried to think of the past, but I couldn't. It just didn't exist. The past and the future folded

[1]Denise Linn, *If I Can Forgive So Can You* (Carlsbad, CA: Hay House, Inc., 2005), 79–80.

into the glowing light to form an infinite present.

I wish with all my heart that I could take you there, if only for a moment, because infused in this exquisite "now-ness" was a most perfect love. It was the love that lies at the very heart of our being, a love that is as natural as breathing. It was a love that goes beyond all boundaries, like a vast, unlimited ocean, penetrating every cell and molecule of my being. The love I experienced wasn't the type that you can fall into or out of. If God is love, then in those few moments beyond death's door, I experienced Divine Love. It was without boundaries and indescribable in its sweetness.

Glowing and shimmering as it flowed to the distant horizon, a golden river of light manifested itself at my feet. Stepping into its warmth, I knew that I would never return to my earthly life when I reached the other side. I wouldn't have to be trapped in a body that was damaged and in excruciating pain. I could escape the trials of my childhood and the abuse of my parents.

As I walked across the river, part of me wanted to let go and dissolve into it. I wanted to surrender to that powerful current, meld my being with its greater force. Where would the river take me? To the far shores of the universe? To the center of the heart of God? I didn't care. Yet I could feel the pull to the far shore. I knew that I had to make it to the other side of the river to be free. Every step took me closer to my true home. But before I could reach it, I heard a deep voice reverberate inside my mind: *You may not stay here. There is something you need to do.*

I screamed, "No-o-o-o-o! No! No!" I felt as if I had been lassoed and was being dragged back to my physical body. "No! I don't want to go back. It's too hard. I'm not ready! No!"

I had a spontaneous memory of my cousins on the Oklahoma ranch practicing their calf-roping skills on me. I know now that the "rope" I felt around my middle was my "astral cord" that was pulling me back to my body. The harder I struggled, the more insistent that "rope" was around my mid-section, steadily yet firmly pulling me back. (In ancient times, it was believed that each person's soul was connected to the body by an invisible cord. As long as it was intact, the person's soul could leave the body; however, once it was severed, the body died.)

Denise endured a long and difficult healing even though her chance of survival was considered by many to be nil. Newspaper headlines and doctors alike hailed her recovery as a miracle. Despite what she went through, Denise believes what she lost on that day doesn't compare to what she gained. Her near–death experience blessed her life in countless, indescribable ways.

Whenever she was in pain, she often felt a comforting hand slip into hers during the nighttime hours when she was alone. She would open her eyes expecting to see a doctor or a nurse, but no one was there. She felt this comforting hand many times during her long hospital stay and now believes the presence was an angel. Angels have continued to come into her life ever since.

Although she has suffered many physical and emotional scars from the assailant's attack, she now knows life does not end at death. We are all connected, and love is all that matters.

. . . .
About Denise Linn

Denise is an internationally renowned teacher in the field of self-development. She's the author of the bestseller *Sacred Space*, the award-winning *Feng Shui for the Soul*, and sixteen other books, which are available in twenty-four languages. Additionally she has a top-rated radio show.

She has appeared on Oprah several times and in numerous documentaries worldwide. Denise gives seminars on six continents and is the founder of the International Institute of Soul Coach, which offers professional certification programs in life coaching and past life coaching certification. For more information, please visit her Web site at www.deniselinn.com.

A Being Named Melchizedek

Martha Cassandra St. Claire, MA
Oregon
Martha@marthastclaire.com
www.marthastclaire.com

In 1974 while I was water skiing with friends, I had an amazing near–death experience that not only changed my life but also gave me a prophetic glimpse into our planetary future. The following is a portion of my NDE experience.

My boyfriend was driving the boat, while his friend was "the watcher." As I skied my last run of the day, the waves were so rough that I was forced to let go. As I fell, my left forearm got tangled in the rope, and I was dragged helplessly behind the speeding boat. This event took place unnoticed by my friends who continued to chat and drink beer, not watching me as they should have.

Struggling to hold my breath, I felt huge pain in my arm. Then suddenly I found my spirit rising out of my body with no more physical pain, and I was looking down at myself being rapidly dragged behind the boat with my face being force-fed river water. I watched my two friends still totally oblivious to what was happening, and I saw my three-year-old son playing on the shore with our other friends.

Without warning, my spirit was soon traveling through a comfortable dark tunnel. It felt familiar as though I had been there before. When I came out of the tunnel, I was in the midst of the most beautiful flowers that I have ever seen. They were all around me, gorgeous and colorful yet with shades and hues not ever seen on earth. It felt as if I was standing on solid ground, yet I was not. I was in the garden briefly and then instantly out in the universe.

There were stars and galaxies, and it was just the most incredible sight imaginable. However, just like the tunnel, this all felt familiar. It was not odd or unusual, nor was it frightening to be in this heavenly divine place. I couldn't have been happier to be there. As I experienced this, I had no concerns whatsoever about my physical body; I had no concerns about my earthly existence.

Many people who have had near-death experiences describe being met by Jesus, God, or a loving relative. In my case a being named Melchizedek appeared before me. He did not tell me his name, yet I recognized him as a guide for me. I knew that he knew me intimately. When we are in this wonderful heavenly place, we know things by telepathy. There is no need for words. Melchizedek was just beautiful with big blue eyes and a gray beard. With a magnificent turban and head scarf he stood about eight or nine feet tall wearing robes of rich burgundy, gold, and deep green colors. He looked ancient and eternally young at the same time. To look into his eyes was to commune with angels.

I knew that I had always known him as he looked at me and simply asked, "Are you ready to come?" I then exclaimed in surprise, "Already?" At that moment I remembered that my soul chose to come to Earth. I remembered who I was before I was born and that we are not here by random accident nor are we here as victims. We come here not only to learn and grow but also to give and to receive love in the physical and so much more. Knowledge such as this had been with me since early childhood (via two childhood NDEs), but my visit with this divine being brought it more fully to my conscious awareness.

As I stood before Melchizedek, I remembered that I had made a previous agreement or contract with him. I also felt as if I had "flunked Earth" and had not yet completed what I had come to do. It was as though my earthly personality was not in complete alignment with my soul. Yet, I was told I could come home; clearly, he saw me differently.

I saw myself fully with my strengths and flaws. But there was no judgment. There is no divine judgment when we die. We judge ourselves because everything that we do is reflected back to us. God is unconditional love, and we are ruled by a universal law of cause and effect. We are also richly blessed with mercy and grace.

Some souls are told that they need to go back because it is not their time, and others, of course, are told that it is their time and continue on to the Other Side. In my case, I was given a choice.

Melchizedek showed me what would happen if I didn't return to Earth. I saw into the future. I saw that my body would be carried to shore where I would be given mouth–to–mouth resuscitation without success. My boyfriend was crying, and I knew he would carry the guilt for the rest of his life. I also saw my young son, and I knew that I could not bear to leave him even though my ex–husband would have cared for him.

In heaven I noticed a glorious border of light, and I knew that I could not go past that border. If I did, I would not be able to return to Earth. I made a decision to come back knowing that I had a life mission to fulfill, as we all do, so I told Melchizedek that I needed to come back even though I totally wanted to remain in heaven and filled with the most glorious golden light of the Divine Presence, which was home. It is very difficult to describe, but all I can say is that this was being in the realm of God. It was beyond any sense of a male or even female God presence, and it was beyond religious doctrine. It was ALL THAT IS. It is peace. It is Divine Light. It is HOME.

Finding myself back in my body, I was conscious and yet coughing up water. I temporarily panicked as I regained consciousness a distance from the boat with my life belt still attached and the rope enmeshed deeply into the shredded muscle of my left arm a few inches above my wrist.

My boyfriend quickly dove in the water and started swimming to me after I tried to yell, all the while coughing and asking, "Can't you see I am drowning out here?" My soul was blissful, but my body carried shock from the trauma. When we finally reached the shore, my son asked, "What took you so long, Mommy? I thought you were never coming back." I knew then that he was intuitively aware of much more than my simply water skiing on the Sacramento River delta.

After this NDE I was never the same. I was filled with Divine Love and Wholeness. I could see auras around people and nature and felt at one with all things. As my spiritual career soon blossomed, I continued to long for the Light and my true home.

After I returned to my life and began to heal not only from the physical damage to my arm, neck, and shoulder but also from the emotional experience, visions of the future seemed to fill my mind and inner sight. I heard things as if a voice was speaking to me, and I had visions. For example, I saw that there would be a twenty-year period from 1992 to 2012 when things would be greatly accelerated on the Earth. Energies would radically accelerate manifested in great changes including earthquakes, floods, tidal waves, and great winds.

I also saw there were areas on the East Coast that could be surprised by earthquakes, and I saw cement rubble in New York City assuming it was from an earthquake. Now, I wonder. It seemed like Japan could slip into the ocean at some point in the future. I was shown something akin to there being three days of planetary darkness. My feeling was that this was not due to a nuclear war but more from natural disasters with smoke from volcanoes that could block the sun.

Yet, I understood that this would pass and that we would always have the Light. I now feel that prayer has helped to offset some of the drastic earth changes that have been expected by many and written about throughout history.

Through my NDE I had an awakening, and I remembered who I truly was. I had access to full divine knowledge which we all have when in heavenly realms in the Light of God. I saw that there is a divine plan for Earth, yet I could not bring back fully the many mysteries of the universe that I beheld while in that heavenly dimension.

There is so much more I can say about this, but my main purpose in sharing my story is to help others to understand that there is no reason to fear death. We simply cannot die. We have so much to look forward to, and it's important to know this because our consciousness attracts consciousness.

I hope my experience will help others to understand that we are actually ascending our spiritual bodies on Earth and that it is no accident that we are here during this vitally important time in history. We all have a purpose. We are beautiful Beings of Light, literally. Truly we are souls that have come to Earth from another place, and we have existed long before physical conception.

Trust your soul and believe in yourself. Know that if you have lost loved ones, they are still very much alive in their spirit body in a heavenly place. You can still connect with your loved ones through clear intention and prayer. Remember, we are one. We are all in this together. There is much, much more than meets the human eye.

. . . .

About Martha Cassandra St. Claire, MA

Martha is a counselor, educator, NDE speaker, writer, angelic-spirit messenger, and healer, including for animals. She has had multiple near-death experiences and has served on the International Association for Near-Death Studies (IANDS) Board of Directors working as the Friends of IANDS (FOI) International Chapter Coordinator. She has also been featured in the media.

Her life purposes are to bridge heaven and earth to bring conscious awakening for others as well as comfort and insight to end of life, death, and dying issues, and to assist in bringing healing and support to the dying and those in grief. She has an MA in Gerontology, has been licensed for assisted living administration, has been trained for the Unity School of Religious Studies ministry, and has been certified for hospice care.

Martha has in-depth experience in shamanic ritual and practice, Tibetan Buddhist and Christian traditions, and with the genuine healing gifts of various Brazilian and Filipino psychic surgeons. She adores animals, has enjoyed traveling to over twenty-four countries, and is looking forward to more international adventure. For more information about her services, visit her Web site at: www.marthastclaire.com.

A Dime for More Baseball Cards

Phil Whitt
Ohio
philwhitt@sbcglobal.net

When I was five-years-old, I liked baseball cards but especially loved the small parcel of gum that came with them. Back then these cards sold for ten cents a pack.

One day my aunt gave my younger brother Rick and me a dime to buy more baseball cards. So when we were alone, I told him that it would be okay if we both ran to the convenience store as it was a short distance away. I reasoned we would go to the store, buy more cards, and then make it back before my mother or grandmother even knew we were gone.

I remember telling Rick that it would be alright if we went to the store and that I would look after him. My brother was a year younger and usually followed me around like a puppy dog. So we made our way across a two-way main road at the traffic light. At that age I understood what the colors meant. Red meant stop; yellow, slow down, and green,

121

go. I figured if I knew, this I would be fine. The only thing was I didn't pay much attention to the cars on the road.

We made it to the convenience store and bought our cards without any problems. Afterward we headed back to the crosswalk and waited for the light to change. When the light turned red for the cars to stop, I started to walk but unbeknownst to me, a driver decided to try to run the red light.

Everything was like a blur and happened so fast, but I remember my body hitting his front fender, doing a flip in the air, and then landing on the road. A neighbor, who had been working in his front yard and saw the entire accident happen, came running to my aid. At this point I kept thinking that I had to get back to my grandmother's house because I didn't want to get in trouble.

When I attempted to get back up, I tripped and fell down again. At this point, the kind neighbor picked me up and carried me over to a grassy area. Luckily, the driver did not hit Rick, and my little brother was unharmed. The driver of the car also came rushing to my side while another witness called for an ambulance.

My mother told me later that when she heard the squeal of tires and the sirens, she knew it was me and hurried toward the emergency vehicles. When she arrived at the scene, I was in and out of consciousness.

The next thing I remembered was being in the ambulance and feeling the EMTs working on me. The sirens still blared but seemed to get weaker. Then I heard a couple of voices telling me to look at Jimmy's face. I refused to look because I didn't recognize any of the voices speaking to me. Plus I didn't know who Jimmy was and had no idea who they were asking me to look at. I learned later that Jimmy was my mother's cousin who had been killed in a car accident just two months before my accident.

There was no pain, no fear whatsoever; I felt nothing but peace and warmth all around me. There was what I would describe as a soft glow around me. I also felt that if I looked at Jimmy, I could never go back. I believe that Jimmy and my other relations who had crossed over were trying to help make my transition to the Other Side an easier one.

I continued to go in and out of consciousness, and the next thing I remember is watching the ambulance doors open as they lowered me to take me into the emergency room. At this point I began to feel pain and looked to my mother for comfort. I told her how sorry I was, but she could not respond through her heavy downpour of tears. I passed out again only to awaken later in the intensive care unit. I spent many weeks recovering in the hospital. But as soon as I was strong enough, I asked my mother to tell me who Jimmy was. She was somewhat surprised by my question and told me not to worry. We would talk about it another time. She was uncomfortable talking about it and was very sensitive about the spirit world and felt I was too young to understand.

After all these years . . . fifty years, in fact, I know that I didn't want to cross over because there was more that I needed to do here on earth. One, I believe, was taking care of my mother when her body was overcome with cancer. Mom passed in 2003 and my brother Rick passed in 2000.

And after all this time, I can still remember that incredible feeling of peace. It was a gift. Life is a gift, and there is no death as many may think there is.

I Was Between Realities

Grace Hatmaker, RN, MSN, PhD student
California
gracehatmaker@netptc.net

The nurse stood by my left and said, "I can't get her blood pressure." All the while I could feel her trying to detect a pressure. A resident doctor was trying to detect the pressure on my right arm. The nurse again, outwardly worried, noted that she still could not get anything.

I then heard the resident exclaim, "&%$@!" Everything suddenly changed. The pain had been released, and I felt a sensation in my stomach as though I had just dropped down from a roller coaster peak. I found myself looking down at my body from the ceiling in the left corner of the room. I could see the backs of the staff, the faces of my doctors, and the Filipino nurse.

I seemed to hover above for what seemed like forever but was actually only seconds or minutes. I'm not sure because time did not make any sense to me. The concept of time no longer seemed to apply. It was irrelevant and unattached to anything. There was no time. Time as we know it is only relevant to life on this dimension.

There I remained for just a moment or just eternity; I cannot say, but it certainly felt like a long time. Somehow I continued to exist even though I was separate from my body. This part of me that continued to exist had nothing to do with my body; it was completely comfortable and no longer felt any pain. All of the distress I had experienced before was gone. There was only peace; it felt like I was bobbing about in a warm bath.

Unexpectedly, I felt myself moving from my stationary spot on the ceiling and bobbing slowly upward and outward. I was aware that I was surrounded, but I didn't know by what or by whom. At first, it just seemed like there was a foggy grayness about me. As the speed of my upward and outward movement increased, the enclosing fog seemed to have a bright ending at a distance.

As I moved ahead through this enclosure or tunnel, I could see the brightness up ahead to my left. Beyond the walls of this tunnel, I could see a shimmering, glowing light that seemed to contain an infinite number of specks. These specks were moving about, some fast and some slow. They were all going in different directions, yet none of them touched or interfered with each other.

If I had to compare this to something, I would say it is like what you would see if you were to look at a sunbeam and notice the dust particles that ride within it. I smiled to myself as I enjoyed this happy, knowing feeling that I was akin to these specks. They were journeying between realities as was I.

I was also aware of being helped through this transition. I was in the presence of an innumerable number of others who were just like me. They were a family that I had either forgotten or didn't know. I'm not sure, but I do know that they knew all about me and were there to celebrate, comfort, ease, and move me ahead.

The tunnel structure thinned along the sides as the Light ahead continued to beckon me. I was intensely attracted to reaching this Light. As the sides of the tunnel became clearer, the Light ahead became brighter and closer as my speed increased.

The joyous anticipation that I was experiencing was indescribable. At this point I had no idea what this was about and didn't even think I was dead. I only felt like a spirit or disembodied person. I knew that the real "I" continued to exist in the absence of my earthly body. I had a sense of heightened knowing, of peace, and of assured expectancy.

As I neared the warm, glowing radiance ahead of me, I felt pure ecstasy. I was in the beginning of the Light. I was part of the Light. The Light was part of me and so much more. Somehow I knew there was more ahead but for now could go no further because something was about to take place. I felt as though I had returned to something I knew before. It was as if I had come home. I had come home not just to the beginning of me but of eternity. This is, I know, very hard to explain but yet so very important. The only thing this concept compares to is the way you feel when you look up at a beautifully clear starry sky.

As you look up, there is an awe of the glimpse we are given of the beginning of infinite space. As I savored my experience, this is what it felt like.

Again, time had no meaning. Time was an irrelevant notion. It felt like eternity. I felt like I was there for an eternity. No remnants of the tunnel remained. There was no cloud or fog. The Light was pure and all good. I needed nothing and wanted nothing as I had everything. I was in communion with the Light around me. I was part of this Light that existed forever. There was an infinite sense of knowing and understanding all. I was completely at ease.

Then from this Light came a message. There were no words, only thoughts. I was reminded of my responsibility to my two children and wanted to disagree. I didn't want anything to change, didn't want to leave, yet I felt like a change had already taken place. I no longer felt that something wonderful was ahead of me. I was being "told" benevolently yet firmly of my duty. This message was the final word and all there was to communicate with me. I wanted to hang on to my experience but at the same time knew it was pointless. I felt like a small child whose loving parent insists and directs him to bed. The directive was the only point. I had to go.

At this moment, I had my last communication with this Light. I saw it all. I saw me as I had been as a baby, a child, a teen, and an adult, all at once. At the same time I saw everything I ever did, everything I ever thought, everything! I saw events and people in my life that I previously considered important. I also saw many things that seemed not so important yet were.

I saw how others reacted to everything that I did. It was all there for me to take in and understand . . . good, bad, or indifferent. For example, I remembered an incident I dealt with in first grade at the age of six. Sister Celine had placed three holy cards on the edge of her desk in the front of the room. The cards were to be given as awards during a spelling bee after recess.

I could see the holy cards so well. The one in the middle depicted a gossamer guardian angel watching over two small children crossing a bridge. That's the one I wanted so badly. Well, as we filed out for recess, temptation overtook me, and I stole the holy card slipping it quickly into my uniform pocket. No one saw me, but I was sick with guilt so I sneaked back into the classroom while everyone was still enjoying recess and put the card back on Sister Celine's desk.

During my NDE, I remembered everything about that time in my life. What was really impressive, though, was that I was aware how very wrong my actions were. Although I had made amends, I "knew" of Sister Celine's dismay at having the card taken. I "knew" that other children saw only two cards on the desk for the spelling bee, not three. What I really "knew" was that my actions carried repercussions that affected many others.

This is the way my life was reviewed. I was deeply aware and had profound insight into everything in my life and all of my dealings with others from my birth until the moment of my near-death experience. All those in the light were witness to my life review. I was enveloped in a loving feeling and given insight to areas of my weaknesses. I suddenly realized aspects of my life that were not compatible with eternity in the light. I also knew now how to correct this. I was charged with the accountability for the remainder of my life.

I knew that more was ahead in the Light that continued forever, but I could not go there now. Seeing my life left me with the impression that my life mattered and was somehow significant as to how far I could go into the Light. My work was not yet finished, and my work was to begin inside me and within my family. I knew I had more to do and now conceded to my impending return since I fully understood the message.

Then I was given a "gift" to ease my return. As the brightness began to dull, the image of my two children were merged into my spirit. As I held their love in me, I returned to my body in the hospital bed. Since then, I have continued on with my life knowing how very accountable I am for my actions, knowing someday I will review my life once more.

. . . .

About Grace Hatmaker, RN, MSN, PhD student

Grace, the author of *Beyond This Reality*, is a full-time PhD student researching childhood injuries in a Hmong refugee group in central California. She also teaches community nursing and conducts a master's seminar at a local university. She and her husband are very active members of their interdenominational church and have done outreach work in Poland, the Czech Republic, and Mexico. In her spare time Grace loves to play the violin.

Total Bliss

Luna
Colorado

In the 1980s I was admitted into the hospital for a routine surgical procedure. Everything seemed to go well, but when the doctors were finished, my heart rate suddenly dropped. At that moment I felt my soul being sucked out of my body like a hand slipping out of a glove. Using the glove as an analogy, my feet were like the fingers of the glove and the top of my head was like the opening of the glove.

My soul rose up through the top of my head going upward above the ceiling of the hospital room. I say above the ceiling because I was very high up. As I looked down at my body still on the hospital bed, I seemed to be only two inches long. So I know I was very high up, yet I had no problem seeing. It was as though the walls of the hospital did not exist because there were no obstacles to block the view between my body and me.

I watched as the hospital workers rushed around me trying to do everything they could to revive me. They were shooting some drug into me as they put blankets on me to keep my body warm.

While this was all happening below me, I was having my own in-credible near–death experience. All I can say is I was in total bliss . . . a feeling I have not been able to recreate since that time. I was at total peace with everything that had ever happened in my life. There were no regrets, no guilt, and no "should haves." It is difficult for me to this day to describe how completely at peace I felt.

I didn't want it to end. I wanted to stay in this wonderful, blissful experience, but I kept thinking about my daughter. As a single parent at the time, I couldn't help but wonder who would raise her and how hard it would be for her to grow up without me. So I asked to come back trying with all my strength to get back into my body by focusing on my intent and desire to do so. It would have been so much easier to remain in this blissful state rather than returning to my physical body.

But apparently I had demonstrated to what I call the Source how important it was for me to come back so that I could continue to raise my daughter. At this point I was allowed to reenter my body.

During my NDE I became one with the All. I stopped taking any type of drugs. I realized that I did not need to alter my energy field in any way to improve it. I had everything I needed to heal myself. All I had to do was ask. For example, asking for a headache to go away is more effective than taking an aspirin.

Also as a result of my NDE, I stopped allowing negativity into my life. After my experience, I realized the importance of being around positive energy. So if someone was complaining or angry, I would just tune him out. I stopped watching the news or reading the newspaper. I even changed my circle of friends to ones whom I felt were more fo-cused on the happier side of life.

About ten years prior to this experience, I had become aware of the fact that I had healing abilities, but my psychic abilities came later as a result of my NDE. It was like a channel of communication directly to the Source was opened up.

I Was Completely Alive

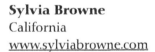

Sylvia Browne
California
www.sylviabrowne.com

I was forty-two and having routine surgery when I flatlined and encountered the following common events:

The tunnel that immediately appeared didn't come from up there somewhere; it actually rose up from my body seemingly from my own etheric substance. Instead of leading up toward the sky, it led across at maybe a twenty-degree angle confirming that the Other Side isn't some distant paradise beyond the clouds. It really exists right here among us only three feet above our ground level in simply another dimension with a much higher vibration than ours.

I didn't just feel completely alive as I moved through the tunnel; I was completely alive. Only my body, the vehicle I had traveled in during this lifetime, had conked out. I felt weightless, free, and exhilarated with the peaceful certainty that everyone and everything I ever worried about would be fine. With my newfound sense of timeless eternity, I knew that my loved ones and I would be together again in what would seem like almost no time at all.

The legendary white Light appeared ahead of me with sacred brilliance and infinite knowledge.

The figure of a loved one stepped into the large opening at the end of the tunnel, in my case my cherished Grandma Ada. The opening was wide enough that I could glimpse a meadow beyond her like any grassy, flower-filled meadow on earth with colors enriched and magnified a thousand times.

Obviously my meadow was in a near-death experience, and two things happened simultaneously to emphasize that point: when I reached out my hand to Grandma Ada, she reached out her hand as well, but her palm was facing me in a gesture that meant stop. And at that same moment I heard the faint, distant voice of a friend I'd left standing beside my hospital bed pleading, "Sylvia, don't go. You're so needed."

The sensation of returning to earth made me feel as if a huge rubber band that had been wrapped around my waist and stretched to its limit was now pulling me back. One second my hand was just inches from Grandma Ada's, and the next second I was snapped away from her and slammed back into the confining heaviness of my body.

Not only was I not glad to be back, but I felt angry, frustrated, and depressed for days afterwards.

It is God's kiss, not of goodbye but only of a brief farewell. We know we're leaving paradise not just for the sake of our own spiritual potential but for Him as well. He assures us, His children, that His perfect, unconditional, eternal life will light our way through all our days on earth and right back through the tunnel that will someday bring us safely home again.

. . . .

About Sylvia Browne

Sylvia is a world-renowned spiritual teacher, psychic, author, lecturer, and researcher in the field of parapsychology. She manifested her psychic ability at the age of three in her hometown of Kansas City, Missouri. She also started The Nirvana Foundation for Psychic Research, a nonprofit organization (now known as the

Sylvia Browne Corporation) to help further research into the paranormal. The newest addition to her ever-expanding organization is The Sylvia Browne Hypnosis Training Center which was formed to teach individuals her unique, proven hypnosis methods.

Over the years she has helped thousands gain control of their lives, live more happily, understand the meaning of life, and find God in their own unique way. Her media appearances include all major radio and television stations; in addition, her talents have been showcased on national and international programs such as *Unsolved Mysteries* and *Larry King Live*. She was a weekly guest on the *Montel Williams Show* for over seventeen years. She has over fifty published works resulting from her research into parapsychology with twenty-one appearing on the *New York Times Bestsellers List*. For more information, please visit www.sylviabrowne.com.

The Rio Guaiba River

Glauco Schaffer
New Jersey
www.ndespace.org

My father took me and my older brothers (ten and eleven) to the Rio Guaiba River in Porto Alegre, Brazil for a day of fun and fishing when I was eight–years–old. It was a beautiful, hot sunny day, and we asked my dad if we could walk up to the river a little bit on our own while he set up camp for us.

At first, he said no but reluctantly finally agreed after all three of us kept begging him to let us go. But, he told us, we had to agree not to go in the water. I remember him repeatedly telling us not to go in the water. In hindsight I wonder if he somehow sensed the danger that lay ahead of us.

We began to walk near the water leaving my father to work with the camp arrangements until we came to a bush that was half on land and half in the water. At this point one of us had the idea of grabbing onto the bush to get to the other side. I remember my brother Marco went first. Within seconds he lost his footing and went under the water. My oldest brother Carlon raced to help Marco, but he couldn't hang on and ended up in the water as well.

Neither my two brothers nor I knew how to swim. But instead of running to get my father after seeing my two brothers plunge into the waters, I jumped in to try to save them without even thinking of my own safety.

I struggled frantically in the water looking for my two brothers. I couldn't see them, and I was so scared. The water engulfed me quickly as I tried desperately to breathe. But there was no more oxygen; I could not breathe. I could only panic as I moved my arms and legs hysterically trying to save my life. My body was hitting things under the water. I don't know what these things were, but I can tell you they were very painful.

The current of the river was moving very fast from west to east towards the ocean. I can't recall how much time went by, but I reached a point when I just couldn't move anymore. I just floated underwater until I came to the bottom of the river. The water was brown so I couldn't see anything, but I didn't need to see to know that I was dying.

I tried to scream, "PLEASE GOD HELP ME!" My mother used to take me to church so I knew about God. And I don't know how, but I knew that He was the only one who could help me. My life started to fade, but then I heard the most pleasing voice telling me just to relax and that everything was going to be okay. I then felt arms embracing me.

Although I could still not see, I knew it was the embrace of a male. He was very kind and gentle. I was happy and confused all at the same time. Soon we were floating in midair and that was when I realized that I was not actually dead. We started moving upward at an extreme speed. All of my pain was gone, and I could breathe easily again. My body was not solid anymore. I could see right through it, but I could still feel myself.

We then began going towards this beautiful Light. As we got closer to it, the Light just engulfed me. It was brighter than the sun but didn't hurt my eyes. The male angel that was with me said, "*Tchau*" and faded away. I was remained there floating for a moment wondering, "What just happened? What does *tchau* mean?"

It's difficult to explain, but I felt connected to everything and everything was connected to me. Then I felt like I was not alone anymore and began to see the shape of a man coming towards me. When he got close enough, I felt the most beautiful feeling of love and belonging that I have ever felt. There are just no words that my human mind can come up with to accurately describe this feeling.

Imagine that you are in an airplane, and then it blows up. Then you wake up and realize that it was all just a dream and that you are not dead. Well, this was kind of the feeling I experienced when I realized that I wasn't really dead. I was so happy to realize that I wasn't dead. But then again, I wondered where I was and why this place felt more real and more at home to me than Earth did.

The male angel appeared again coming closer to me and speaking telepathically. He told me he was there to help me and answer my questions. Boy, did I have a lot of questions. But before he answered them, he showed me my life, and it played before me like a movie. My life was going backwards. I remember thinking, "How bad can this be? I am only eight." The first thing I remember seeing was an incident when I used a key to scratch a car. I could feel the pain that I caused because of my actions.

Then I remember thinking, "Oh, no! I'm in trouble!" But at this point my angel surprised me by saying, "Don't worry; these are just lessons." Instead of being comforted by his words, I was a bit unnerved by the realization that he could read my thoughts. All this was going on as the movie continued to play showing second by second of my entire life. And again, I could feel what I caused as a result of my actions.

Everything that I had ever done seemed to have a life of its own. For example, I felt the pain the owner of the car experienced. Then I felt the pain his wife experienced when he told her about it. This was all a very unpleasant feeling.

In addition to the not so pleasant times, I was shown the good times as well. I was shown the things I had done out of love, like the time I had brought this homeless boy to my house. We showered together; we ate together, and then I gave him some of my clothes. My angel was very happy about this and told me that these are the things that really matter—the things we do out of love for another person.

The "movie" continued as I now saw myself as a baby in my mother's womb, then just as a molecule of life . . . really small but very much alive. Today, whenever I hear of a woman having an abortion, it makes me want to cry. They don't understand that God gave them this child for a reason; they were chosen by that child. I don't know how I know this, but I just do.

The scenes of my life finally came to a stop, and then he said two words. Everything I ever wanted to know was answered by these two words. In an instant I knew everything. Then suddenly I started to miss my mother, the sun, the rain, playing soccer, and everything that made me happy. I started to think of my mother, and I could feel her pain when she would find out that all three of her sons had crossed over. But I also knew that I was being shown this because it wasn't my time yet. I sensed my mission was not complete and wanted to go back.

My near-death experience helped me to understand just how beautiful and fragile the Earth really is. I could sense the Earth breathing as if it was alive. I could see a light around everything that was alive: trees, flowers, grass, animals, volcanoes, and humans. Humans are in control over every living thing. Everything has an aura. I don't know why, but the angel told me not to tell anyone and that in time it would reveal itself. To this I said, "What?" But then I felt a jolt and realized that I was suddenly back in the water. Only this time I was being held by a different angel who was pushing me out of the water. I was human again and back in my body. What a feeling this was! Being human is a beautiful gift!

I felt somewhat drunk as I reached the surface of the water and could see the breathtaking blue sky above. I began to breathe again but panicked as I thought of my brothers. "Where are my brothers?" I uttered in alarm. I looked to my right, and there they were safe and sound right next to me walking out of the water. I then rejoiced thinking, "OH MY GOD! THANK YOU! THANK YOU!" I have tears in my eyes now just thinking about it.

People were running towards us; some were crying; some were smiling and hugging each other. They were as happy as I was, but why? I couldn't figure it out. Then I heard this police officer talking on his radio saying, "I found them. I found the kids." He told the other officers to come up the river. After a few minutes the other officers arrived and remarked in astonishment, "This can't be them. They couldn't have survived twenty-two minutes in the water and lived to talk about it!"

The medical personnel, who were at the scene, agreed, and all went back down river looking for other kids. I was standing there in a state of shock. I wanted to tell them that it was indeed us. I tried to explain what happened, but I could not get any words out of my mouth. I just couldn't speak. My mouth was moving, but no sound was coming out.

I then looked up at the sky and said, "Please give me my voice back; I won't tell anyone! Slowly, I got my voice back! I do have a stuttering problem today, but I don't care about that. I'm alive, and that's all that matters. I don't know which is better: being back here or having the knowledge that we never die.

My experience changed my life. I try to do everything out of love. Truthfully, though, this is not always easy. We live in a world of uncertainty. People don't know who God really is and don't always understand the importance of love.

Since that fateful day at the river, I have asked my brothers what they remember about the experience. Marco told me that an angel told him not to talk about it. A week went by before I asked Carlon. When I did, I was told we died, and an angel saved us. He said he also saw a movie.

We never really discussed the incident in depth probably because we were all afraid that something would happen to us if we did. Though as the years went by and I got older, I began to have the urge to tell the world that both God and heaven are real. I pray that one day the human race, the sons and daughters of God, will live on earth with that same love and peace I felt on that day. I hope that one day we will all come to the realization that we are all one.

About Glauco Schaffer
Glauco played professional soccer while living in Brazil before coming to America in 1978. He is also a former musician and the owner of a painting business called Aura Painters. According to Glauco, he named his business as such because he used to see people's auras after his near-death experience.

Today he runs a networking site for people who have had NDEs and other spiritual experiences called www.ndespace.org. Please visit his Web site for more information.

A Blow on the Head

---•◦⟨∞⟩◦•---

Joyce Hawkes, PhD
Washington
www.celllevelhealing.com

While I was cleaning the house, a leaded glass window encased in an oak frame (24"X18" and about 20 lbs.) fell off the mantel and whacked me on the head. I remember catching a glimpse of it coming toward me and feeling the impact as it drove me to my knees. At first, I felt incredible pain and then no pain as I separated from my body.

In 1971 I earned a PhD in biophysics from Pennsylvania State University and was a postdoctoral fellow with the National Institutes of Health at the Oregon Regional Primate Research Center. At that point in my life I was immersed in science and research on the ultrastructure of cell pathology in organisms exposed to environmental pollutants. I published several manuscripts in scientific journals and had no spiritual beliefs, no belief in an afterlife, God, or any religion. I had never heard of near–death experiences nor had any interest in what I would have, then, called fantasy.

I was not thinking about any of this as I whizzed down a long dark tunnel toward a Light that was drawing me to itself. I was not thinking about anything at all nor was I afraid. I was just there with all this happening so fast.

I remember slowing down, without my choice, at the entrance to this beautiful lighted place and was amazed to discover my mother and grandmother standing to the right and greeting me with so much love. They communicated to me in some way, certainly without words or hearing, but clearly inside my mind. I was astonished to see them healthy, happy, middle-aged, and so full of love and recognition for me. I would have taken any blow on the head to have had the assurance of their consciousness. What a gift!

I then passed into the place of Light: rolling hills, grass, flowers, and blue skies vibrant with color. What amazed me were the intensity, brilliance, and clarity of the color. It seemed to be coming from within each aspect of the landscape. The grass glowed green. It was so beautiful. It was so very beautiful.

Suddenly I was in the presence of a Being of Light. I could not see the face. I could communicate not in words or pictures, but rather by a direct connection. I was one with this Being of Light. I experience that connection in meditation frequently though I cannot describe it very precisely. It is beyond words. The emotions are always enhanced. I feel joy so deep that my whole self leaps with gratitude. I feel peace; I feel awe and belonging.

I did not have a specific life review but felt everything about me and my life was known, understood, and not judged. I was profoundly loved. It seemed that I was there forever in this Presence.

Without discussion or warning I was suddenly back in my body with a very sore head. A mat of dried blood was all over my hair, and I was really woozy. My physician's service asked if I had lost consciousness and I said no. How dumb! So I went to bed propped up on pillows because it hurt too much to lie prone. This was Friday night.

By Monday when I returned to the lab and work, a colleague took one look at me and hustled me off to his doctor. I had not been in Seattle that long, and I had only an OB/GYN, not a family physician. After a CT scan and neurological testing (I had no toe curl response on one side and was very wobbly), I was sent to bed and asked to not work for several weeks. The hematoma on my brain was small enough not to require surgery; the gash on my skull was sealed by now. The doctor said, "We would have stitched that for you had you come in earlier."

So for the first time in my life, I had some time to myself without some external "busyness." The images and feelings of my NDE kept coming back to me.

As I recovered and was up and about, I wandered into a bookstore. Raymond Moody's first book about near–death experiences *Life after Life* seemed to hop off the shelf into my hands. I read much of the book, maybe even all of it, standing there astonished. He described case after case of similar experiences. I could not discount what happened to me and the visions I saw. From that day I was launched on an exploration of consciousness and expanded reality that continues to this day.

After years of meditation, learning, meeting teachers and people who have had similar experiences, I had a vision that called me to healing. In 1984 I turned the lab over to one of my assistants and left my career behind to pursue a life of counseling, studying spiritual traditions in shamanic cultures, and facilitating spiritual aspects of healing. Now I continue to offer private sessions, teach, present seminars, and have published the book *Cell-Level Healing: The Bridge from Soul to Cell* to make the information I gained available to others.

. . . .
About Joyce Hawkes, PhD
Joyce Hawkes is a respected researcher and scientist in the field of biophysics, a Fellow of the American Association for the Advancement of Science, and an internationally recognized healer, teacher, and lecturer on the art and science of healing. Her book *Cell-Level Healing: The Bridge from Soul to Cell* continues to touch lives and inspire people to explore the power of the body and mind to heal. For more information, please visit www.celllevelhealing.com.

A Very Risky Transition

---··◀◁∞▷▶··---

Diego Valencia submitted by his wife Dina Valencia
Colombia
valenciana444@gmail.com

Why? I wanted answers to why my life had been so very difficult and decided to ask for them one day while in a state of deep meditation. I have had many spiritual experiences since I was a child and have the ability to foresee the future. This has caused me much distress and isolation over the years. As I meditated, I wondered what the meaning of my suffering was. Suddenly I left my body and flew to a place which was still and felt as if it were on the first floor before beginning an escalation into the higher realms. It was cloaked in a dark dimness.

I talked with some beings who told me that I was in a very risky stage of vital transition from which I might not be able to return. But I could ascend still further to talk with someone who would decide whether or not I could come back to my body. They said that the more I ascended, the greater my experiences would be and the less likely would be the possibility of my return.

It was probable that the same beings who were talking to me now would bring me back. It was like being in a train station where many beings chattered and the colors of that dimension were brownish. Farther away there were grayish entities that were helped by guides to definitely leave their terrestrial life. There was not any true color besides the tones from black and brown to white.

I saw people I knew on earth who greeted me and continued their ascension.

The guides told me I was on the threshold of death. I wondered if the persons who were dying and leaving their bodies at that moment knew where they were.

As they accompanied me, these guides were kind, tactful, and VERY COMPLIANT but impenetrable when certain questions were asked. When they did respond, it was only with a smile. The communication was by telepathy, and they knew instantly what I was thinking, but their answers were essential, concise, and certain.

They were very calm, unadorned, and with a tender sense of humor. It was then that the judgment began—but I was the only one who judged me.

Although they considered everything self–evident, they helped me understand all the contradictions, actions, guilt, and non–guilt which I was feeling from the events of my life. They comforted me with precise words and calmed me. When I felt within myself a violent dialogue that justified or blamed me, they made me understand that it was all within the game of evolution and that in the long run the events of my life were not as important as they seemed.

Then I had the sensation that I was still in a foggy place near earth.

They told me I could make the decision to continue, but it was with a maximum risk for my physical body or life. Then, identifying myself with my Diego ego in the earthly realm, I agreed to continue since the guides were willing to accompany me. I worried because of the risk. Nevertheless, I agreed discretely and humbly although there was haughtiness in my earth identity that wanted to have the experience. At the same time my cosmic conscience allowed me to make the decision without panic.

We then began to ascend at great speed without friction or effort as when one is falling but instead we were climbing. I was in quite a state, hearing a zooming sound and feeling a little dizzy as though in a car traveling at a great speed.

The guides then seemed to have disappeared. In that moment I understood my panic. I asked myself if I could resist the situation.

Suddenly with a great number of voices, I began to judge myself, blame myself, and make decisions that belonged to their own code of existence. In that moment, everything was valid and excusable because it was understood that my own position was that of a small humble spot in the opening game of evolution. If other proposals seemed more valid, they were humbly accepted because in the depth there was no real guilt.

After simultaneous cultural, legislative, and theological ideas exploded within me, the answer of the guides was "intranscendence," and they pronounced that word with a smile. All the actions I considered so important were not.

Suddenly, my mind was allowed to rest in a quiet place in order to further ascend through a translucent tunnel with a light that had a rather yellow murkiness. Then I saw many beings; some ascending, some descending. Two of them were known to me on the earth realm, and I had not seen them for more than twenty years. I also saw people unknown to me then, whom I met many years later in their bodies in the earth realm. I asked one of the two persons I did know what he was doing there, and he told me that he had had a very serious health problem and had almost died. Now the health problem had already been solved by the doctors. This is the reason he was going back to his body. Nevertheless, another person, who was a friend of my family for many years, was leaving the earth realm in a definite way, so was I told.

Then came some guides to take the friend, who had been ill, back to earth through a tubular shape. I also observed other tubular shapes through which other souls were ascending, and among them was a lady known to me and my family whose body had died. I inquired if the lady could go back but they said her time was over and that she had definitely left her body. I felt the energy of the lady perturbed, because she was confused since she did not know she was dead, but I avoided meeting her. In that moment my guides smiled.

A different lap started in which the path was transparent, silent, and accommodating. I felt the pleasure of having my conscience in total calm, escorted by the gentle but distant company of the guides and other entities whom I could not see.

Suddenly I saw another path where all the dead members of my family appeared and among them was my father.

I then entered another stage with a moment of unconsciousness, but I recovered quickly. It was as though I had crossed a purifying sauna, plunging into unconsciousness, but I soon noticed my consciousness was revived.

I understood I had undertaken a risk of no return and with repentance asked to come back because I knew I had already crossed the threshold of death. In that place everything was brighter although still not so much. I felt that only the realization of the affection I had for my family on earth motivated me to come back to my body.

I, then, had a slight but intense sensation of unrest and anguish because I understood again that I had traversed the threshold. I, therefore, asked my guides for an answer. They told me that the decision did not depend on them anymore because we found ourselves in realms that were out of their reach. The answer made me feel dazed. I asked them if they could keep on accompanying me because I wanted to have a dialogue with someone, and they kindly accepted. I later had the sensation that they took my hand.

We then shot ourselves out at a great speed with acute cosmic sounds, pure and deep echoes, and the brilliance of a light—so white, almost metallic—in which I felt that we were flying within an agreeable and refreshing wind. There were warm and exquisite odors and suddenly a fog as well as a flat floor on which I saw the guides standing.

From the white fog appeared a tremendously golden luminous figure—an androgynous Being radiating a light as bright as the sun, but not hurting my sight. The Figure, which was well delineated, began approaching me and becoming bigger in size until I saw that it was a little larger than I. Standing in awe with such WONDER for this beautiful Being, my mind almost could not comprehend the meeting. I almost lost awareness of myself as I became one with him in that immense consciousness. I was soothed by this compassionate Being.

In that amazing happiness and with only a thread of consciousness left, I turned towards my guides and whispered that I deeply thanked them for this immense experience but that I had to go back to the earth realm to undertake unfulfilled small tasks. They answered that my life would go on, nevertheless, as tortuous as it had been before with only a few attainments and that my life would last only for the time that was planned by destiny. Almost nothing of what was planned could be changed.

In my great pride and haughtiness I remained before this wonderful BEING who transcended me, of whom I felt a small part within me, and for whose kind and definite answer I waited. I turned again and looked at the Being of Light directly as he stood at a distance of about half a meter. He was a powerful and beautiful entity of extraordinary energy, but I could not see his face. I had the feeling that if I did, it would be the equivalent of staying.

Suddenly the Being made me feel an infinitely tender and noble embrace which is impossible to describe. I understood and thanked him, because everything now was possible, even refusing to stay, for I had reasons to go back to earth.

In wonderment I saw how he extended his right arm. Between us there was a dark abyss which I could pass by jumping if I took his hand, except that no return would be possible. He told me I was free to make my own decision, an offer for which I looked at him thankfully and satisfied. Inclining my head, I breathed exquisite and refreshing air.

The Being of Light slowly lowered his hand and went away, becoming smaller and smaller. He was a being of pure love, wisdom, light, and energy. The curious and kind guides then appeared again and were ready to take me back.

I jumped and fell down at horrendous speed with the sensation of a fire ball. I could not stand the friction and the unbearable noise. At the moment of maximum friction and sound, I accepted that I would die rather than stand this sensation. But to my surprise, the guides told me telepathically with luminous words to relax because I would soon arrive.

I then felt an explosion of white and red marmalade and traveled through it contrary to its flux. I finally fell with a dry and heavy fall, weighing tons, to see myself sitting on my bed with my eyes open and burning. I felt a deep pain near my heart, a pain almost unbearable, and had great difficulty breathing.

My body was rigid. My arms could not move. My feet were frozen, and I could not move them either. I could only allow threads of air to enter my lungs or else they would hurt. I felt a little dizzy and the pain in the chest was still intense. I was unconscious for a moment, but when I managed to move my waist, I closed my eyes and lay down. I was still hearing internal and external noises and zooming.

The pain in my heart lasted with intensity for one-and-a-half hours. I managed to go to the bathroom, feeling as tired as I ever had in my life. I then went back to bed and slept for twelve hours. When I woke up, I remembered the guides told me how my wife, my daughter, and I would die. I saw my complete future and that of my daughter. I was told I would remember only fragments of it at certain moments. The guides reminded me that my life would be painful but with a few moments of happiness. It had to be like that because it was programmed that way, and the purpose, although unpleasant, was very constructive and evolutionary. I could not change it.

. . . .
About Diego Valencia
Adventure was always Diego's passion growing up in an educated rural town in Colombia. As a child he picked up a paintbrush and never looked back becoming one of today's foremost artists with exhibitions around the world. He is also an accomplished poet and musician.

As an artist, he is known by the pseudonym, "WALCOPZ." To view his masterful art, please visit www.fineartamerica.com/profiles/walcopz-valencia.html.

He can be contacted at valenciaana444@gmail.com.

Dave's Transformational Experiences

David Bennett
New York
www.Dharma-Talks.com
Facebook–Dharma Talks
Twitter@DharmaTalks

In this lifetime I have had three very transformative experiences. The first was a near–death experience that I'd rather call a "new–life" experience. Before my near–death, I was a very brash young man who liked to challenge everything. I would put my life on the line for the thrill of the adventure. I think in that stage of my life I was an adrenaline junkie. My philosophy as a young adult was rather simple: enjoy life, learn how to survive, and cut your swath in life to get where you want to be. At that stage of my life it served me well. I became chief engineer on a research vessel and a commercial deep–sea diver. While on this job, there was an accident at sea and I drowned.

As you probably have heard from others who have died and returned, I went into the Light. There I was met by others, and it felt like coming home. I experienced love and acceptance such as I have never felt before. While I was in the presence of these other beings, I went through a life review. This was not just a review of what I had done in my life. I also experienced not only how my actions had affected and influenced other people but also how their feelings and emotions were connected to my actions. It is hard enough to explain this experience plus the intensities and details of the life review without judgment. There was a feeling of growth and evolvement while I underwent this review. The review continued, and I started seeing things that were unfamiliar to me—things that I had not yet lived or experienced. The group around me was very supportive through this process although there seemed to be more of them at this time. Even with their support it was still disorienting. At that moment I was told that this was not my time and that I still had purpose in my life. I then realized that I was seeing parts of my future. I also realized that I had to return to my physical body, an act that was more painful than the actual experience of drowning. Somehow I was given the strength to accept this, and I returned to the body. It was emotionally draining and mentally staggering besides being physically painful. It was a bit of a miracle in how I was revived, which only proved to me that again I was meant to experience more of this life.

After I came back, I was connected with the Light for two straight days. One part of me was in a state of shock; another part was in the body feeling the actual pain, while a third part was in the Light experiencing the physical healing of the body. During those two days I realized that I was given three incredible gifts. The first gift was acceptance. I knew who I was and could accept that I had faults and strengths. I no longer needed to beat myself up over failures. Instead I could learn, accept, and make myself a better human being. I now understood how my life could touch others without them knowing it. I also know that I am in the perfect place at all times. The second gift was tolerance. This attitude was very new to me. As I said, I liked to cut my swath through life. Suddenly, I now had a way of respecting and recognizing others' beliefs or practices. I can now see that others on their life path are experiencing what they need for their growth. Tolerance allows me to allow them to walk their paths. The third gift was my truth.

The two days after my near-death were the most powerful because it was not just the physical shock; even more it was the spiritual shock of knowing my truth. Those two days I was living with my heart wide-open. I was experiencing everything through an open heart. When I say an open heart, I mean the Light that you experience when in the presence of that unconditional love. That feeling of coming home is present in your heart, and your heart feels as though it has expanded beyond the physical body and is in touch with everything. Facing my own truth for the first time was very emotional and painful because I had to truly face myself. I had to face my faults and my strengths honestly and clearly. Then I came to recognize that everyone has his or her own truth and that it is very different from factual truth.

With these three gifts my new life started. I began to change. I didn't view anything the same way anymore. I started to work on myself. As a young man growing up in Arizona, I had gained an understanding of the Native American natural way. I tended to follow that path of observation while working on myself. Some of my greatest growth would come during times of communing with nature. My spiritual side now communicated by giving me information that I had no way of knowing. At first I didn't trust this knowledge, so I would test it. I would argue with this newly awakened spiritual side of myself until over time I grew to trust and depend upon it.

I continued to work, play, and live my life with my newfound truths until about ten years later. I went on a spiritual retreat back in Arizona where I had grown up as a teenager. My agenda was to hike some of the old trails and enjoy myself. I figured I had come a long way with my three gifts, and I thought I was doing very well. The first day of the retreat the whole group was to meet for morning meditation. I went off, away from the others, to meditate in a little grotto that I knew of. My intention was just to meditate for the purpose of calming, relaxing, and centering. Little did I know! Spirit and the Light of my near-death overcame me. I began reliving my near-death experience over and over again. But it was much different. This time Spirit was now talking directly to me, not just projecting thoughts and information. I had never tried to return to the Light or to open my heart since that original experience ten years ago. It was something I had packaged up and put far back in my memory. At that time my human self could not accept that connection with a universal all-knowing God, Goddess, All That Is. I realized it was something that I had repressed. I came out of the meditation, and I was once again in that space with an open heart. I lived half in the Light and half in the physical presence for three days. All that time I kept reliving the original experience again and again.

So this became the second transformational experience. This second experience left me knowing that I can connect with the Light at any time. I learned that we can all connect with the Light. It is a matter of allowing ourselves to listen and to quiet our minds. It has also made me recognize that we are all a part of whatever we call God. We are all co-creators of our life's path and everything in our experience. I needed those ten years of integration to be prepared for this second transformation which forced me to face all this. These understandings caused me to change my life even more. Before, I worked on myself to become a better human being; now I have to walk my talk. I started what I now call my quiet ministry. Others began to come to me to seek help. Spirit many times would communicate through me some aid or assistance often in the form of a spiritual seed for those individuals. I think what people were drawn to was the way that I expressed love and compassion. By being able to touch the Light, I experienced unconditional love. Because we are all human, our human self naturally puts conditions on our love. Whether it is the love for a girlfriend or a love for a snack, we have expectations. We expect love in return or at least certain behaviors. Unconditional love doesn't work that way. By living your life without expectations of others and by unconditionally giving your love, you build a true compassion that others can feel and are drawn to. But it can also cause trouble. The human side often misunderstands unconditional love. The human side creates expectations. It caused me some troubles before I recognized this fact.

Within the last few months, my third transformational experience has surfaced. In my life review, I was shown parts of my life that I had not yet lived. Dealing with cancer was one of them. I have recently been diagnosed with Stage 4 lung cancer with a poor prognosis. This came at a time when I was dealing more with my human self than my spiritual self. Yet because of my ministry and experiences, acceptance of the cancer was immediate. It brought me back to my center and balance of self and Spirit. It has given me new insights on how to deal with all the aspects of coping with a terminal illness. Gratefully, Spirit has been communicating many ways of dealing with the physical pain, the drug induced highs and lows, and the mental aspects of healing. I was shown practices of visualizations and meditations for relieving physical pain and to help in re-centering when the emotional anxieties and mood swings occur. Eventually these will be found on my Web site so that all may benefit from them. Spirit has indicated that this is my future path. I am to work with others who have a terminal illness to further my life ministry. This third experience was not like the others where I was given specific gifts. This has brought the gifts together with even more balance and clarity. It has also acted as a confirmation that I am again in that perfect place on my path. I now know that it is time to communicate what I have learned through experience and how I am using the knowledge to cope with my terminal illness. Now I am to begin to share it in a more public way.

I think if I were to say what came through the strongest in these three life-transforming experiences, it would be that we all chose the path we are on for the potential of growth and evolvement; we all have access to God's light and love; we just need to stop, listen, and be open to it, and finally we all have obstacles and experiences that we must overcome and learn from for the growth to occur. God hasn't abandoned us when things seem tough. It is necessary to experience what we perceive as good and bad in order to grow. God's light and love is a part of each of us, and we don't have to go searching for it. We just need to open up to it.

This article was written by David Bennett. Visit www.dharma-talks.com for more original content like this. Reprint permission granted with this footer included.

. . . .

About David Bennett

David is a public speaker, author, and teacher. He has made several radio and TV appearances and has also lectured at the international conference of IANDS (International Association for

Near-Death Studies). He continues to share his inspiring message of hope across the country including the well-known Lily Dale.

At this writing, he is serving as the leader of Upstate New York IANDS where he runs a monthly experiencer support group and a bi-monthly public meeting. David also serves on the planning committee for www.NearDeathExperiencers.org helping to coordinate Near-Death Experiencer Spiritual Retreats in St. Louis, Missouri. He is also an advisor to the American Center for the Integration of Spiritually Transformative Experiences (ACISTE.org) in San Diego.

Since recovering from cancer, David has retired and devotes his time to writing and spreading his message. For example, he writes columns for *Metaphysical Times*, a bi-weekly blog, and various Web sites. He also posts daily reflections on Facebook and Twitter. For more information, please visit: www.Dharma-Talks.com, or log onto Facebook-DharmaTalks and Twitter@DharmaTalks.

The Mystery of the Moment

Tim Freke
www.timothyfreke.com

Excerpted with permission from Tim's book, *How Long Is Now: A Journey to Enlightenment . . . and Beyond*, (Carlsbad, CA: Hay House, Inc., 2009).

I'm sitting with my dog on a quiet hill, overlooking my small hometown and all its insignificant busyness. I'm twelve years old and I'm thinking about some big questions that fascinate me: Why are we here? What's the purpose of life? What happens after death? What should I do with my life? Why is there so much suffering in the world? How can I be truly happy? How can I really help others?

I'm convinced I've been born on the wrong planet, because I clearly don't belong here. Being alive is so profoundly strange, yet the grownups around me seem to just take everything for granted. It's as if they've fallen into some sort of coma and don't notice that they're alive. Or perhaps they've secretly agreed never to talk about the big ques–

155

tions of life, but to anesthetise themselves with trivia.

Everyone goes about their daily business as if they know exactly what life is all about. But I can see that actually no one's got a clue what's going on. Most people just go along with whatever ideas are currently in vogue, whether they're about makeup, music, or the nature of reality. Something inside me rages against their inane, unquestioning "common sense" approach to life. I refuse to believe that my purpose in this extravagant universe could be to climb a career ladder, buy a house, and get a pension plan. Life is too important to waste just making money and acquiring things. Life is like an enormous question that demands an answer.

And then, unexpectedly and inexplicably, it happens . . .

My train of thought jolts to a halt and the whole world starts vibrating, sending seismic shudders through my soul. I feel as if the top of my head has just come off and the sky has poured in. I'm overwhelmed by awesome, unfathomable, breathtaking mystery. I don't know anything. Nobody knows anything. Life is a miracle of such enormous proportions that the mind can't possibly comprehend it.

I seem to have inexplicably slipped into another reality in which the colours are brighter and the birds sing symphonies. I'm immersed in wonder. I feel a bizarre sense of Oneness with everything around me, as if I'm the universe looking at itself, and amazed at its own beauty. I'm utterly happy for no reason at all. I feel certain beyond doubt of the goodness of all that is.

The humdrum world has peeled away like a superficial veneer, revealing a secret garden that I've always suspected lay close by. I know this place. It feels like home. But how can this be so familiar when it's unlike anything I've ever experienced? I've no idea what is happening to me. But I know my life will never be the same again. And I know the answer I'm searching for so desperately is not a clever theory about life. It's this experience of wonder in which all my questions dissolve.

And then there is sudden deep silence. I'm consumed by the sensation of sinking, as if I'm being engulfed by an ocean of bliss. Spasms of relaxation ripple through my young body, and I feel embraced by such a love that tears of relief spring spontaneously to my eyes. The whole vast universe is pulsating with limitless love. It's held together by love. And I am that love. There is only love. I've been born to experience this moment.

. . . .
About Tim Freke

Tim has an honors degree in philosophy and is an internationally respected authority on world spirituality. He has spent his life exploring the expanded state of consciousness he calls "the magical mystery experience" or being "deep awake" or "lucid living" . . . and he has a unique talent for helping others to experience this amazing state for themselves.

He is the author of over twenty books that have established his reputation as a groundbreaking scholar and original freethinker. He is best known for his revolutionary work on Christian Gnosticism with his close friend Peter Gandy, including *The Jesus Mysteries*, which was a top 10 best-seller in the UK and USA, and a "Book of the Year" in the *UK Daily Telegraph*. The founder of The Alliance for Lucid, he is often featured in documentary films and chat shows broadcast by the global media such as the BBC and the History Channel. For more information, please visit his Web site at www.timothyfreke.com.

God Energy and Remote Healing

————•⊷⟨∞⟩⊶•————

Mike
Colorado

As a result of being struck in the head by a playground slide at the age of five, I was knocked unconscious and remained in a coma for two weeks. When I finally awoke, I was completely paralyzed on the left side of my body. I was in such bad shape that I remained in the hospital for one year undergoing shock therapy to my then shaved head and a host of other treatments. Shortly after one year I just got up and walked out.

How was this possible? I simply said, "That's enough. I am getting up and going home." I did get up. I walked out of the hospital completely cured.

I knew that I could be healed simply by willing myself to be cured. No doubt this is due not to the shock therapy but to where I traveled while I was in my comatose state. At that time, I experienced myself out of my body. I went to a room filled with light that had a long white table within it. It appeared to be about fifteen to twenty feet long and

seated around this table were children my own age. They were all pay-
ing very close attention to a Light Being who was at the head of the
table speaking to them. This entity was luminescent in nature. As his
mouth moved, he was making hand gestures to those in attendance. All
the chairs of the other children were pulled up to the table, and the
entity was explaining something to them.

All the other children seemed to be hearing what was being said, but
I couldn't hear anything. My chair was not pulled up to the table; instead, it was pulled back about three feet. In what appeared to be only
a few minutes the Light Being (who looked like white radiating light)
came around the table and said to me, "It's your turn to go back." Then
poof, just like that, I was back in my body awake.

After I came back from what I later learned was called a near–death
experience, I was given a special gift of hearing and seeing. For example, I could hear what other people were thinking about but not
expressing. I was aware of intention and approaching danger. I could
see both into the future and back into the past. And as noted above, I
knew I could cure myself just by asking to be cured.

Around 1965 I was on a date with a girl from high school. We were
driving to go to dinner when I got the feeling or sense of what it felt like
to be in a car accident. I blew it off choosing not to take it seriously.
About twenty minutes later, I was in an accident.

Later in 1969 I was serving in Vietnam as an Airborne Ranger Staff
Sergeant leading my men in combat. The enemy had their hands full
with me. In all twenty–three contacts (battles) I fought in, I "knew" they
were coming about twenty–four hours in advance. I would simply tell
my RECON team, "Dig your foxholes deeper."

Then in 1997 I was going on another date and felt that same sense or
notion I had experienced in 1965. This time, not wanting history to
repeat itself, I decided to change history. I pulled over and waited for
one minute. My date was confused and wanted to know what I was
doing to which I replied, "I'm changing the future."

We continued on about sixty seconds later and met with another
couple. As we were pulling into their development, right in front of us
at the light was an auto accident that had occurred one minute earlier.
So I really didn't change the future, but I did change my position in it.

Instead of being a participant, I became an observer.

In 1996 I learned how to remote view (the ability to relay information about an unseen object some distance away using extrasensory perception). Two years later I became a remote healer—one of 120 members of The Monroe Institute Dolphin Energy Club. We work on remote healing cases worldwide, and I have worked on about one case a month for the last ten or so years to help participate in healing intervention and interaction.

The following year, in 1999, I was traced down by a subcontract group called on by the U.S. government to see things remotely and effect not only collection of data but to cause a positive outcome to manifest. For example, when there was a spy at the National Security Agency (NSA), I was asked to help find him. They knew there was a spy then because information was found that had come from a source within NSA.

I was able to remotely identify his car, where he sat at work, and where he lived. I was able to describe the distance between his home and work. Likewise, when there was another spy case at the DIA (Defense Intelligence Agency) and leaked information was discovered, I was again asked to help. Again I was able to remotely describe his desk and the department he worked in.

During yet another case, a man was missing and I was approached to help find him. I was able to time travel and revisit the point in the past when he was murdered. I became an observer of the events that unfolded and happened in the past. I described everything I saw in detail giving descriptions of the people involved. Not only could I see the crime, but I could also set in motion events that would lead to the criminal making a mistake and getting caught. Using my ability, I was able to locate evidence at the crime scene that linked the criminal to the crime. All of this was done at a remote distance of several thousand miles away.

In yet another interesting case, I was asked to locate a suitcase containing a nuclear bomb. After locating it remotely on a ship in one of the harbors in the United Sates, I then remotely and mentally disabled its trigger mechanism so that authorities could board the ship and confiscate the suitcase before it was detonated.

While the above covert program is going on behind the scenes in my life, in real life and in public I am called on by everyday people who want to be healed. I can see the issue and heal it, not only by seeing and observing but also by effecting outcomes remotely.

In 2005 I became a reverend in the Universal Life Church and was given an honorary Doctor of Divinity Degree (under the laws of the State of Colorado, a reverend is permitted to do healings openly without having a medical degree).

Two years later, in 2007, I became a Reiki master. Afterwards, I was able to use Reiki to heal cancer. Reiki is a Japanese word that means God Energy. My teacher studied Reiki in Japan and was able to heal three AIDS patients who were bedridden in the hospital. All of them got up and walked away after treatment in a 1998 study.

Mikao Usui (1865–1926) was a Buddhist monk who meditated and prayed in the forest for twenty days and emerged with the knowledge of how to heal remotely by applying God Energy though the hands. Usui called his healing Reiki and wrote seventeen handwritten manuals for his students, one which I have studied. Over the years I have healed many incurable diseases, illnesses, and cancers.

In conclusion, I think all of this is a gift that I brought back to earth when I had my near-death experience. Since then, I have put my skills and gifts to good use in order to help and benefit mankind. What else can we call this skill or ability that was brought forth after an NDE other than God Energy? It is a blessing.

Your Little Mother of the Sky

Nadia McCaffrey
California
www.North-CA-IANDS.org
www.PatrickSpirit.net

At the young age of seven, I was a lonely child with unending questions about life and an immense desire to learn. Each summer I would spend my vacation from the convent school I attended with my mother's parents at *Le Prieure de Beauvezet*, their estate in the Province d'Auvergne, France. The property is beautiful with the main building on Le Prieure being at least four centuries old. It was once a chapel and later a monastery with a surrounding cemetery. Some of the walls are one-and-a-half meters thick. Over the years, the monastery became the large, elegant house encircled by an incredible park of lilacs, rare plants, and trees that it is today.

The master house, now occupied by my grandparents, is located on the very top of a hill that was once a *tour de guet* (a tower designed to provide a view of anyone or anything approaching the property from far away). At the foot of this steep hillside is a grove of wild cherry trees nearby a dry, stone retaining wall.

On this momentous day I was standing at the edge of the wall. I had been playing in the meadow picking flowers. I simply love flowers and especially loved the wild sweet peas that grow in colorful profusion among the tall golden stalks of wheat. So I began looking into the wheat field seeing bright spots of color—red coquelicot, blue bachelor's buttons, and the sweet peas which seemed to be beckoning me into the field.

Feeling overwhelmed by the wheat, which seemed to tower over my head, I ran into the field feeling like I couldn't resist the flowers and stopped suddenly. I had disturbed a red aspic or asp viper. It stayed perfectly still for a long moment but then curled on its tail in a perfect circle before staring deep into my soul. I was petrified but couldn't move as a horrible pain overtook me. The snake quickly moved away as two tiny spots of blood appeared on my left ankle. I began screaming long, piercing, and extremely loud sounds of death.

I tried to walk up the steep hillside but dropped down on the grass just as my grandmother came running to me. Not wanting to frighten her, I said, "Un serpent m'a mordu." (A snake bit me . . .) But I didn't have to say anything as she already knew and began taking off her black apron to rip it into long narrow rags. Grabbing a nearby stick, she made a tourniquet around my leg and then began to suck out the venom as I drifted in and out of consciousness.

Having done everything she could, she carried me back to the house where I began to vomit nonstop before slipping into an unconscious state. This was 1952, and my grandparents did not have a car or even a telephone so at the sound of my screams, my grandfather Leon left the house on his bike racing to the nearest public telephone more than two kilometers from my house. When I did finally regain consciousness, I could see two doctors attending to me. One younger doctor insisted on giving me an injection of Pasteur serum while the other felt it would do no good.

After a long argument, the younger doctor prevailed, and the injection was given; afterwards I slipped into another coma which lasted ten days. While in this coma, I was oblivious to the real world around me and realized that I had left this dimension. I saw this beautiful Lady of Light hovering above me. She said, "*Je suis ta petite Maman du ciel.*" (I am your little mother of the sky). She was so beautiful and was glowing with a bright and powerful light that filled me with warmth and engulfed me with a sense of serenity. Mere words cannot describe the love and well-being that I felt in her presence. Somehow I knew that this love is what will save us; we must care for one another and spread compassion in our world of sadness and destruction.

At this point, I left my body and began floating in her direction. She then smiled at me holding up the palms of her hands helping me understand that I could not go towards her as she said in French, "Be strong and let's love one another. Share this love I have for you with others. There are many ways to love. Do not fear as you will be guided. I will be with you always. You cannot stay with me now. You will show the way. You will be home. In the middle of a garden you will see a rose, more colorful and beautiful than all the others. When the time will come, you will open yourself to others and share this message of love. To speak to me is prayer and to pray is love."

She then returned later one last time with an additional thought, "And you will now return to life. You have a lot to learn and a lot of accomplish. My love will always be with you. Never forget." I was then told that I would be okay and that I would get better.

I wanted so very much to curl up into her arms and remain with her rather than return to my body, but I had no choice. My body claimed me and was immediately overwhelmed by pain and sadness. Unable to completely understand what had happened, I remained in bed for several weeks with my leg swollen to three times its normal size. This frightened me a great deal because my leg was the same mottled color as the snake that had bit me. I refused to talk to anyone and was filled with resentment about having to come back to this dimension into my painful and disfigured body.

My grandmother was a healer and applied several natural remedies and herbs on my leg which did help. My recovery was called a miracle. My body took several months to recover, but my spirit did not heal as quickly. I could not forget about the beautiful Lady of Light and wanted to find out more about what I had experienced. But when I told my grandmother, she told me not to tell anyone.

Years later at seventeen, I was popular and many felt that I was beautiful and bright. But what people did not know was that I did not want to be alive. After my near–death experience, I felt isolated and different. I could not talk to anyone about what had happened and rejected offers of friendship. I wanted nothing more than to go back to the beautiful Lady of Light.

My teenage years were neither happy nor good. I was a rebel fighting everything and everyone. The sisters at the Catholic school I attended didn't know what to do with me. My grandmother and I constantly fought. I was also very resentful of my own mother whom I seldom saw and was determined not to accept any comfort or support from her.

In an attempt to end my misery and return to the Lady of Light, I overdosed on prescription drugs that had once belonged to my great-grandmother. Apparently no one had thought to remove them from the house. So I decided to get back to her. I calculated how much of a dosage I would need to end my life. Oddly enough a friend Antoinette and her boyfriend stopped by hoping to borrow a scrapbook. She found me on my bed showing no signs of life and rushed me to a small local hospital.

From the time I had taken the pills to the time I had arrived at the hospital was approximately two hours. As I was being wheeled into the emergency room, I was out of my body. I floated above for awhile looking down at my now lifeless body on the gurney. My true spirit self was now a glowing shape. I watched people crying while the doctors and nurses were trying to revive me for awhile before turning my attention to a long dark tunnel. At the end of this tunnel or what looked more like a dark hole was a very bright light, and I moved toward it with extraordinary and effortless speed.

My thoughts at this time were dominated by one clear thought, "Oh, the Light, the peace, the extraordinary feeling of love. Once more I am in it." Then, suddenly I heard an extremely powerful male voice telling me to go back because I still had work to do and had not even begun. I began returning to my body and there was nothing I could do to stop it.

The next thing I knew I was lying on the gurney overcome by terrible pain and sadness as one of the nurses, an older kindly woman, was crying thinking that I had died and was not coming back. I later learned that the doctors could not detect a pulse for approximately ten minutes and had given up on me. But as they began to remove the tubes from body, I began to show signs of life. Surprised, they quickly resumed their efforts to stabilize my condition.

In the hours that followed I again felt incredible sadness, not for what I had done but for what I had failed to do. I was a young, beautiful, intelligent woman on the outside but on the inside I felt like a prisoner in a gilded cage of flesh and bones.

As much as I wanted to feel that Divine Love once again, I was forced to realize that I had a reason for being on this earth and my job was not yet done. I was not going to be allowed to shirk from my responsibility. My choice was simple. It was as though I simply flipped a switch and turned on a new light. Since that day, I have never contemplated suicide again. My last NDE changed my life completely. Once I understood that I could not go back on my terms, I stopped fighting with the world and began trying to pass on the love that I received from the beautiful Lady of Light to those around me.

I will forever remember her words, "Share this love I have for you with others. There are many ways to love. Do not fear as you will be guided. I will be with you always." Today, I try to share this love in my work with the terminally ill. I draw upon my own experiences for the benefit of those who are making their transition to another dimension. In fact, I experienced a third NDE more than thirty years after my second one while sitting at the deathbed of a person dying in a nursing home.

This time I experienced an empathic NDE which is said to occur when you feel another person's death as though it were your own. Suddenly, I felt intense pain in my solar plexus as I sat there and realized that my hair was glowing. I then found myself in another dimension as I was being shown pictures of the past, present, and two different futures. One was of destruction and the other was peaceful.

I again heard a powerful voice ask, "Do you want to come home?" At that time, I was seeing pictures of a healing center that I was being called to build. I saw lines of people waiting to be helped. I then heard the voice ask again even louder, "Do you want to come home?" To my amazement, I replied, "No, I can't. I must help these people and fulfill my mission."

Having lost my own fear of death long ago, I know with every fiber of my being that love can never fail us. It is this certainty that I can pass along to people who are dying or have lost loved ones and to those who are troubled or in turmoil. Love is the only thing that matters.

ABOUT NADIA MCCAFFREY AND THE LOSS OF HER SON PATRICK

Nadia's war began in June 2004, the day her only child Patrick died in northern Iraq. At a time when the Pentagon was trying to keep photographs of returning coffins out of the media, Nadia invited the press to the Sacramento airport when her son's flag-draped coffin was flown home. The scene attracted international attention.

She was outspoken about her opposition to the war as well as her son's growing reservations at the time he was killed. She has appeared at dozens of vigils and peace rallies. She gives aid to families of other soldiers killed in action or wounded as well as war veterans suffering from PTSD (post-traumatic stress disorder) or TBI (traumatic brain injury).

In December 2004 she traveled to Jordan with a humanitarian aid delegation for child victims in the Iraqi city of Fallouja (plans to travel inside Iraq were cancelled due to security concerns) and met with Iraqi mothers who had lost children in the conflict. "All I wanted," she said, "was to be able to find at least one Iraqi mother who, like me, suffered a loss and to be able to have an exchange about the way we felt. I wanted to talk about what to do to start working for peace and to do it mother to mother with no governments.

The basic meaning of the mission is peace. It's a first step, and I hope that other people will follow.

I asked myself why I was still alive while my only son is dead. When I thought of this and of Patrick, I would have taken his place with joy, but that's not the way the plan was. I think there are no coincidences, no accidents. Things happen because we are meant to do certain things. It's totally up to us to fulfill what we have been left to do. Both Patrick's death and the war itself drive me to do something.

I have opposed every war, always. But with this war it became stronger. I won't stop anymore, never. I also believe that the road to end the war goes from people to people, and from mother to mother, not through the government. For mothers especially, there is a very important task in the struggle against the war. What we need is a worldwide alliance against the war. We, the people, have to unite our powers. To me, the concept of human rights is the highest priority."

. . . .
About Nadia McCaffrey
As with many NDErs, Nadia's message is about the importance of love and the hope that exists for a world abundant with love. She views her life as a testimony to the joy that can be experienced by connecting with one's life purpose. For more information, please visit:
www.ValleyForgeCenter.org,
www.PatrickMcCaffreyFoundation.org,
http://patrick-mccaffrey.memory-of.com,
www.PatrickSpirit.net.

Author's Note: Nadia was shown that she would build a self-sustaining center according to specific plans involving sacred geometry. The center would be volunteer based and would be a haven providing assistance to war veterans, healing and educational services in order to show people how to reconnect with the earth. At this writing, she had land set aside and was in the process of recruiting volunteers including an architect who deals with sacred geometry.

Dying is the Easy Part

Mindy
Idaho
http://waitingtowakeup.com

After being in a serious car accident, I found myself on the side of the road, curled up as close as I could get to a fetal position. I could not breathe and was in a state of shock not knowing exactly what had happened. Later I would find out that I had multiple breaks and fractures in my chest and ribs in addition to three intestinal ruptures. And on top of all that, my heart and lungs were bruised. So there I was on the road trying to find the strength to breathe; but each time I did, I would black out from the intense pain.

When I did black out, there was nothing but blackness . . . no color, no thought, nothing. But each time I came out of this blackness, I thought of my kids and my mother. I couldn't help but wonder what would happen to my kids and how my mother would handle it if I died. I began to literally panic as all these thoughts rushed through my head.

Moments later I began to calm down and assured myself that my kids would eventually be okay without me. I then prayed that God would give my mother the strength, one day at a time, to take care of my boys and then told Him that I accepted death as my fate.

As my prayers ended, I began to relax even more and said, "Thank you, Jesus. I'm coming home." This time instead of the typical blackout I was experiencing, I saw nothing but the brightest white Light you could ever imagine. My body or really my spirit was traveling very fast and seemingly very high within all this brightness. I was one with this Light. There was no pain, no sadness, and no regrets. I was going home!

I could still hear the sirens below me, and I had no interest in looking down there again, but then the woman who had been sitting with me started screaming, "She's not breathing! Get the paramedics over here! Oh dear God, she's stopped breathing!" Suddenly, I slowed down and turned my head and shoulders down and to the left to look again at the scene unfolding below me. I wanted to go back and tell her, "It's okay. I want to go." But I didn't get to. The next thing I remember was the paramedics strapping me down and taking me into the ambulance.

Although I never did get to heaven that day or even hear God's voice, I know without a doubt that that's where I was headed in the midst of that beautiful white Light. I was in a hurry to go home and was not scared or in any pain whatsoever. I can honestly say that I would have been happy had I died on that day as I knew I was headed to heaven. But thanks to the panic in that woman's voice and my desire to reassure her, I am here today to raise my boys. I am thankful to be alive!

Dying, as painful as it was, was the easy part. Coming back was the hard part.

God and Love: The Only Reality

Linda
Connecticut
el-stewart@worldnet.att.net

When I finally gave up my will to live, relinquishing my life to death was sublimely easy after my long debilitating illness and loss of everything that had made life worthwhile. The decision to leave this world hung suspended in an extended moment of absolute quiet.

Passionless, I watched my spirit leave my body as a feeling of "otherness" engulfed me. I felt a strange detachment from my physical body and the life I had created. I was no longer connected to a pitiful, suffering mass of flesh. I was not that body, and yet I still existed but in a new state of being. Gone was the wrenching pain that had accompanied my every waking moment. The strain of expanding my lungs to gasp for air had disappeared. Fatigue, which had weighted my life for years, had lifted. Depression no longer drained my mind of hope. Sight and sounds did not sear my head with pain, leaving me emotionally bereft. And yet, I still existed. I felt weightless and calm.

Although I knew I was not in the lifeless body lying on my bed and that the eyes and brain I had previously identified as mine were in that inanimate object with which I no longer identified, I was still aware of sight and thoughts and sensations. I observed my new reality with tranquility. Slowly I looked around, and below me I saw a vast, endless blackness. Like a void or black hole, I was irresistibly drawn toward the darkness. Gradually, I felt myself sinking toward it. I thought without fear or any emotional reaction, "Isn't that strange?" I had been so afraid I was going to be judged and sent to either heaven or hell. But it appeared I would simply disappear into the dark nothingness. As even my new awareness waned, I yielded to the heaviness overtaking me as darkness filled my mind. My vision became obscured as I began to merge into the blackness.

Offering no resistance, I released my hold on any remaining shred of consciousness and personal identity. At the very moment that I felt the last of me disappearing into nothingness I was suddenly buffeted by a powerful, energetic force that swooped beneath and lifted me, carrying me upward.

Barely conscious, my only awareness was a sensation of rising. I seemed to be traveling upward at an unimaginable speed. A clean sensation of wind rushed over my face and body with tremendous force, and yet there was no discomfort. Vast distances seemed to fly by me, and the higher I rose, the more my head cleared. I became aware of a deep sense of peace and warmth that permeated my senses. Confused because the energy that had enveloped me had a definite presence, I tried to see what was happening and who was carrying me. Who or what cared so deeply for me? I felt peaceful and loved immeasurably. I knew I was in the arms of a being who cherished me with perfect love and carried me from the dark void into a new reality.

As my mind cleared, scoured of the remnants of mortal, past associations, I was finally able to open my being fully to spirit and my vision cleared.

With the eyes of my soul body, I looked to see what held me in such love, and I beheld a radiant Spirit Being so magnificent and full of love that I knew I would never again feel the sense of loss. I have no way of explaining how, but I knew the Spirit was Christ. It was not a belief, perception, or understanding, but my recognition of Christ came from my new perspective of spirit.

I did not see the Spirit as I had seen Jesus of Nazareth depicted in paintings, but the innate knowing of my heart remembered and acknowledged Christ. The radiant Spirit was Christ, the manifestation and expression of pure love. Because of my Christian education, I knew no other name to call what I felt as I looked at him.

Others might have called him Buddha or Yahweh or Great Spirit in the Sky, but the naming did not matter; only the recognition of absolute love and truth was important. Safe in the gentle yet powerful embrace of His love, I rested secure that everything was okay, exactly as it was supposed to be.

Ascending ever farther, I lifted my eyes to see a great Light in the vast distance. With Christ as my guide, I rapidly approached the Light. Ecstasy filled my soul as I looked at the radiance, manyfold brighter than a sun. The Light was everywhere and everything—the brightest I had ever seen and dazzling beyond description. It was brilliant enough to blind or burn, yet I was not harmed.

The Light moved over and through me, washing every hidden place of my heart, removing all hurt and fear, transforming my very being into a song of joy. I had thought the love I felt from Christ was complete; yet, the Light toward which we were soaring was the fulfillment of my search, the loving Source of all that exists, the God of truth and unconditional love, the origin of creation.

My understanding of love was forever changed. The majesty and glory of that vision was an ineffable moment that defined forever more the direction of my new truth. I was home, and I wanted nothing more than to remain in the Light of God. Christ had delivered me into the Light, and I stood in the presence of God. I was filled with complete knowing: The Light was love and love was God. Waves of consummate love which emanated from the Light obliterated every burden I carried and every thought that kept me from knowing God. I was made aware of my purity. With new clarity I realized I had been walking through life ghostlike, wrapped in a shroud of fear, and huddled against illusions. I stood like a lover open to the liquid flow of golden Light that filled my empty shell to overflowing.

There was no limit to the outpouring as I came to the rapturous awareness of the infinite nature of God's love. There was no place that God did not exist and I was within God. I am an inseparable part of the Light. The truth of who I am, indeed, who we all are, is perfect love as a creation of God. All of God's creation is one creation, and I am one with creation. God and I are one, Creator and created.

I had spent a lifetime in fear of judgment, and now, standing with God, I had been known completely and found faultless. I knew God regarded me as perfect. God loved me because love is the totality of God. God loves without limit. Finally it all made sense. God could only love me because God is only love, nothing other than love. The only reality is God; there cannot be another and GOD IS LOVE.

I had reached my true home. I turned to Christ and said, "This is beautiful. I am home. This is where I want to be. I want to stay." And Christ answered, "You can stay for a little while and then you must return."

AFTER HER RETURN FROM HEAVEN

I couldn't believe I had to come back to physical reality. After a life-time of confusion and fear, I had stood in the presence of an open, receptive, nonjudgmental, totally loving God. I wanted nothing more than to remain in that presence but was told I had to return.

As a result of my near–death experience, I no longer have a fear of death. In fact, death became my favorite subject overnight. Where I had once forbidden the dreadful word in my home, now my family and friends couldn't get me to stop talking about my amazing experience.

Surprisingly, I was sad and angry, even defiant. I was confounded that after my lifetime of fear, I had made it to heaven and then had been sent back. "Why?" I asked, "Was I too little a fish or what!"

For almost a year I would often lie in my bed at night crying, sob-bing, and begging God to let me come home. I was not one of those lucky people who experienced a spontaneous remission of her illness with her near–death experience. I was still very sick, and I didn't under-stand the point of my having to remain on earth when I could make no contributions and had barely any interactions with my family or other people. I found myself whining, questioning, and begging God. "Please, please, please, PLEASE let me come home."

Bargaining with God, I urged, "If I have to stay here, why can't you cure me so I can do something?" Pleading with God, I cried, "If you aren't going to cure me outright, what if you let me be just well enough to paint even just an hour a day? If I can't do anything, why can't there be some way I can be around people? I'M LONELY!"

Although I felt waves of love wash over me constantly when I stopped complaining long enough to remember my experience, I never got the answers to my pleas. At least not the answers I wanted.

After about a year I prayed a new prayer from the sincerest depths of my heart. Once again I relinquished my will and efforts to direct my own life as completely as the night I gave up my hold on life and died. I said to God, "My dear God, I give up. I do not know what is right for me. I don't know what I am supposed to do, who I am to see, or what I should say. I don't even know what to think. I am always requesting what I think would be best for me. God, I don't know what is best for me. My life is yours.

Whatever you want for me is fine. If I am to lie here in this bed, sick and disabled for the rest of my life, whether it is twenty minutes or twenty years, that's fine. Whatever happens is fine. I know you love me." And then I added, "I make one request, however. Please, if I am to live, let me be useful in some way—for YOU."

HER GIFT FROM GOD

A curious manifestation after my near-death experience was that I began seeing a white glow and glint of lights around people and objects. Because I had had so many physical anomalies during my illness, I assumed the "lights" were another optical side effect of the illness. I was later shown that the lights were far more than that.

As my health had slowly improved, I occasionally drove myself short distances to appointments. One day as I was driving down a busy street, I stopped at a red light and watched an odd scene unfold before me. A delivery truck had parked on the right side of the street about half a block ahead. The truck was one that opened from the sides rather than the back. I watched as the driver walked around to the traffic side of his truck and began unloading his cargo with oncoming traffic approaching. Inside my car, I said out loud in my little southern voice, "Oh honey, you shouldn't do that; it's dangerous."

On this notable day I watched, stunned, as the familiar dancing lights around the delivery man swirled and quickly coalesced into the form of a breath-taking, translucent, beautiful woman-spirit, glowing with light.

Perhaps it was because I had sent a loving and concerned thought about the delivery man's well-being that the spirit turned her loving gaze on me. For a brief moment, our eyes met. She smiled at me and then hovering over the unsuspecting man, returned her attention to her charge who was oblivious to the heavenly presence and was busily going about his business. I was thunderstruck.

Barely breathing for fear the vision would leave and mesmerized by the vision, I was reluctant to take my eyes off the beauty of the scene; however, from my peripheral vision I became aware of even more compelling lights. When I was able to tear myself away from the spirit, I glanced slowly at the vista around me, and everywhere I looked, every single person in my view had beautiful, loving spirits attending them. People walking nonchalantly down the sidewalk were accompanied by spirits. From within cars unfettered by physical barriers, I could see the glow and form of beings around the occupants. I saw joggers with flutters of light streaking behind them as their spirit kept pace. As people entered and left buildings, light beings followed them. The view before me was filled with brilliant, white light.

From the limited understanding of my human mind, I struggled to comprehend the meaning of what I saw. I knew the lights were connected to the individual people, although more *of* them than *with* them, almost as if they were an extension of their existence—a light connection to an aspect of their Higher Self. The lights, which were a connection to the humans, were glinting off the beings so brightly and expansively that they interconnected forming a sort of light grid. I remembered reports in books on the near-death experience of people seeing grids on the Other Side that they didn't know how to explain.

As I looked at the network of light before me and felt the immense outpouring of love coming from the beings, I realized the connection of human beings to the Beings of Light was through love and that the love itself was connected through this grid.

The metaphor represented by the image I saw and perceived was absolutely clear, and I was overwhelmed with the knowledge that WE ARE ALL ONE. I understood that our Oneness is interconnected by love and is an available, much higher level and means of communication than we normally use but to which we have access. This love is available to anyone who is willing to do the hard spiritual work that will allow us to open our hearts and minds and eyes to Spirit. I remembered the love I had felt in the presence of God and experienced a total sense of love for all existence as an interconnected Oneness and a manifestation of God.

Over and over this single truth was being driven home to me. Only God exists, God is everything. All that I gaze upon is a representation of God—not the physical mirage but rather the shining brilliance behind the mask. I was startled back to everyday awareness by the blasting of a horn. I looked down at my speedometer and realized I was barely creeping forward in the car. With sheets of tears streaming down my face and all but blind with emotion, I pulled to the side of the road until I could take in all that I had witnessed and regain my composure. I don't know how long I sat taking in the wonder of that event, but I couldn't move until the spectacular vision slowly dissipated returning to the more familiar form of lights around the bodies of the people I watched.

I was reluctant to leave because I hoped the angels would return, and I called them angels because I didn't know what else to say. But when I gathered my senses enough to drive, I made my way home. Anxious to tell my husband, I still wondered what he would think. Would he think I was hallucinating, getting sick again, or perhaps even losing my mind? Much to his credit, he listened with open ears to my tale. In fact, after I told my story, his response was, "Can you see anything around me?" Looking deeply into the lights around him, I discovered that by focusing on the glinting lights, a form emerged taking the appearance of a beautiful spirit. When I described his spirit attendant, he was thrilled.

Encouraged by Ed's response, I told my story to my children and friends, and they related the information to their friends. That initiated the sometimes timid and skeptical but always curious inquiries from friends. They, too, asked if I would mind telling them if they had beings around them.

Would I mind? It was my joy to share the love I felt coming from the exquisite inhabitants of a dimension where love reigns. Eagerly I shared with anyone who wanted to know if they, too, had angels around them.

Eventually, news of my ability to see the angelic realm spread via a newspaper article, television appearances, college lectures, and most significantly, word of mouth. Today I devote my time to readings, counseling, and lectures. As I talked to more and more people, I garnered new insights. In the beginning I called what I saw angels because I didn't have any other word to explain what I saw. The beings were always loving, luminous, and had otherworldly presence and beauty. Curiously, as my ability to discern spirits progressed, I began to see a different type of spirit hovering around people, and they compelled my attention. I felt responsible to describe exactly what I saw and only what I saw around the people who requested a reading even if their spirits did not look like the stereotypical angel that they expected.

For instance, I once told a woman of an older man with ears that stuck out, wearing little round spectacles, and with a goofy smile that revealed teeth that had spaces between them. The woman looked amazed and with tears in her eyes, she said, "Oh my gosh, I recognize him. That's my uncle who was killed. I've always wondered if he was okay." The spirit grinned and related telepathically with me. I was able to let his niece, whom he still loved, know that he was fine and had been with this unsuspecting woman all the time. The first time this sort of thing happened, I was taken by surprise. Confused and with a knot of apprehension in the pit of my stomach, I thought, "Oh great, now I'm seeing 'dead' people!" If I had not had my near-death experience, I might have thought I was going crazy. But I did have a near-death experience. I could now see angels, and evidently I could also see the spirits of people who had died.

There is no death, but I could report on the presences from the other realms where spirits reside after leaving their mortal existence. I also discovered I could, on occasion, see the spirit form of people who are still alive on the earth realm. I quickly resolved my apprehension about this ability when I saw the happiness and comfort it gave people to hear the encouraging stories of love beyond the grave.

Author's Note: Linda owns and operates the highly successful Internet discussion group: http://groups.yahoo.com/group/nde/. She can also be contacted via e-mail at el-stewart@worldnet.att.net.

My Missing Five Minutes

--◦◦◦◦∞◦◦◦◦--

Ray Morose
Australia
www.themindofconsciousness.com

In November 2008 I was admitted into the hospital for a popliteal aneurysm bypass in my left leg. I never made it to the operating theatre, though, because the anesthetist who gave me the lumber/spinal block killed me. The hospital discharge referral read as follows, "Unfortunately, Raymond's operation could not be performed as pre-operatively bupivacaine was accidentally injected intravascularly, resulting in a systolic arrest. He was resuscitated in five minutes."

Normally lumber/spinal blocks do not take much time. After the two injections, one simply waits until the numbness sets in to be moved into the operating theatre. I was lying on my side with the anesthetist at my back administering the injections and a male nurse was facing me on the other side. As I watched the male nurse, he suddenly disappeared. I went from seeing him standing in front of me to seeing what can only be described as being in an "awareness disconnect bubble."

This transition occurred instantaneously. One second I was looking at the male nurse, and the next second I was in this "awareness disconnect bubble." I refer to it as such because it felt contained and restricted. Hence, the feeling of being in a bubble emerged, but of course there was no bubble, just containment as I moved beyond it. My first thought was, "Shit, I'm dead."

Then I noticed the background or what I was submerged within. The environment was of a blue/grey color and appeared to be perforated with an endless number of very small and dim or subdued sparkles. This is very difficult to describe. My next thought was, "Can I see myself?" And, of course, I could not. The thought made me aware of the absolute purity/clarity of that awareness. This is also difficult to describe as it was the normal awareness one uses in daily life but yet a more clearly defined, concentrated version of that normal awareness experienced as being personally absolute—meaning it is what it is and nothing can alter or change what it is.

Naturally, I could not see myself as my "self" (awareness/consciousness) was what was seeing. Simultaneously with that thought I recognized that I could know. By this, I mean that I was still connected to the mind as I could think and thinking is a biological function of the brain. Therefore, I knew I was somehow still "alive" but could not do anything with that "aliveness" as I was technically dead and was experiencing nothing outside my awareness bubble.

At this juncture I notice a single row of lights, with each light being similar to the illumination that a small torch (flashlight) would produce. It began as one single light, then a black space; then two lights clumped together, and then another black space; then three lights clumped together, and another black space. And on and on it went. I became entranced by the sequential numbering of these "clumped lights" and began to follow the sequence until I got to around number fifteen and then something compelled me to look back to the beginning of this row of lights. Upon turning my vision back to the beginning, I noticed a pair of translucent crossed hands moving up and down over the first of these sets of lights. I thought, "They are using CPR to revive me." But then I noticed how dim those first few sets of lights appeared as compared to the sets of lights from the fifteenth set onwards appeared, and because the illumination was not very powerful at the first light as compared to the brighter illumination as the sets of lights increased, I thought, "No, he won't make it."

However, for some reason, I was still drawn back to the beginning of those sets of lights. When I arrived at around number five, I was absolutely certain that whoever was doing the CPR would not succeed as the closer I got to the first set with the pair of translucent crossed hands over it, the greater the dimness density increased, creating the feeling the other direction that contained more light was a better option. But I was still inexplicably drawn toward the first set with the moving translucent hands. Then just as I arrived at the first light, my (biological) eyes opened and became aware that I was back in the body. The first thing I did with great effort, as it felt like lead, was lift my right hand and point to a tube sticking out of my mouth. I could not talk or did not have the energy to talk, but I really wanted that tube out of my mouth so I could breathe. The next thing I remember was waking up in the intensive care unit.

The entire experience took five minutes; during which time CPR was continually applied creating a "slow" pulse that both kept me alive and, I assume, moved around whatever injected pharmacological agents were used to neutralize the effects of the block that shut my heart down. Later I began to ponder what these sequential lights meant. First, the increased illumination moving outward was greater because the number of lights was greater making the "area" around the first sets of lights appear to be dimmer. In other words, just because the lights were greater, moving outward does not imply "moving to a greater light" as that increased illumination may impart. Secondly, the pair of moving up/down "translucent crossed hands" at the beginning of the series of lights is a clue to understand what those lights meant: they were the number of compressions taking place.

With each compression, a light was added to indicate its number creating a row or series of lights which means that the mind was still receiving information from the body, but that information could not be translated into understanding because the knower of consciousness was "disconnected" from the body. Therefore the knower could not know that was occurring to the body. However, consciousness could receive information through its observer as the observer is the visual aspect of consciousness. That is what occurred as I witnessed the background, the lights, and the "translucent hands" which is the mind visually demonstrating what it cannot explain in any other way as its knower is not present to understand those occurrences as it was locked within its "awareness disconnect bubble."

WHAT IS THE MEANING OF THIS AWARENESS DISCONNECT?

The observer-knower forms the two self-referencing aspects of consciousness (awareness) that provide the foundation for your existence, but it is the biological mind that provides all the information to make it work. This "little" episode in my life has confirmed those self-referencing aspects. For all the pain (broken and cracked ribs from the CPR) and suffering it has caused, it also experientially confirmed what could be confirmed only following the death of the body. I was technically dead for five minutes, and those minutes were sufficient to experience the separated absoluteness of consciousness confirming its indestructibility. How you appreciate or understand the terminology of "absoluteness" may be different from how I experience that term. However, when the human body dies, the terminology of "absoluteness" will be held in common confirming our nonbiological heritage and our commonality.

The "bubble" that I was confined within felt contained. There was no form (body), just pure awareness as an observer-knower of consciousness. The disconnected aspect of that containment is one of the more difficult aspects of this experience to define. Its "bubble" felt like a temporary position, sort of a holding pattern waiting to see what would happen: to stay or move on. However, what it did expose was the thought that when consciousness is disconnected from the body, everything in the world, and I mean everything, simply evaporates as if it never existed. There is simply no memory connection to an earthly existence. When consciousness is disconnected from the body, apparently all of its earthly connection memory goes. As alarming as that may sound, it is also liberating as consciousness does appear to subliminally have access to information that "exposes what it is" which allows one to be aware that one is indeed aware, which is the meaning of experiencing subliminal self-awareness. That disconnected "bubble" was experienced as knowing and seeing (observation), as pure awareness, or awareness of that awareness, but it was also free or liberated from all earthly connections (memory) making it exceedingly peaceful. However, as it was "somewhere in–between here and there," it was also totally isolated or alone: there were no other entities and no noticeable environment other than the blue–gray background and the series of lights.

Attempting to describe the clarity of that isolated and/or disconnected subliminal self-awareness "bubble" is also trying as there is no earthly experience to compare it with. The clarity contains an unfettered expansive freedom that defies comparative description. That internal vision of oneself (subliminal self-awareness) reveals a sense of absolute purity ("stainless" transparency) which is the core or essence of existence. In other words, that is what we fundamentally all are. The mind is what adds spirit value to the core essence or detracts from it, which is a free will decision, bringing individual consciousness into permanence or making it a short-term acquisition.

Experienced in isolation, that awareness "bubble" was a little disconcerting, and I thought I would sit down to have a think about it. However, the moment I had that thought, I realized I could not sit down as there was nothing to sit down with and nothing to sit upon. The situation became quite humorous and the concern dissipated. It was at this time that I was beginning to be drawn back to the first of those "lights," which eventually brought me back to experiencing my body and where that body was located. It was an interesting experience that confirmed some of the aspects that I write about—not all, but most of them. The rest may have to wait until the disconnection is permanent. Until then my "missing five minutes" will have to suffice.

. . . .
About Ray Morose
Ray is an author whose books masterfully combine psychology, philosophy, and religion into one. His books: *The Heart of Silence*, *Presence*, *Resolution Psychology* and *The Source-code of Consciousness* were a progressive process which led to *The Mind of*

Consciousness and *The Source-code of Existence*, which contains essential data from all his previous books. For more information, please visit: www.themindofconsciousness.com.

I Could Not See
His Face

Stanley A. Wilson
Texas
stanleyawilson@hotmail.com

Even though my health was not great, I had refused to go to the doctor. I felt so overtly tired all the time and I knew something was not right, but I stubbornly refused to get medical attention.

One night as I lay on my bed, I stopped breathing. Suddenly, I found myself in this really bright tunnel full of white light. The brightness of the light was intense, but it did not hurt my eyes. My body began moving at an extreme speed upwards. As I moved, I noticed that the tunnel was about twelve feet wide with white light permeating everywhere up and down the sides. This magnificent light was penetrating through the walls; it was serene and beautiful.

I realized then that I was out of my body, but all of my senses were still intact. I was still me. There was neither gravitational pull nor any G forces. I was travelling at the speed of light until I began to slow down. At the top of the tunnel, I saw about twenty-foot long objects hanging down and completely filling the space. They resembled white, silk punching bags, yet they were very clean.

As I ran into these "punching bags," they wadded up and stopped me. I then began to automatically push them apart and move upward through them. The next thing I remember I was holding onto the edge of a hole in the floor. It felt like I was being birthed again into a new world as I looked around and realized I was in this great big room. Off to the right about ten feet in front of me was a wide and long table.

At the end of this table closest to me was a man sitting in a throne-type chair; he was clothed in a white robe. I was at his back left side and could see his dark, wavy brown hair shine. It was more like a mahogany color and came down to his shoulders. He had a pronounced nose resembling a Middle Eastern influence. He was the begotten son of God Jesus Christ. He never looked around at me, but I knew He was aware of me. There were also four other men sitting to the left of Jesus. They wore white Jewish caps, and I knew they were some of his disciples.

I then floated out of the hole in the floor and moved passed Jesus on His left side never looking at Him again. I was floating above the man closest to Jesus; I noticed he had curly hair. I was so close that I could smell his scalp.

Without warning I heard my wife yelling at a distance, "What is the matter with you?" Immediately, I was back in my body. She later told me that I was not breathing and had no pulse. I have no idea how long this experience took place. But I do know that I was so excited when I came back and couldn't wait to tell my wife what had happened. I had been without oxygen for so long, however, that I just could not get my lips to form my words.

After some time I came to believe that the reason I did not see Jesus' face was because of Exodus 33:20 which states, "You cannot see my face; for no man can see me and live." If I had seen the Lord's face, I don't think I would have been able to come back.

My Four Near-Death Experiences

Tina Michelle
Kentucky
tina@tinamichelle.com
www.tinamichelle.com

My first near-death experience occurred when I was only five. I had gone swimming in the family pool. The people who had adopted me were having a rare family gathering. Everyone was laughing, and smoke was drifting off of the barbecue. The new family took great care for my pool safety; they even installed a fence around it so that I would not accidentally fall in. What they failed to observe, however, was that the inflated ring I wore that day was not an actual lifesaving device. In fact it was more like the "Ring-O-Death."

One moment of lifting my arms too high and down I would go. And that is exactly what happened. Perhaps they were testing the buttermilk to see who had the best, or looking at family pictures, or telling tall tales. I don't know what they were doing when I found myself in the pool alone.

Suddenly all I heard was silence as I went down. I remember coming up for air a few times. Maybe I didn't make enough noise to get the gathering attendees' attention, but I went down again. I recall hitting the bottom of the pool with my backside, and I was twisting and turning. Then all I recall feeling was serenity. All I recall hearing was absolute silence.

Then it was like someone or something pushed me up from the bottom of the pool. Later I was told I was actually "fished" out of the pool (I don't know by whom). Someone knew enough to resuscitate me, to bring me back into my body. To this day, no one in the family can recall who actually helped me.

I do know it was a moment in time that changed me forever. As I opened my eyes, I looked up from where I laid on the patio to see my new parents, aunts, and uncles all looking at me with concerned faces. It is what I saw around them, however, that really startled me. I mentioned it to everyone, but no one really listened, or maybe they were just too concerned about my welfare to hear what I was actually saying.

Around each person looking down at me were other "beings"; I called them "sparkling people." They were multicolored, in constant motion, and glistening. They stood behind each person, and as my family looked me over, so did "they."

I still see them to this day, and I call them angels.

Life became different after this. I was very lonely and scared all the time as I was the only child in the home, and visitors were rare and usually were adults. But the beings, the angels, came to me and played with me for hours on end. Many times I would hear my new mother telling her friends that I played for hours by myself. Well, I wasn't really by myself. I had legions of angels with me at all times. They provided the comfort I so desperately needed at the time.

Mediumship began with me when I had my second NDE (near–death experience) due to rheumatic fever at age nine. The hospitals were filled to capacity with the flu and a round of various illnesses in the early '70s. I was extremely ill and can barely remember the ride to the hospital. I do recall mother being upset and worried that my pediatrician was out of town, and the on call doctor was not very responsive to her appeals that I needed to be hospitalized.

So she did the only thing she could do and that was taking me home and putting me in "the big bed." I don't remember a lot of what happened during this time and can only recall waking up for brief moments from time to time to see her sitting by my bedside. She would wipe my forehead and tell me not to worry. Apparently I was delirious more than once and recall "seeing" and "feeling" snakes and bugs crawling all over me. What I do remember next, however, I don't believe was a result of delirium at all.

According to my adoptive mother, I had a temperature for nine days, often reaching as high as 103°. Sometime during this period I awoke to find myself alone in the room. Well, almost . . .

At the foot of my bed stood a man dressed in what I referred to as "nightgowns." He walked toward the side of my bed and stood silently next to me. He looked just like the man (Jesus) in the picture above my bed. To this day I cannot recall if he said anything, but I guess it doesn't really matter. It is what (or rather whom) he brought with him that matters.

The room began to crowd with other people. Some wearing "nightgowns," while others wore strange regalia. All in all it looked like a costume party. Those standing in the room began speaking at once. The problem was they spoke in different languages.

These people, I later came to learn, were the deceased. And apparently they wanted to talk to me. So, how did this affect and change my life? In so many ways!

For starters I had a difficult time reclaiming my body. In other words after this near–death experience, I was weakened for many months. I was in such a weakened state that I couldn't even open the heavy glass and steel door to my schoolhouse.

For weeks after returning to school, someone needed to assist me. I lost most of my hair, and my appetite didn't return for nearly six months. This was also the beginning of my chronic, lifelong migraines, fatigue, and body pain.

While in elementary school, I began to see and speak to the deceased (in school, at home, everywhere). But I soon learned not to discuss what I was seeing with others as I knew they would think I had lost my senses.

I was married (for the first time) at age seventeen. My new husband Richard and I took our first trip out of state. During our stay at a hotel, Richard and I went swimming in the heated indoor pool. We were the only people in the pool that afternoon, and it had been recently cleaned so the safety lines with their bright white and blue floats had been removed. Still Richard was an EMT (emergency medical technician), so I felt fairly safe. That was a mistake.

We had an argument about something silly, and he turned his back to me while he stayed in the 3' area relaxing. I walked away from him down the middle of the pool and was verbally telling him how I felt about something. Just then I stepped over an area that went from 3' to 10' depths. I was unprepared and began to panic.

The next thing I recalled was Richard holding me while I coughed and vomited water. He told me he had revived me, and from the bruises that developed on my chest, I believe he did. This was my third near-death experience. And to this point, it had been the most dramatic.

My second marriage to my current husband Jay was early in 1986. I had a terrible case of pneumonia in October of the same year, and I just happened to be 8½ months pregnant at the time. I was released at noon from one hospital and went into labor early that same evening. Jay and I had just ordered a pizza (as I had suffered from the horrible hospital food during my pneumonia bout). Our daughter was coming into the world. Her birth was horrendous for me and actually took my life for the fourth time!

My baby turned sideways during the birthing process. I had to have a Caesarian section, but I couldn't be put to sleep as I had just had pneumonia and my lungs were not healed enough to withstand it. This is the only death experience I can recall that had the "floating above the body" type of experience.

The contractions were horrible. Being a mother once already, I knew something was wrong. I wasn't screaming (I didn't want that to be the first thing my child heard in this world) and probably didn't even have the strength or the energy to scream out in pain.

I heard a nondescript voice deep within me ask, "Do you want to go?" Instantly I was seeing outside of myself or of my life actually. It was like an episode of *It's A Wonderful Life*. There were two screens (similar to picture–in–picture): one showing how my loved ones were affected if I stayed with them and the other showing the effects if I were gone.

I recall thinking that they both looked okay. I recall seeing Jay caring and raising our newly born daughter, so I was assured of her care should I not return. There was another contraction, and I told my adoptive mother (who was by my bedside) that I was going to die. I became unconscious.

I awoke to a room filled with doctors and nurses. I do not exaggerate when I tell you there were at least twelve medical staff members there. Every breath I took was agony. I was embraced by pain to the point I couldn't even focus on their words; I just wanted it all to stop. The baby was in trouble, and emergency surgery was all I recall them saying. It hurt too much to focus on their words; I just wanted to slip into the darkness again.

My spinal block anesthesia wore off in the midst of surgery. Through sheer and intense pain, my anesthesiologist's face took on the face of my husband Jay. I remembered telling him "good–bye"; his appearance then morphed into the face of my oldest daughter Danielle, and I again said "goodbye." The last face I recall was my adoptive mother to whom I had also said "good–bye." I thought I was dying, and apparently I was correct. I **know** that we are given "visions" of those we love to be able to say good–bye before we pass over. My family obviously wasn't in the OR with me, but it soothed my soul to have those final connections.

I began to see colors. Being in so much pain and feeling irrational, I must say that when I saw the bright red before my eyes, I thought it might be blood. I thought I put my hands up before my eyes attempting to touch the bright swirling color but later realized I was actually paralyzed due to the medication and couldn't have touched anything as my arms wouldn't move!

Just as I "touched" the living, moving red, it dissipated, and with it came a loud sound in my ears, a "whoosh". The red was replaced by a living, swirling orange. As before, I tried to touch the color (in my mind, I suppose), and once again it dissolved beneath my palm with a whoosh. It continued with color after color, each processing faster and faster, until the last color ended with a "pop" that reminded me of a champagne cork being popped at a New Year's Eve party.

Right before this or perhaps during (it is difficult to explain how it all occurred during the same moment), my life reviewed itself instantly. You would think it would have been major events, weddings, births, first big job, and so forth, but it wasn't. Not at all! It was small things such as helping an elderly person load groceries in his car as I walked by him at the market or calling a friend in need and checking on her, and even feeding a stray cat or dog. All of these things made it to the "big show" of my life. None of the things I would have thought important ever showed. Interesting, huh?

Suddenly I was free. I was free from pain and free from "heaviness". I soon came to understand I was out of my body. I was drifting in a cloud, an ocean, a field of white substance. I liken the consistency to heavy cream as it did have a consistency. It was a sensation of being warm and embraced. I looked down (for whatever reason) and saw myself lying on the operating table, and I was cut open. Blood was everywhere, and the attendees were scurrying around while machines beeped.

I tried to hear them talking, but it sounded like the teacher on the Charlie Brown TV specials. Another metaphor would include listening to a 78-LP record on a 33-LP album speed. They spoke in such slow motion that I couldn't make out what they were saying. Hindsight being what it is, I now realize that because I was out of body, my vibration had increased to a point where human language was just too slow, too dense, and well, too . . . human.

As I continued to watch the comings and goings of the people below me, I was oddly detached from them and from the form on the operating table. I saw the bloody mess that was my body. I remember thinking, "Oh, that's gross". To me, this proves that you carry on your slang, your beliefs, and your mindset (e.g. I cannot stand to look at medical pictures, as they make me ill). I turned away from the sight just like a swimmer turning in water. I turned to the Light.

When I did, I experienced heaven . . . the Elysian Fields, the Summerland, Nirvana, or whatever you wish to call it. It was an intense, everlasting sensation of warmth and nonstop love. But once again, I came back knowing it was still not my time. I wanted to be there for my two children. I wanted to complete my purpose on this earth. But when the day finally comes that I do go back "home" for good, there will be no regrets, only euphoria.

. . . .
About Tina Michelle

A professional psychic, angelologist, and workshop leader, Tina travels the country speaking about the near-death experience, awakening your psychic self, angels, and more. She is the creator and founder of Discovering Your Enlightenment Spiritual Learning Series (DYE), an on-line learning environment for psychic arts and metaphysical studies.

Tina is passionate about teaching and helping others recognize the power within. She shows others how to open themselves to their own personal power through the remarkable unconditional acceptance of our angels. For more information, please visit her Web site at www.tinamichelle.com.

My Heavenly Garden

Jen-Irishu
Australia
inharmony7@hotmail.com
www.jen-irishu.com

I remember my near-death experience as though it was yesterday. I was in surgery having another one of many operations. I am not sure how long I had been under the anesthesia; it doesn't really matter. I remember "flying" up into the clouds at a great speed and almost being sucked up into the heavens. The air was cold around me. Clouds whisked by like watered-down cotton wool.

Before I knew it, I was sitting on a park bench in a beautiful garden. The colors were so bright. There were stunning flowers everywhere. I wasn't cold anymore; it was warm and balmy. I wondered why I was there and looked around me for someone to ask. I felt a deep sense of loss as if I knew I had "died" and was sad I had left my children behind. Yet, I felt a deep sense of peace knowing I had come home.

A voice in the distance, yet not in the distance, vibrated all around me. I was asked if I would like to see a movie. A screen appeared before me. I was shown a coffin. Beside the coffin were my two children who were quite young at the time. They were each putting one single red rose on my coffin. They were crying. The voice asked me if I wanted to leave my children without a mother as they still needed me.

Crying, I told the voice I felt torn as I so much wanted to stay in heaven. But I looked at my children again and realized I couldn't leave them all alone. I told the voice I had made my decision; I would return to my body. The voice said I had made the right decision as I had a lot of work to do for God. I had been chosen especially to do this work; it was my gift only.

I asked what the gift was. I was told it was too early to know; it would unfold as my life progressed. I was not to be daunted or afraid; it was by birthright. This was the reason I incarnated on earth at this time.

Suddenly, I felt myself wrapped in a blanket shivering uncontrollably. There were nurses all around me saying, "She's back! She's back!" I tried to open my eyes, but they seemed glued shut. Sleeping beauty (me) didn't wake up again until two days later.

I know something important happened to me that day—something I just can't fully explain. But all I can say is I have never felt love as I did in that heavenly garden. I am sure I will never feel that same unyielding love until the day comes for me to go home again. It has a name I am sure . . . God.

. . . .
About Jen-Irishu

Jen is an author, spiritual counselor, and speaker. Although she always had the gift of "knowing," she never truly understood it until later in life when a deceased loved one returned to her to share a glimpse of his life on the Other Side and to prove that love has no end. Jen shares their true, unforgettable story in her book, *Messages of Love: My Spiritual Awakening*. Her children's books *The Angel in my Dreams* and *The Adventures of Angela and Eli* were given to her in her dream state. She is also the publisher of an e-magazine called *Spirit Whispers*. For more information, please visit her Web site at www.jen-irishu.com.

The First Crossing

Reece W. Manley, DD, MEd, MPM®
Texas
www.spiritthinking.net

During a five-month battle with MRSA, an infection caused by Methi-cillin–resistant Staphylococcus aureus bacteria, I experienced a pro-found near–death experience. There was no sudden happening that let me know I was passing. I remember listening to the mechanical sounds of the ventilator and hearing the murmur of loving voices. The ventila-tor was rhythmic and calming. This calm seemed to totally surround me. There was no flash of light. There were no bursts of joyous angels. It was just calm, quiet, and gray. Here is how my crossing began:

The calm, quiet noises seemed to have had an effect on me. I felt better—rested. I remember trying to open my eyes. However instead of my eyes opening, I simply became aware of a calm, quiet gray mist. The mist was everywhere, and while I began to hear the rhythm fade, the calm expanded.

At this point I became aware that I wasn't hurting. My feet had been so painful lying there in the hospital. The suffering had been so intense when I was aware of them. They were the least of the physicians' concerns, and the pain medication was being used very sparingly so as not to interfere with my respiration. The pain had become so harsh and so constant that I knew something was happening.

My feet weren't hurting. And quietly the ventilator began to fade in the background. I did not feel movement. It was as if things were simply fading away . . . fading away into this calm, gray mist.

However, I felt very much alive. I felt energy coursing through me. I felt as strong as I ever was since my weight training summer with my brother in late 1980s. There was a pause, a moment.

And then I was lifting weights with my brother. The first sensation was the smell. If you've ever been to a gym where the focus is on free weights, you know the smell. This is an odor that is a combination of sweat and disinfectant and leather from the gloves. The gloves on my hands I now felt. The smell, the feel of a glove on my hand, and then—pop—my eyes were open, and I heard my brother cheering me on. In a voice so much younger than it should have been, I heard Ross saying, "Three, Man! You can do it, now four." Along with the sound and understanding of Ross' voice came the feel of the weight against my hands. I felt the intense load on my hands and the muscles of my chest contracting.

Another pop, an audible pop, occurred this time as though a speaker amp had come on. My sight formed, and I was indeed pushing up a full load of weights in the middle of a bench press. My brother was standing above me urging even more strongly to "push, push." I could see the determination on his face, and I quickly felt my pulse quickening wanting to make the "one more" lest the whole damn bar come down on me! The energy coursing through me doubled, and I let out a little laugh that came out more like a grunt. The noise surprised me. After all I was in a hospital room in Plano in 2008, not in the gym circa 1989. But, I was wrong about the hospital room. I was, indeed, at the gym and the only thing in the world that mattered was getting that weight up and onto the bar bench.

Next, suddenly, my mouth was filled with taste. I have no idea what I had eaten the day before I got to the gym, but it was still on the taste buds of my mouth. Then I felt another pop. It was water I tasted. It all came together. I was at the gym, smelling the smells, seeing my brother, hearing his voice, and tasting the swig of water I had taken from the water fountain a few minutes earlier. It was a point in my life when I had felt wonderful. I had felt strong and powerful. I was with the one person in my life in 1989 I would trust to lift weights off of me at just the right time. It also came to me that I was **not** going to get that weight up without Ross' help. I made another noise, and my brother smiled broadly and feigned dropping the bar toward me. Then he finally said, "Good job, bro," and the bar lifted up and into place. I jumped up from the bench and clapped Ross on the shoulder. Ross took his place at the side of the weight bar and began removing the weights to where they were right for his work out. I was sliding a weight off the bar and then . . .

Again, there was gray mist and calm with no smell, no taste, no noise, no touch—the only "sight" was this simple gray mist. I still felt energized and was feeling more so by the moment. It was an amazing sensation. I was feeling completely well, young, and strong. Yet in the hospital lay a thirty–nine–year–old body ravaged by MRSA pneumonia and the cumulative years of neuropathy causing pain sometimes so severe that walking was impossible.

Ross' stayed in my thoughts, no in my experience, for a few moments, and then, pop, I felt sunlight on me.

It was a wonderful warm light. The sensation of the touch of the light was immediately joined by the visual knowing of sunshine. The gray had faded away, and I was in the sunlight. Next, in the back of my mouth a taste began to take shape. It was a fruit and it was good. It was unusual. Not something I had every day. Yet another pop happened followed by a spark, and my mouth was flooded with the taste of pineapple. But it was not just any pineapple, but a mixture containing coconut and the smooth burn of rum. I was in sunlight, and I was drinking a piña colada. This was getting a bit closer to heaven! I **still** had so much energy. I felt so incredibly good and so incredibly strong. My thoughts began, "Rian, that looks great; now try some blue." My eyes were suddenly reporting right along with my thoughts, and I was sitting outside by a pool at a Mexican resort somewhere in either Cancún or Playa Del Carmen. Rian is one of my wonderful nephews. He was eight. His skin was tanned with a bit of red from the sun, and I had had the honor of being the center of his attention for a few moments. He was dutifully painting in the activities area outside by the pool. I looked over at him, and he grinned and nodded as he admired his work and then reached for the blue.

Rian continued on his work as I lifted my eyes out to the ocean and swallowed a taste of the frozen drink in my mouth. I looked down again at the table and was aware of everything in the scene. The newspapers lay out to catch the glob of paint which did not quite make it onto the ceramic. Rian was painting enthusiastically, and there were several splotches of spilled paint about the paper. A cup set up with water was holding the brush in place which had been bearing red paint only a moment before. I was lost in the scene and thought about how wonderful it would be to be young like Rian was right then.

Pop.

The sunlight was still warm, but this time it was staving off a cool wind. The little boy with me was much younger than the young boy I had been with only a few seconds ago. And it was a different boy. I was back with my brother Ross. He was three or four, and I could tell I wasn't much older. There were adults talking next to us as we walked past them on the way to the ducks. Ducks! The lady whom I called out to was a tall pretty woman, and when she turned, I knew she was Momma. Momma and Ross and I were feeding the ducks on a perfect day full of sunshine and cool winds.

Pop.

I was still running at high speed toward a body of water. But instead of ducks I was sneaking up on Angi Culp with every intention of knocking her into the pool before she noticed me. My very good friend Richard was there wearing the impish, sly smile he reserved for such times and places. Wearing red swim trunks and pulling off the kind of "cool" only sixteen-year-old guys can pull off, my hands made contact with the softest thing I had ever, ever felt—the skin of Angi Culp. She screamed wildly as my body made contact with her carrying us both into the water. The water was cold, and Angi was hanging on to me. And, again, pop.

It was cold, so very, very cold. I scooped her up and headed down the mountain. She was the lightest thing in the world, and she was safe in my arms—safe against the wind, safe from the hurtling snowmobile which had just cast her upon the snow. I enjoyed making her safe. I was feeling quite the hero. I was feeling so proud of having saved milady from her dangerous steed.

Pop.

I was still feeling proud, very proud indeed, as I held a piece of paper in my fat little hand and shoved it right in front of a man's face saying the words, "Pay up!" It took a minute for me to figure out where I was when I heard my voice say "Pay up, Daddy," and it sounded again so young. My hand held the latest report card from Ms. Garcia's sixth grade class. It was full of As from top to bottom with the exception of PE. I watched the smile across his face thick with whiskers as he took the report card and studied it dutifully. The smell of his cigar filled the air. It was a familiar smell still present when . . . pop.

It was New Year's Eve, and my family and I were on our first cruise. Dad was smoking his cigar on the deck complaining about how he could only smoke it there or in the casino. My head begin to swim, and my mouth tasted of champagne. My sister-in-law was wearing the most beautiful shimmering dress, and the wind on the deck was blowing hard against her body. We were on our first trip since having the "new" money my father's and brother's business had brought to us. Dad and his wife were laughing, and I couldn't get my eyes to focus. I just noticed the stars going so far out into the heavens. The ships' lights paled in comparison to the stars' brilliant shine.

These "pops" would recur another twenty or thirty times. Each time I shifted, I was awestruck by the reality of the scene I found myself in. Each time I relived a different time in my life. Every one of the human senses was involved sharply and completely as the scenes changed. It seemed to go in the order of smell, sight, touch, sound, and taste. But that is an observation I make here back in my body.

I have no doubt whatsoever that I was actually revisiting these times in my life. I was not simply reviewing them or remembering them—I was there again. It seems impossible, but it held true for each session. There was no dreamlike quality. It was sharp. It was in focus. I learned about half way through the experiences that I was consciously able to will myself to be there by simply remembering the event.

I did not visit any of the darker times of my life. I don't know if I would have been allowed to have done so even if I had tried. But the gloriousness of the experience was so overwhelming that I thought I had very much found what awaits all of us on the Other Side. This was the ability to go back and enjoy the full experience of every moment of our past lives while in our human bodies.

As I recall these things, tears stream down my cheek. The moments in time were perfect for the instances in which they were made. However, today the scenes do not connect in such happy ways. Dear friends I revisited during moments in my life are lost to me now through my own carelessness of not keeping in touch. Sad moments would quickly follow many of the happy ones on the path I had visited. But to be able to visit just the precise moment, without having it relate to all of the other moments in my life, was priceless.

Each memory was picture perfect by itself and separate from the others. My relationship with the people at these various times of my life was exactly as it should have been for that moment of time. Another tear is shed as I realize how much I miss the relationships I had with some of these people whom I no longer have in my world. Yet it is comforting to know that those we love and care for are never really separate from us. In actuality, they are but a thought away.

. . . .
About Reece W. Manley, DD, MEd, MPM®
Reece has been helping and counseling clients for over fifteen years. He credits his near-death experience as the most important moment of his life. He is the author of *Crossing Twice: Answers from the Source* and *Spirit Thinking* in which he shares his new insights on spirituality and the love of an accepting, compassionate, empowering God. For more information, please visit his Web site at www.spiritthinking.net.

Grandfather Dean's Visit

Hal Cope
Arizona
zebuone@aol.com

Grandfather Mitchell Dean husking corn 1930s

Malaria is a vector-borne disease transmitted by mosquitoes and is widespread in tropical and subtropical regions. Each year there are approximately 350–500 million cases of malaria killing between one to three million people, the majority of whom are young children in sub-Saharan Africa. The most deadly form of malaria is *Plasmodium falciparum* which is normally found only in the female *Anopheles* mosquito. My forty plus year relationship with sub-Saharan Africa exposed me to malaria many times.

Even though I took the necessary precautions against malaria (there is no malaria vaccine), I found myself hospitalized in Harare, Zimbabwe (Africa) in 2000 with a life threatening bout of *Plasmodium falciparum* malaria. This was my fifth bout of malaria and by far the worst. I had been in the hospital for several days semiconscious alternating between states of freezing cold one minute followed by burning fever the next while shaking violently from head to foot. Fortunately the Avenue Clinic Hospital was one of the better medical facilities in Harare and well prepared to deal with malaria.

One night I awakened from my semiconscious stupor to see my deceased Grandfather Mitchell Dean standing at my bedside. To me it seemed perfectly natural for him to be there. He said to me, "Grandson, it is time for you to go. Follow me." I got out of bed and followed him down the hall to the elevator. This was not a dream; I remember literally getting up out of bed and walking with him, feeling no pain or discomfort whatsoever. It was all much too real.

My grandfather appeared happy and exactly as I remembered him working on his farm near Alda, Nebraska. When my parents divorced, my sister Rosella and brother Erwin and I were raised by my grandparents until my mother remarried. So I spent a lot of time with him out in the fields plowing and harvesting the crops. He would always let me ride Molly, one of his favorite horses, whenever we finished our work. After unhitching the horse, he'd put me on her back and turn us both loose. All I had to do was hold on to the reins; Molly always knew her way back to the barn.

These happy memories came rushing back to me as I looked lovingly at my grandfather. I was so happy to be with him once again. When we walked out to the hall, there were no windows, and it was dark and cloudy. It appeared to me to be almost like a tunnel setting. I looked around and didn't notice anyone else in the hallway. Then suddenly during this short trip to the elevator, my IV dropped to the floor. We stepped into the elevator which had two buttons, UP and DOWN. Grandfather Dean pushed the down button. When the elevator came to a stop and the door opened, he said, "It is not yet your time. Go out of the door."

I think it is important to note that when he told me to follow him in my hospital room and when he told me it was not my time in the elevator, he was not contradicting himself. When he asked me to follow him, he meant that I was simply to get out of bed and follow him. Likewise, when he said it wasn't my time to go, he meant I was not dead. This is why I believe he pushed the down button rather than the up button signifying heaven.

Strangely, I don't remember anything after that point. I just walked out of the elevator door, and then the next morning I was discharged from the hospital. I remember waking up feeling well enough to go home.

My experience was as real as sitting here writing this story. Maybe one of the reasons my near–death experience was so natural to me was the fact that I had adopted a strong belief in the afterlife and reincarnation since the 1970s. The idea that life never ends has been my philosophy in this life; it is my guiding star.

No Fear of Going There

Mary A. Ale
California

It was March 1956, and I was almost three months into my pregnancy. I had awakened with stomach cramps and decided to call my employer to report that I wasn't feeling well. By the time the evening hours came and my husband Ernest returned home from work, I was bleeding profusely. He rushed me to the emergency room at St. Mary's Hospital in Jamaica, Long Island, New York.

My obstetrician met us at the hospital and began to order tubes and other medical fixtures be placed into my body. I heard the doctor say several times, "Oh my God, Oh my God." I wasn't concerned. I was comfortable and not feeling any pain. As I lay on the table, I felt myself dissolving into a comfortable dark area.

I remember looking down at my body on the examining table and seeing many lights in the ER. The next memory was of Ernest in the barren hospital hallway; his arms were folded against his chest and his back was pressed against the wall with his left foot raised behind him resting on the wall. A nurse approached him and asked him to come to the office.

The next memory was of me wearing one of my favorite dresses—a red-and-white checkered blouse with puff sleeves and a black princess style jumper. I found myself in a dark, tunnel-like hallway with a bright light at one end. Standing in that light were variously sized people: short, tall, and childlike. I did not see their faces. Then a voice from the opposite side of the light seemed to ask me, "What do you want to do?" I replied, "I am young, and I want to have a baby."

Suddenly, I felt I was dropped back on the examining table. Shivering I heard a voice close to my face repeating, "Can you hear me? Can you hear me?" I struggled to emerge from what I felt was a hole so I could respond to the question. I recall moving my head up and down to signify "yes". A male voice shouted, "She's back! She's back!" I opened my eyes to see hovering over me a priest praying in a rapid mode.

The next morning Ernest was at my bedside with my parents. They were consoling me about the loss of our baby. In my weakened voice, I asked Ernest what the nurse had wanted when she asked him to come to the office. Ernest was startled and with a stammering, halting voice asked, "How did you know she wanted me to go to the office?" I explained that I had seen him in the hall when the nurse came to talk to him, and now I wanted to know why he had to go to the office. Ernest continued to stare at me in disbelief. He said the office wanted me to pay for the blood transfusion.

Was it a near-death experience? Did I have the opportunity to enter the hereafter? Had I been given another chance at life? I cannot verify it; however, fifty-three years later I still have vivid recollections of the experience, and it still confirms my belief in the hereafter. I have no fear of dying and no fear of "going there."

My Most Glorious Time

Metro Sinko
Ohio
metro351@sbcglobal.net

While preparing for prostate surgery, I was required to fast for four days on a liquid diet. The three-hour surgery went well, and I was given a morphine drip and ice cubes for the next three days. I remember that while I was on the morphine, my hearing was so incredibly acute that I could hear papers being stapled down the hall during the night shift.

While I was still on my ice diet, the nurse told me that it was time for me to get some exercise and go for a walk. I sat up on the bed and proceeded to move into the chair next to my bed. Suddenly I became completely overcome with exhaustion. This was followed by dizziness and cold sweats as I slumped into the chair and dropped my cup of ice.

The next thing I remember is being in a beautiful place of serenity and comfort. Although it is difficult to describe with mere words, I will say that it was wonderful utopia. Everything was beautiful—no pain, worries, or troubles. There was only peace, happiness, and calmness.

In a split second I appeared to have this panoramic view of the Other Side and felt nothing but contentment. Oddly while this was going on, I could hear the nurse's voice in a distance repeatedly calling my name,

"Mr. Sinko!"

But I was enjoying my newfound world and didn't want to listen to her. I was too busy taking in my surroundings and enjoying my state of bliss.

"Mr. Sinko!!"

Looking back now, I would have to say that I was kind of in-between two dimensions, two worlds. The nurse yelled forcefully for me to come back for the third time,

"Mr. Sinko!!!"

And this time I did. I was dragged away from my utopia and pulled back into reality. I was so upset. I did not want to leave that beautiful place. I did not want to come back to the unbearable pain.

My blood pressure was then measured at 88 over 60, which is low. The doctor said this was because more fluids were going out of my body than were coming in. I have seen a glimpse of heaven, and I am no longer afraid of death. I know it will be a most glorious time.

A Birth and Awakening to the Other Side

Angelyn Ray
Oregon
www.araypress.com

The anticipation of the birth of our second child was something we looked forward to as pros. After all, hadn't we already been through this once? Apparently that was not to be the case. Nothing could have prepared me for the medical twist that was to occur as I delivered our second child or for the excursions out of my body.

There was a mix-up between the doctor and the hospital personnel. I had received a preparatory injection which served only to muddle my thinking. It did not take away or begin to dilute the pain. The doctor was delayed by several births in other locations, and by the time he arrived in my delivery room, he had forgotten that I was not prepared to deliver by natural childbirth. The planned pain medication was not administered, and throughout the delivery I remained strapped down on my back with my wrists and ankles shackled and my head seemingly going around in circles. As the labor contractions intensified, I reached the point where I could no longer tolerate the wrenching pain that gripped me in its vise.

Suddenly I found myself shot out of my body, out of the hospital, off the Earth, and zooming into outer space. Just as suddenly suspended in the dark limitless expanse, a cube-shaped room appeared out of nowhere as if to catch me in my trajectory. The room looked like an ordinary waiting room with transparent walls. It was without furnishings—without my body I wouldn't need a chair, would I? A tall luminous being was in attendance observing my approach. As I neared the room, the being turned his back to me as if my arrival was not expected, and I catapulted back into my pain-consumed body only to shoot out again.

Until Leif was born, over and over like a yo-yo on the end of a string, I rocketed between my body and the waiting room with the same result each time—the luminous being turned his back just as I reached the room.

I have called this being "him," but it may very well have been androgynous or gender neutral. The apparel was a long white glowing gown over a straight body. The glow emanating from the shoulders and heart area lent a hint of the appearance of wings. The shoulder-length hair was light and luminous. I was not close enough to see the face before he turned away. I sensed that he had his own agenda which served a much greater purpose that transcended my physical condition and that his task at this juncture was to keep me attached to my body, distracting me from the pain, and then sending me back repeatedly until the labor was finished.

Leif is now a healthy thirty-five-year-old, and as I write these words, the image of the being in the room out of nowhere surrounded by the expanse of space is as vivid in my mind as it was then. The birth of a child puts one in touch with "the Other Side" often in subtle, indefinable ways. The birth of this child put me in touch with "the Other Side" in ways that have changed me completely and in ways that have been written about by others who have been temporarily admitted to the Beyond.

As I look back at that early morning in the hospital delivery room, it seems as though I was allowed a glimpse of a different kind of room, a minuscule piece of heaven, just enough to relieve my pain so that I could survive the labor and the birth experience, but it would not hold me there. Primarily I gained there an acute awareness of our tiny, though very critical, human presence in the cosmic scheme of things. There was a pervasive sense of comfort in the universe and in an overarching goodness that teams in perfect order just beyond our ordinary consciousness.

By the time I experienced my second visit to the heavenly realms, I had studied the NDE phenomenon and had read everything about it that I could find. Reassuringly, and not surprisingly, features of my experience during Leif's birth turned out to be typical, though nothing in my life up to that point had prepared me for it.

Just over six years later I was driving Leif's older brother Miles to a school event on a Saturday morning. A light rain was beginning to fall, and I underestimated the slippery effect on the dry, dusty pavement. Accelerating after coming around a sharp curve, I lost control. Along the road were a series of boulders that marked the edge of a parking lot. Hitting one of the boulders, the car somersaulted into the parking lot which was, fortunately, empty. Landing on its wheels, it shuddered to a stop. Dazed, I turned off the engine and saw blood coming from Miles' scalp.

We clambered out of the car, and people appeared helping us to a cement stairway at the entrance of a restaurant where I sat with my son's head in my lap. Someone gave us an ice pack to slow the bleeding until the ambulance arrived. As I stared across the road, the landscape looked backward to me as though a mirror image of the familiar scene.

The wound on Miles' scalp was closed with stitches, and I was diagnosed with a concussion. The concussion, if not the trauma, would explain the daze and the scene reversal. But neither the concussion nor the trauma would explain what I experienced during the moment or two that the car performed its acrobatics. My known vocabulary doesn't offer a fitting term for the space or dimension I entered.

Time was suspended, or it would be better stated that "space" was not subject to time. I found myself looking into a tunnel of arms reaching toward us as if to catch us if we entered the tunnel. There were scores of them. The beings to which the arms belonged remained in the unseen background. The nature of those beings was defined by the character of the outstretched hands—infinitely open, welcoming, blessing, comforting, and healing. There was a dear familiarity about every one of them as though they waited to welcome us to a home that we had forgotten.

By the time of the car accident, I had learned about others' experiences of luminous beings, but I had never heard of a tunnel of loving, welcoming arms. So I was surprised again. My brain would have been forever relieved of all fear of death if any had remained after the glimpses I'd been afforded six years before.

While we sat waiting for the ambulance on those cement steps with Miles' head in my lap, he repeated over and over, "Are you okay, Mom? Mom, are you okay?" The pure, undiluted love that emanated from those welcoming arms echoed through the love in his words and also peeked through the responses of the unidentified observers who had furnished the ice and called for help.

About Angelyn Ray

Angelyn is a licensed clinical social worker with a private practice in Oregon. Her work as a therapist combines a three-fold approach: integrating the losses of one's life, building healthy, self-nurturing skills, and developing one's unique creative expression.

She is an award-winning author, poet, and artist. Currently her books carry her own imprint ARay Press. She writes an Internet journal based on questions that come from her readers or through her work. She is a longtime member of the Association for Research and Enlightenment. Angelyn can be reached through her Web site, www.araypress.com.

Encircled by Weeds

Rick Bunch
Indiana
rick@rickbunch.com
www.rickbunch.com

My near–death experience (NDE) occurred at the age of five while on a family reunion at a camp ground in Nebraska. My father had taken my sister and me fishing at the end of a long pier. I recall asking my father to cast my line out for me because I was unable to do it on my own. Every time I cast the line out, I would keep reeling in weeds. This was entertaining for me and kept me occupied while he was busy teaching my sister to fish. Because she was three years older than I, she could cast the line out on her own. I remember seeing them together at the end of the pier hunched over trying to fish.

Then it happened. I was not just in the water but under it. I was surrounded by many weeds, and within these weeds were dead frogs and a turtle. He appeared to have been caught or tangled in the weeds. At the moment I realized I was sitting on the bottom of the lake. I observed bubbles going up and up as my eyes followed them going towards the surface far above me. The reflection of the surface sparkled as the sun shone down upon it. I recall feeling the dirt in my hand. As I lifted the dirt, I was fascinated with the feeling of it. It was soft and silky and made swirling clouds as it resettled back down to the lake floor. It was beautiful. I never felt any danger nor was I gasping for air as the water filled my lungs. I was at peace. The last time I glanced upward towards the surface I noticed that the light was different. This time the reflection from the sun was more like dancing colored lights performing for me. The lights resembled the colors of a rainbow and were forming some sort of a pattern above me.

I felt safe, and I also felt that I was not alone. Next, the rainbow-colored lights came together in a circle pattern, and as they did, the colors became white. This white light was brilliantly bright. It illuminated the darkness of the lake floor. The Light began to surround me. I was in the Light and part of it. Somehow I knew I was not alone; I was protected. I felt like I was no longer in or under water at all. In fact, I was no longer wet but dry. Beautiful, calming voices within this Light were talking to me.

Then bam! The next thing I knew I was sitting on the floor of the cabin's shower. The room was filled with steam from the hot water, and people were running around yelling. I began to cry and cough at the same time. All of this excitement was overwhelming, but then I felt pain coming from within my cold body.

Many years later I recall my parents talking about the accident. My dad described that moment in detail. My dad and sister did not realize I had fallen into the water. Apparently, I fell in the lake in such a way that I made no splash. They never heard a thing. Once they realized I had fallen in, my dad dove into the lake. But the lake water was very dark. He could not find me. After several attempts of searching, he yelled at my sister to run to the cabin to get help. He searched and searched continually coming up for air and back down again. There was no sign of me. Then he noticed something at the bottom of the dark lake that looked brownish white; it was my t-shirt. He swam down and pulled me up by this shirt. He, then, tossed me onto the deck.

My lifeless, cold pale body with dark blue lips lay upon the wooden deck. I was not breathing nor was there a pulse. This was before the day of CPR. He got up on the deck, threw me over his shoulder, and ran up the hill towards the cabin. As he was running, water was pouring out of my mouth. He was met by frantic relatives as they put me in a hot shower and kept slapping my cold hard face. I guess everyone thought it was too late. Then to everyone's amazement my eyes sprang open, and I began to cry. My family estimated that the total time from when I was under water to when I awoke in the shower was approximately fifteen minutes.

How I managed to be without oxygen for so long and to come back to life, I don't know. But I can say that this experience forever changed my view of life. I've known that life has no end since a very young age. To me this experience has been one of my greatest blessings.

. . . .

About Rick Bunch

A gifted medium, Rick says he has been drawn to the supernatural realm for as long as he can remember. Whether his gift was due to his near-death experience at the age of five or to the fact that his grandfather was also a gifted clairvoyant, he does not know. But he is a strong believer that we **all** have some form of psychic senses. The only difference is that some learn to use these senses while others don't.

Rick helps people understand that life does continue and that death is not to be feared by conducting not only public and private Spirit Circles, his demonstration of mediumship, but also workshops, conferences, lectures, and readings. He is a member of the American Association of Psychics, the American Association of Psychics and Mediums, and of Find Me, a team of dedicated law enforcement detectives, canine search and rescue personnel, and psychics dedicated to locating missing people and solving cold cases all over the world. All members are volunteers. For more information about Rick, please visit www.rickbunch.com.

A "Snow" Departure

Mark Jacoby
California

December 17, 1979, a school day, brought an abundance of fresh snow to North Lake Tahoe. Although I had hoped school would be canceled, this would not be the case. Placer County and the State of California stepped up to the task and soon had the main roads cleared enough to drive school buses. One of their mandates, it seemed to me, was to clear the main school bus routes first. This task they nearly always achieved, to their cursed credit, and on this white morning they had done their job.

I was a seventeen-year-old senior at North Tahoe High School and by this time had been driving myself to school for about a year in either my parents' cars or in my own car equipped with studded snow tires. Without a four-wheel drive, I learned that any self-respecting local would use studded snow tires. To me it seemed that the use of tire chains was a sign of weakness and inexperience.

The roads were in pretty good shape considering the rate of snowfall. I had no problems with the drive to school that morning once the shoveling was done to release my car from its white prison in the driveway, but I do remember thinking that there sure was a lot of snow coming down.

When school officials didn't call a "snow day" in the morning during such storms, students of North Tahoe High and a great many other schools, I suppose, would look out the window or step outside to see the fluff pile up in between classes. Even though our morning pardon had not been granted, we did hope that the vice principal's voice would come over the intercom at any minute announcing our reward of early release. These half days were in some ways better than snow days because we wouldn't have to make them up at the end of the school year as we did snow days. There was the added benefit of being with our friends and knowing each other's plans for the rest of the day. I would never learn whether or not they let school out early that day.

Pink Floyd had released one of the most popular albums of the decade entitled *The Wall*. I was the first kid on my block or even in the whole school, it seemed, to have this album on cassette tape. I had been listening and playing it for my friends for a few days and asked a friend if we could go "crank up a couple songs" at his house during lunch. Tim, whose father was a real estate developer or some such professional, was one of my many friends with wealthy parents. Friends with wealthy parents were as common at Tahoe as friends with pets are in the other places I had lived. Their condo was on the lakefront with a very powerful and expensive stereo in the living room.

Tim also had a brand new Jeep CJ Wrangler. This jeep had great tires and four-wheel drive, the ultimate snow toy for young drivers. The lunch bell rang, and off we went across the school parking lot to the Jeep. I was quite comfortable with the walk to the Jeep in my new down jacket. Having a down jacket was like having four-wheel drive or studded snow tires on one's car; it was part of the Tahoe survival kit for locals. Some of the "more local" types were fond of patching holes and tears in their puffy down jackets with duct tape. My goose down jacket had no duct tape as it was new.

The Jeep had no problems with the conditions once Tim adjusted his speed to be safe on the lethal surface. Once at the lakefront condo, we listened to Pink Floyd from Sansui speakers with oversized woofers as we ate sandwiches and drank sodas. The time had come to take the cassette back to the Jeep and drive back to school.

While we were lunching at the condo, another winter road condition emerged. A snowplow had visited Lake Forest road. When a snowplow equipped with a normal, straight plow blade encounters this packed snow condition, it doesn't remove much snow. Unable to penetrate the rock-hard white ice, the machine simply peels the rough layer from the surface just as a razor blade removes dried paint from glass. This peeling action leaves a clean scraped road of ice resembling polished white marble. This type of road surface is so slippery that one can barely stand or walk on it. The storm then added, perhaps, another a quarter inch of snow to this polished white surface; we might as well have been driving on an ice rink.

I assume Tim saw what he thought was a good place for an e-brake turn about a quarter mile down Lake Forest road. This stunt consists of gaining speed as quickly as possible, then cranking the wheel one way or the other while slamming on the parking brake. The result would be an exciting 180° sliding turn that sends snow flying in restless billowing clouds. I don't think either of us expected what happened next; on the deadly slick ice, once the slide began, the Jeep actually seemed to accelerate. The Jeep slid completely out of control. It was a familiar feeling—to slide out of control in the snow; I had done this many times before. But this slide was different. We slid to the right side of the road with the driver's side first towards a driveway. The speed was probably around thirty-five mph, but we were not slowing at all.

As I looked in the direction of the slide, I saw we were headed for a telephone pole. In my mind I saw the pole snapping with comical insignificance like some of the orange, wooden snow poles lining the mountain roads to guide the plows, which my friends and I had run over before in malicious vandal sprees. I, then, envisioned us being stuck in the deep snow bank afterward, having to dig out. In my mind I thought, "Great; we're going to get stuck and have to dig out; then we'll be late back from lunch." The Jeep continued to slide as time seemed to slow. It wasn't difficult to turn in my seat to watch the slide; I wore no seat belt. As we slid, I continued my strained glance over my shoulder toward the pole, and it seemed that we might miss it. What did happen was very different, indeed. My last memory of this situation was little more than a loud sound and more of a rustling blur really than a crash, which was similar to newspaper being quickly wadded up and stuffed into the woodstove. That sound was accompanied by a brief flash of light, then darkness, or more accurately, nothing at all.

The next sound I heard was Pink Floyd's *The Wall* playing from the Jeep's stereo. The motor was no longer running, but I could clearly hear my favorite band as the stereo was turned up high. I awoke slowly and felt quite numb. My whole body was tingling, similar to the way it felt when a leg would fall asleep from sitting cross-legged for too long. There was a ringing or hissing sound in my ears as well. As my vision faded in, I was surprised to see I was lying on my back directly under the rear differential of the Jeep, staring up at the rear axle. I don't know how long I had been there. I was very confused by this; I really didn't know what to think. In trying to rationalize this situation, I thought I had crawled under Tim's Jeep as I had been under cars before for mechanical maintenance and such, but didn't remember doing it or why. I don't remember whether I was dragged out or got out from under the Jeep on my own, though it does seem I somehow pulled myself out. I do remember being on the street behind the Jeep and standing up only to immediately fall down in darkness again.

Awake again, I felt the numbness begin to change to pain as Tim and a stranger held me by my arms and began to drag me out of the street. My feet slid obediently across the slick snow while Tim and the stranger struggled for footholds supporting their load. There were knives and daggers inside my left arm; I could feel grinding and something very loose and sharp inside my arm or my shoulder or my chest. I couldn't tell what was happening, but I knew something was broken. I told Tim to let go because my arm was broken and he was hurting me. He released my arm and grabbed around my waist, while I leaned more of my balance into the lady on my right. I began to realize I could not breathe. It felt as though the arm around my waist or the weight of my body in the arms of these two dragging me had somehow knocked the wind out of me. This sort of labored breathing was familiar to me because I had played football; I had been winded by blows to the abdomen before. I was sure that I would eventually catch my breath as I had done on the football field. They took me into the home of the lady and laid me on the living room sofa. The pain faded to darkness once again.

Suddenly awake, I heard voices. Tim was there along with the stranger lady and another man. I must have been moaning or crying because they were talking about what to do to help me with the pain. I heard that they had called for an ambulance and that the highway patrol was on the way as I drifted in and out of consciousness. I knew I had been in a car accident. I knew we had hit the telephone pole and that it did not break. I heard the man and woman talking to each other, and they had decided to light a marijuana joint for me as it would help ease the pain. When the man handed it to me, I had to tell him I couldn't smoke because I was having too much trouble breathing. In fact, my breathing seemed to get more difficult with each breath. I was to learn later that my right lung was collapsing.

When the highway patrolman arrived, he started asking me questions. By this time I could not draw enough breath to speak above a quiet whisper. I know he asked me my name several times, and after each time I answered him, he would repeat, "Do you know what happened? Can you tell me your name?" I would tell him, "I'm Mark Jacoby, and we crashed in the Jeep", but apparently he could not hear me. I went back to sleep again as Tim and the highway patrolman discussed the accident. Tim told him who I was. I honestly cannot say how long I lay there; it seemed about forty-five minutes, but it could have been ten minutes or an hour; everything was quite distorted. I remember drifting in and out of consciousness desperately trying to escape the intense pain. There was more commotion, and I heard the medics arrive.

Two Tahoe City fire department medics were kneeling beside me, and I thought it odd that they asked me the same questions as the highway patrolman, "Can you tell me your name? Do you know where you are? Do you know what happened? Where does it hurt?" I gave them the same answers I gave the patrolman, but since they kept repeating their questions, I assumed they were playing some kind of game with me. I could not for the life of me understand why. It hadn't really occurred to me that they could not hear me. I grew frustrated trying to talk to them. They fussed with one of the bags they brought in and produced a pair of scissors with which they began to cut off my new jacket. I was desperately trying to get them to stop as I had just bought this jacket. It seemed that I was successful in getting them to pull it off, though I don't remember seeing the jacket again.

Next they cut off my shirt. I was fond of this blue–striped knit shirt and watched sadly as they peeled it away from my torso. When they removed the scraps of cut fabric, I began to understand for the first time what had happened to me. As I looked down at my chest, I saw that my left shoulder was grotesquely dislocated to near the center of my chest; my shoulder seemed to be under my nipple. Every movement had become painful. Everything the paramedics did to me, hurt beyond description. I tried to scream but could not draw enough breath to make a sound.

As I looked at my deformed body, I began to feel as though I was not looking at my body at all. This confusion may have been due to shock or something else, and at this point things began to get very strange. I remember concentrating all my energy on breathing as I simply could not breathe enough. My vision was strange as well; the air seemed fuzzy as though I could see the air. I looked at my twisted body and noticed that my perspective had changed. I was coming to the realization that I was hurt very badly. It was with more than just a broken bone. I also seemed to be looking at the paramedics and at my shoulder from just above where my shoulder should be; it was to the left of and just above my left ear. This compounded my confusion as I was pretty sure I could not sit up. I had tried to sit up earlier and found that I lacked the strength to struggle through the intense pain.

Quickly after, I remember talking to the paramedics and looking at them eye to eye, but this could not have been as they were standing over me and I was lying flat on my back. The sight of my body, the pain, and all of the confusion was overwhelming, and I tried to go back to sleep. This time, though, the breathing was harder than ever.

I liked the sleep; it was the only escape from the pain. To be awake meant to feel the pain, and pain seemed to have replaced every sensation. It hurt to breathe; it hurt to try to talk; my mind hurt from the inability to communicate with the medics. My shoulders hurt; my chest hurt; my neck hurt; my back hurt, and my stomach muscles hurt from trying to suck air into a crushed chest.

This was not like any pain I had ever felt before. It was a dry, sharp, stinging pain, just like a cut that kept on cutting or a burn from the inside that did not feel better when the heat went away. This pain was getting worse, and this pain was there to stay. There was no lying still to make it go away. The paramedics were also moving me around and running their hands over my body to search for injuries. There was no waking relief from this pain.

I had to put so much energy into breathing that it was wearing me out, and it hurt to breathe. I just couldn't breathe no matter how hard I tried, and it was becoming too hard. I really didn't know why; it was so very confusing. The rhythm of my breathing dominated my awareness. It was becoming impossible to breathe adequately. I was exhausted, not the way a hard day at work or play exhausted me, but this was the exhaustion of a lifetime. In sleep this body stopped hurting. Yet, there was something else in the sleep. It started quietly from a faraway place deep inside and moved closer and closer the longer I "slept."

I may have thought I was sleeping, but I was actually passing out due to a combination of pain, the hypoxic effect on my body, shock, or more than likely, all of the above. But I was aware somehow. I could feel the labored breath coming in and going out. It began to slow as each breath seemed to take a long, long time. One breath in particular I remember. I don't so much remember it coming in, but I do vividly recall it leaving.

This breath seemed to exhale too much. I don't know where that much air could have come from, but it seemed I exhaled slowly and completely—more completely than any breath I had ever experienced before. In fact I kept exhaling after all the air seemed to have left my one semifunctional lung. I felt a sensation of movement with this exhalation. It was as though somehow I could feel the air once it left my body. In fact, I was the air that left my body. I could feel myself peeling away from the body. This sensation, while difficult to describe, was quite disorienting at the time. I rode out of my body inside this last breath. I could feel myself leaving the body on the sofa in a kind of tingling, whooshing sensation. This new feeling was concentrated in my head as though I had been sucked out of my face by some vacuum-like force attracting this last breath.

The pain had left me, but I was not asleep, and it was not dark as when the pain was gone before. I could see. I could still see the medics talking to me. They knew I had stopped breathing, and they were talking to each other as one of them was telling me to stay with him. By now I was looking eye to eye with them. Slowly I saw that their faces seemed to sink below me; soon I was facing downward toward the medic who was doing most of the talking. This was very confusing; I was becoming aware that something very strange was happening, strange indeed, though somewhat familiar. I knew that this scene was very wrong because I knew I was lying on the sofa. I knew this because I was certain I did not stand up. I also knew this because things had become progressively worse since my last attempt to sit up or even move at all. I also knew that I was no longer asleep nor was I unconscious. I willed myself to turn my field of vision toward the sofa. I saw a familiar face though I could not immediately recognize it. I had the distinct feeling that I knew this person very well but could not quite put a name to the face. A bizarre realization forced itself upon me, though irrational at first, when I began to recognize the face as my own. What I find strange to this day is that I was not surprised to see my face on the body below me.

This "awareness" changed things. I don't believe I knew I was dying just yet, but I did know that this was serious. I was certain up to this point that I would somehow regain the ability to breathe. I just needed to "catch my breath." Now that I was floating in the room, breathing was no longer a priority. Once I realized that I was not in my body anymore, there was a moment of panic, but not one of fear, more of disorientation. I felt unstable as though I was standing on ice and had slipped unexpectedly. My arms were flapping for balance, and just as I regained my feet, I became afraid to move for fear of slipping again. There was a sense of weightlessness just as during the top of the arc of a roller coaster or the moment of surprise when an elevator starts to descend unexpectedly. I was experiencing some feelings of vertigo as well. These strange sensations seemed to linger for a moment that was just long enough to be noticed when the scene continued to change yet again.

I had a sense of movement, and the room began to distort around me. I could see the medics and me as my field of vision was growing to include the whole room. I could see the others and the California Highway Patrol officer, but the scene was distorted. It seemed like the room was elongating as though I was on the ceiling, but the ceiling was rising. It was just a normal room with an eight or nine foot ceiling, but my view was of this room as though the ceiling had risen to maybe thirty feet. At this point the sensation changed from my field of vision altering to one of movement. I felt as though I were being drawn away. It was not that I was gaining in altitude, but that I was separating from this scene. It was as if the world was moving away from me and I was becoming a part of something else that was reclaiming me.

The people in the room looked different as well. It was as if their outlines had been traced with a crayon of light producing an orange glow around the lines of their bodies. The air had become lavender-hued fuzz as if the air molecules were a translucent purple. I could see the air, and then I sensed a kind of hissing sound and a strange perception of fuzzy darkness as I floated through what would have been the ceiling. I was in the storm now; I could see purple-hued snow falling as I continued to merge upward with something to which I was connected. There came a sensation of great attraction. I would not call it speed exactly; it was more like the world was moving more rapidly away from me than I from it. The scene below me seemed to stretch away in an infinite distortion.

Though difficult to describe, it seemed as if the room, building, and snowstorm were projected onto a cloth sphere. I ascended to the top of this sphere which distorted just like lifting a sheet from a bed between pinched fingers; the scene draped away from me and changed as my point ascended. As I was lifted higher, the fabric of the world dangling around me distorted further and further as the point lifted higher.

I was returning from whence I came. I cannot adequately put this feeling into words, but I knew of this place; it was familiar, and I had been there before. It was not that my body and the world were unfamiliar or a place that I didn't belong; they were familiar as well. But this place I was moving toward felt like home, not like my home today but like a childhood memory of home when Mom would take care of me as a small child. This was a warm, nurturing feeling of complete trust. I felt as though I was expected, and there were open arms awaiting me.

At this point I was aware of a great journey—a great distance to be traveled, only a portion of which I had traversed. My senses changed in this motion as well. I no longer had a sense of sight, of temperature, or of movement. I could not feel pain nor do I recall hearing. The only sense I do recall at this point was a deep sense of love. This sensation was felt deeper than I had ever experienced before though it was a familiar feeling. I recognized it as love, which seemed to emanate from all points towards me and from me outward. It was a warm feeling, a comforting feeling, a sense of perfect well-being.

There was also the sense of a great burden having been lifted from me. I had been here before. I knew where I was by now, though I cannot name this place. I had returned from whence I came, and I don't know what it is called. Though I have heard many labels applied, this could have been heaven or some kind of Samadhi, a collective of souls. Personally, I don't know what to call it. I try only to describe it as I remember because I believe to label the place is to call it something that it only partially is. I had been in this place before. This was a place of pure grace expressed in love, radiating from all points to all points.

I was no longer alone as I sensed the presence of another. I was aware of being myself, autonomous and complete, yet inside of this awareness I felt the presence of the other in the same way. I was there; the other was there; we were separate, yet I could feel the other as though the other was a part of me. It was as if somehow my feelings, emotions, and knowledge had merged with those of another. Then I heard a voice. My use of the word voice is interesting as I had no sense of hearing and I suspect no ears though I do not have a good description of what my "body" in this place might have been like. This was more of a thought in my mind which was not a thought of my own. It was the thought of the other. This sort of thought communication was odd at first but quite natural to me as it was also familiar. Not only was this style of communication familiar, but I also recognized the particular other whose thought I was sharing. I had shared thoughts with this other before.

It is unclear how we started, yet the result of this first thought exchange was for me to begin a series of feelings about my life. These feelings resulted from numerous actions in my life. The difference was that not only did I experience the feelings again, but I also had an empathetic sense of the feelings of those around me who were affected by my actions. In other words, not only did I have feelings about my actions in life, but I also sensed the feelings of others resulting from my actions. The most overwhelming of these feelings came from my mother.

I was adopted as an infant. As I grew, I had become somewhat of a troublemaker. I sometimes hurt other children when I was smaller and had taken to drug and alcohol abuse, stealing, crazy driving, bad grades, vandalism, cruelty to my sister, cruelty to animals; the list goes on and on. All of these actions were relived during these moments as were wonderful moments as well with the associated feelings of both myself and the parties involved. The most profound, however, was a strange sense coming from my mother. I could feel how she felt to hear of my death. She was heartbroken and in great pain, but it was all mixed up with feelings of how much trouble I had been in. I got a sense that it was such a tragedy to have had this life end so soon without really ever having done much good.

This feeling left me with a responsibility of having unfinished business in my life. The grief that I felt from my mother and friends was intense. In spite of my troubled life, I had many friends; some of whom were very close. I was well-known if not popular, and I could sense many things being said about my life and death, but it was the sense of my mother's grief that was overwhelming.

There were other feelings as well from school friends; in fact nearly the whole student body reacted to the news of my death. I could feel a great many thoughts: sorrow, grief, and prayers. I could feel the thoughts of extended family members as well. People I didn't even know were affected: community members, people who read the news of my death or heard it on the radio. Through a sense of empathy I could feel all the repercussions of my death at once. Each thought was an individual feeling, but more significantly they were summed up as one overall feeling. It was not so much a judgment of what my life meant, but more like what I, and others, felt about my actions in this life. The other did not judge these feelings as we experienced them together.

I became aware of the thoughts of the other again. This other had experienced these feelings at the same time and in the same way I had just done. It was like we had just watched a movie together, and we were discussing our feelings about it. However this movie was one that we could not only see but also feel. I cannot say whether this other was God, my spirit guide, an angel, Jesus, some spirit guide, or some relative of mine. My sense of it is that these terms are so similar in this place that it is not entirely relevant to apply such a label to this other. The other actually felt more like a very close friend at the time. I can say with certainty that this voice and I were together in some profound way then as we have been in the past and will be in the future. In that sense it did fit in with some of the things I have read about in the Bible. I have also read similar writings about guardian angels, spirit guides, the Higher Self, and a great many spiritual entities. However, during this exchange I was not so concerned with labels.

I must try to explain that which cannot be put into words. This place was a part of me, and I was a part of it. We are not and were not separate even as I write these words years after the experience; we are still one, this place and I. The experience of being there is to exist as love, inside love, and knowing only love. It was as if the emotion of love is what in the end and in the beginning I have always been. Love is what I have only been. And to extrapolate that to human existence, we are all connected in this way inside this place, which is all things and all people; life is love and love is life. Every atom in the universe is connected in this way.

I recalled that as I floated away from my body, I was somehow aware of the air molecules, not in a scientific way, but such that there was a connection between the air molecules and what I had become, or rather, what I had always been. In this frame of mind I am always connected to all things. I have also said in conversations about this experience, and continue to assert, that what is really going on is so much bigger than anything I had ever experienced in church or in literature through any medium. It transcends the human capacity for expression. In my awareness I became or returned to being a part of this.

After summing up the feelings of a short lifetime, the thought exchange continued. The question was put in my mind, "Do you want to stay?" The voice seemed to actually ask many questions at once. In the question I sensed a great many different meanings: "Are you done with this life? Do you want to finish the work you were to do in this life? Do you want your loved ones to experience this grief?" All of this was asked in an instant in a single thought. It is my recollection that the choice was mine, totally of my own free will, but I also have a sense that within the question the repercussions and results of either decision were also known in vivid detail. My mind was able to encompass infinite details reaching throughout all of existence regarding the repercussions of my actions and this decision. For each version of the question, the feelings and repercussions of my decision were felt. The feeling of grief my mother felt at the news of my death dominated my feelings. Somewhere beneath this overwhelming feeling of grief, however, was a sense of duty and of work to be done.

While the dialog and images of this exchange were at times difficult, I must emphasize the context of overwhelming compassion and love in which the exchange took place. This was, in fact, the most peaceful and tranquil moment of my life. I cannot adequately express how natural and wonderful this experience was. In this place with this being everything was more than okay; it was almost a celebration. Acceptance and understanding of all my feelings were shared instantly with this being who understood and loved me unconditionally.

The specifics of whatever else was asked in this singular thought are now lost on me, but my response to the question was, "If I go back, will I be able to come here later? Will it always be like this?" The answer was immediate; apparently I had decided and the result was instantaneous. There was an oxygen mask on my face, and I was struggling to wake up, or more honestly, not to wake up. I knew they were planning to start CPR on me, and I did not want them to do this as my chest was in extreme pain again. I awoke to a medic holding an ammonia inhalant under my nose after having slipped the oxygen mask up and slightly covering my eyes. I awoke to such pain that it defies description. I screamed a weak and wretched groan. This time the medic could hear me; he stopped asking me the same question over and over again. This time the medic was actually talking to me. I remember his new mantra as clear as day, and the rest of my experience is very clear to me. He said, "Don't go back to sleep, Mark." He was to repeat this mantra in a well-practiced tone all the way to the hospital.

The oxygen was apparently just enough to restore some level of brain and motor skills. In spite of the trauma to my chest cavity, I still had one good lung. I believe the working lung was not enough to sustain me due to the pressure of my shoulder joint and associated hemorrhaging on top of my "good" lung and ribs. The oxygen, however, had given my desperately starved brain and blood the boost it needed to remain alive. The medic had saved me from death though I would live to regret both his actions and my decision in the coming months. The pain had returned with a vengeance.

I remember trying to escape the pain of them putting me on the gurney; I tried to sleep but could not. I just hovered between mind-numbing pain and the desire to leave my body again; it was as if I were rocking back and forth between the two. The oxygen had become a double-edged curse and blessing because though it kept me alive, it was in unspeakable pain. The next thing I recall was snow falling on my face as they wheeled, dragged, and carried me from the house through the snow to the ambulance. The medics struggled to get the gurney through the deep snow between the house and the ambulance. At one point I felt a hard jolt when they either dropped me or the wheels on the gurney hit a large bump.

I cursed loud at this new pain, and I vividly recall the situation because of the reaction of the medics; this was probably the first time they had heard my voice form a word. They stopped and one of the men bent down close and put his ear to my mouth. I don't think he heard anything else because a couple of times he said, "What?" The purple fuzz returned; I looked into the storm and could feel myself leaving again. I think what I was trying to tell him was that I would die if they kept dropping me. In a way I wanted him to know that I was quite angry and would leave if he kept hurting me. No sound came from my lips, though; I was busy leaving my body again while he put his ear to my mouth. However, the oxygen kept me from floating away.

They started moving again. The pain was incredible. A few more bumps, and I was in the ambulance. Normally, it is a half-hour ride or less from Lake Forest to Tahoe Forest Hospital in Truckee, but today the ride was very long and rough. It went on for an eternity. I wanted to sleep so badly. The roads were horrible; we were in the middle of a blizzard, and the four-wheel drive ambulance had snow chains on which shook and rattled my fragile twisted body beyond torment. All the while my paramedic friend repeated his mantra, "How you doing, Mark? I need you to stay awake for me. Okay, buddy? We're almost there." After about a hundred more times of "Don't go back to sleep, Mark," even the other medic started to join in when the oxygen gave me the strength to put up a protest. I think I managed to get out, "It doesn't hurt when I sleep." To which the chorus chimed, "We need you to stay awake. Okay, buddy?"

But I wanted to go back from whence I came. I wanted to go back to sleep—to a place where there was no pain, only love.

. . . .

About Mark Jacoby

Mark is a computer systems engineer, inventor, entrepreneur, search-and-rescue emergency medical technician, and near-death experiencer. He has spoken before groups across the country regarding his experience. His story has been featured on the Discovery Channel and *CBS Evening News*. His book *Qualified to Speculate* is scheduled for a 2011 completion.

A Lifetime Guided by Lessons Learned in a Childhood NDE

Pamela M. Kircher, MD
Colorado
www.pamkircher.com

The day began in anticipation of my first Halloween party. I had just turned six and eagerly awaited my first party without my parents' presence. The nagging sore throat was ignored in the excitement of getting dressed in my Halloween costume for the party. My sore throat intensified, making bobbing for apples excruciating. Later that evening I developed a terrible headache that progressed to a stiff neck and dizziness the next day as I sat in church. By the time the doctor's office opened on Monday, I was in agony with meningitis from a ruptured abscess of my tonsils. Penicillin was given, and my parents were warned of dire consequences if I walked. I was sent home to live or die. Such was medical care for meningitis in 1950.

My NDE began as an awareness of intense pain that was suddenly and completely relieved as I left my body, and my consciousness rose to the corner of the room. In that place was perfect peace and perfect quiet. I felt myself surrounded by God and perceived myself as pure soul without age or sex. I felt complete, perfectly loved, and a part of God. In the next instant I noticed the girl in the bed, recognized her pain, and then realized that she was me. At that moment I returned to my body. That simple brief experience was the most profound moment of my life.

From that moment on I knew that death was not an enemy but a reward at the end of my life. I knew that my soul existed before this life and that it would exist long after life had ended. I knew that a universal love and sense of Oneness was all that I wanted from life.

How did that early experience serve me? It led to a private life because I decided that my parents wouldn't be able to handle the experience and that they might try to fix me in some way, especially since I did have meningitis, an infection of the brain. I was even more certain that I didn't need to be fixed; I had merely seen a glimpse of how things actually are. It was good news, but it didn't fit into the strict Missouri Methodist culture of my family, and I lacked the courage to try to change their minds. Instead, I kept the experience to myself for the next thirty-two years. I never told a single person about my experience until I was forty-two-years-old. It felt like a private experience, not one that required sharing in order to make it real.

It was only after books began coming out about NDEs that I realized how profoundly I had been affected by the experience and how frequent such experiences actually were. After reading Ken Ring's book *Heading toward Omega* in 1987, I realized that not only did I have an understanding of Oneness from my NDE, but I also had the sensitivities and psychic abilities common in people with NDEs. As a child I had interpreted the sensitivity to the pain of others as a "birth defect" in which I had been born without the protective shields that allow souls to traverse a lifetime on earth. I thought that my NDE had been given to me to remind me of my soul and life before earth birth so that I could bear to be a human and could be certain that I could go home to Oneness when this life was over. It was a shock to learn that it was the NDE itself that had created the sensitivity, not the "birth defect."

By the time I decided to go public with my NDE, I had already become a family doctor and was aware that the medical profession and the general public would be more likely to pay attention to my NDE than to someone else's without my credentials. In addition, my NDE had occurred some thirty years before, and I had long since gone through the initial adjustment period which is often so fraught with confusion and radical changes that convince friends and relatives that the person with the NDE has simply become unbalanced.

When I began to talk about my NDE, I had no idea how profoundly it would change my life. Suddenly most of my friends became people with near–death experiences in their histories. We were friends not just because of the shared experiences of trying to explain ourselves to people who hadn't had a similar experience, but more importantly because we had so much in common in terms of values and ways of looking at the world.

As I spoke about NDEs to groups, more of my counseling practice became grief work. Within a couple of years that led to a shift in career toward hospice work where my values and beliefs were quite welcomed. I was comfortable being a midwife into death for people in their last stages of life. I connected at a deep level with the patients who were looking back at their lives to see what had mattered to them and were wondering about what lay ahead of them. Many of them had NDEs themselves which reinforced my growing understanding that NDEs and other spiritually transforming experiences are available to everyone if we are open to them—and sometimes even if we don't think we are.

From my years in hospice I kept stories and wrote the book *Love is the Link* about NDEs in both acute and hospice settings in order to show doctors how common these experiences are and that if they aren't hearing about them, it is because they don't appear to be open to hearing about them. The book led to the incredible opportunity to talk to groups all over the country where people shared their most profound experiences and how those experiences have changed their lives.

Another aspect of my NDE was that I have never been particularly interested in material possessions or success in conventional terms. It is that lack of interest that allowed me to change from being a family doctor to the less prestigious hospice doctor in the early 1990s. With that switch I also started to bring complementary modalities into conventional hospital settings in the first years of the new century and to be a champion for bringing T'ai Chi to older adults and those with chronic illnesses in the past few years. Each of these career changes has been bold. The theme of each of these careers, though, has been the goal of bringing a greater sense of Oneness to the world. When people know themselves better through counseling and taking good care of their bodies, they are more likely to be kinder and more present for loved ones. When people are comfortable and deeply contemplate their lives in the hospice setting, they heal not only their own lives but also those of their loved ones. When I speak to audiences about other people's NDEs and share my own, it causes participants to reflect on their own lives and those experiences that were out of the ordinary and possibly ignored. When a hospital caregiver uses energy work to elicit a patient's own healing response, the person feels what it is to be both at peace and empowered. It opens his consciousness to the rest of the world. When people learn to know their own bodies through the gentle movements of T'ai Chi, they make friends with their bodies, perhaps for the first time. When they are friends with their bodies, they are more likely to be friends with strangers.

My NDE has been the theme of my life. The ebb and flow of family life and several careers have woven around the central theme of recognizing that the reality of Oneness is such that we are not merely our brother's keeper, we are our brothers in a very real sense. My life's goal has been to help to create a world that more closely resembles the reality that I experienced when I first felt myself in the presence of God and universal love.

. . . .
About Pamela M. Kircher, MD
Dr. Kircher is a family doctor and a board-certified hospice and palliative care physician. As a family doctor, her passion has been bringing complementary therapies into hospital settings.

She is the author of *Love is the Link: A Hospice Doctor Shares her Experience of Near-death and Dying* in which she discusses both her NDE and hospice care. Since that time, she has traveled the world educating both doctors and students about death and dying.

A T'ai Chi practitioner and master trainer, she has also led numerous instructor workshops in T'ai Chi for Health for seniors and people with chronic diseases such as arthritis and diabetes. For more information, please visit www.pamkircher.com.

The God Spot: Our Connection to the Divine

Melvin Morse, MD, FAAP
www.melvinmorse.com
www.spiritualscientific.com

We all have a God Spot—an area in the brain that permits communication with a source of knowledge and wisdom outside our physical bodies. Everyone seems to have his own definition of the source of Universal Knowledge. The Hindu religion calls it Brahman. Theoretical physicists call it quantum nonlocality. The children I resuscitated from death simply call it "God."

We use this God Spot on a regular basis when we use instincts or gut feelings to make decisions. Our instincts are immediate and not fear or anxiety driven. They involve a sense of knowing and are not born of the logical analysis of a problem.

How do we know that this God Spot is real? Medical scientists have actually located it within the brain. A process called Controlled Remote Viewing (CRV) proves it is real. We use this God Spot to have near-death experiences, spiritual visions, and spiritual experiences of all kinds

as well as in prayer and meditation. Mediums use it to access information in their work.

Even those who don't believe in a God or that consciousness can
exist outside the brain accept these new scientific findings of a God
Spot. Atheist Mathew Alpert wrote a book called *The God Area of the Brain*
and argued that this area of the brain explains the "human delusion"
that there are spirits and Gods or a God that can affect our lives. The
human dilemma for many of us is: Do we as human beings create spirits and Gods to bring meaning to an otherwise random uncaring universe? Or can we look to a source of wisdom and love outside our
bodies to find a greater meaning to our lives?

As a pediatrician, I have attempted to resuscitate hundreds and hundreds of critically ill children. Unfortunately, most attempts were unsuccessful. I was surprised to learn in documented studies that most of
the parents of critically ill children see those children again after they
have died. Typically a child will tell his or her parents, "Don't cry; I am
all right. I am safe and loved. We will meet again." Yet parents typically
dismiss these visions, as intensely real as they may be, as meaningless
hallucinations.

Over the years, with many of my patients having died, I have witnessed so many grieving parents that I've often reached that point of
"burn out," a frequent occurrence in critical care physicians. One day, as
an infant lay dying after yet another futile effort at resuscitation, my
fellow physicians and I were making the sort of callous jokes and dark
humor that serves to insulate us from the reality of yet another hi-tech
death. While the parents sat in a nearby waiting room, we were thread-
ing intravenous lines and using heroic medicines in one more useless
exercise in preventing death. Instead of permitting the infant to die in
those parents' arms, instead of welcoming them into the process, we
isolated them from the final moments of their baby's life. We made
jokes while they longed to hold their baby one last time.

The nurses confronted me angrily and ordered me to talk to the
parents and apologize for our behavior. I did so with lead feet and a
callous heart. To my surprise, they took my hand and said, "We forgive
you. We know you were doing your best to save our baby. At first we
were horrified that you would laugh and talk about the 'Grateful Dead'

while our baby was dying. But then, we realized that life goes on. Your laughter taught us that there is still laughter in this life even with the horror of our baby's death. We thank you; we saw our baby's angel in the room with you. We pray that his angel will always be with you."

Since then, I have had an obligation to those parents and all parents who grieve from the death of a child. I have spent the rest of my career attempting to answer the immediate question I had that day: "Was this a real angel that these parents saw, or were they creating a pleasing fantasy in their minds to help them to cope with the death of their child?"

This is my answer after twenty-five years of studying the spiritual experiences of children who have died.

CONTROLLED REMOTE VIEWING: THE FINAL PIECE OF THE PUZZLE

My wife Pauline slowly reads me a string of eight numbers. I quickly write them down on a blank sheet of paper: 7349 2303. Suddenly my hand jerks, and I make a quick scribble on the page.

My hand is moving up, curving over, curving under, moving across, and now straight down. Images come to my mind: metal, thin, open. I suddenly know I am attempting to draw a structure.

My wife prompts me, "Melvin, what do you see next?" I tell her everything I think and see. She helps me organize my thoughts. For this viewing, she is the monitor of the process to insure its scientific integrity, and I am the viewer.

If what I think has something to do with my five senses, I write it in one column on the paper: hard, rough, curving, bright, dark, moving, rocking. If what I think has to do with anything else, I write that on the right side of the paper. "I think this is silly. It is a subway train." "Why did I agree to demonstrate Controlled Remote Viewing for a science reporter for NPR?" "I am going to be embarrassed when I get this wrong."

Every thought I have I write on the paper. "Objectify all mental data!" says Paul Smith, the great guru of Controlled Remote Viewing.

Soon I am filled with a sense of awe and amazement! "An incredible invention of man," I tell my wife. It is in a city; it is both scary and amazing!" This is my first glimpse of the unknown target; it has an emotional or aesthetic impact on me.

Suddenly I start sketching. Within minutes I have sketched a wheel with spokes and a thin rail surrounding the central wheel. I draw small round booths which are attached to the wheel.

Now it is time for the target summary. Neither my wife nor I know what we are attempting to describe. We have just been given a string of numbers. We must commit ourselves in writing with a detailed description of the "target" before our session ends. I write that the target is an invention of man located in a large city. It is made of metal, is circular, and moves in a rhythmic manner. It has two elements: a central moving core and attached hollow elements that rock.

I thoroughly describe the colors, shapes, textures, smells, and other physical sensations I identify as being part of the target.

I have just described the London Ferris Wheel. My wife and I were giving a demonstration of Controlled Remote Viewing for a science reporter from National Public Radio (NPR). I instructed him to choose six targets of any sort from anywhere in the world. They could be land, water, or man–made structures. He was to choose an eight digit number for each one of the targets and then randomly decide which target my wife and I would describe.

We have absolutely no way of knowing which target out of all the thousands of possible targets anywhere in the world he has selected. We are only given the number he has arbitrarily attached to that target. That number is the target's address in the mind of God.

I could see from the dropped jaw and look of astonishment on the reporter's face that we had scored what the professional remote viewers call a "direct hit."

IT ALL STARTED FROM THE STORIES
OF CHILDREN WHO NEARLY DIED

I am a pediatrician, still practicing in the state of Delaware. I started my career as a critical care physician working for Airlift Northwest out of Seattle Children's Hospital. I flew hundreds of flights bringing critically ill children from a four–state area to Seattle.

A few children defied the odds and were saved from death. Contrary to what their medical condition indicated, these miracle children told me that they never died at all! During the time we thought they were dead, they thought that they were leaving their bodies and taking a journey to another realm which they typically called "heaven."

The entire experience was completely real to them. For example, one young man described his experience of drowning and being underwater for forty-five minutes as follows: He was riding in the back seat of his parents' car when it hit a patch of ice, flew off the road, and plunged forty feet into a river below. He told me that "the car filled up with water and then everything went all blank." He was describing his own death, the end of his brain function, and the end of input from his five senses. But he was still conscious and alive!

He said that suddenly he was in a "huge noodle." The noodle had a rainbow in it. He describes a journey which to us seems so fantastic that it must be a hallucination. Yet he insisted that it was "as real as we are talking now." He traveled down the huge noodle, through a rainbow, made a brief detour in "animal heaven," and then went to the "human heaven." He met his grandmother who had already died. He was disappointed to return to "life."

At Seattle Children's Hospital our research team undertook a scientific investigation of these experiences and proved that they are "real." By "real" we meant that they did, in fact, occur at the point of death and are not hallucinations. They are not caused by drugs, or a lack of oxygen to the brain, or from the psychological fear of nearly dying. They are not made up by the children after they are returned to life. They are a real part of the dying experience; we will all have a similar experience when we die.

Most of these children meet some sort of a "God." They are typically told and shown that life is about learning lessons of love. We went on to study near-death experiences in Japan and Africa. We learned that the common elements to all these experiences is that the children are conscious at the point of death, meet some sort of a God, and are taught lessons of love about living. Life, according to these children who have touched this Light, is about loving and learning to be loved.

In other words, we learn things about living when we die. The children told me that they entered into a world in which they suddenly "knew everything that ever was and ever will be." There is no time or space in this world of the dying, only love and knowledge.

As part of my obligation to understand these experiences, I participated in the National Institute of Discovery Science (NIDS), funded by aerospace entrepreneur Robert Bigelow. Colonel John Alexander of the United States Military, a long-time mentor of mine whom I have known for over twenty years, told me about Controlled Remote Viewing and invited me to join NIDS.

As he explained it, I realized that he was describing a process in which we could access this source of Universal Information, this "God" as my wife believes it is, and obtain real information about this current world from it.

For example, the London Ferris Wheel is a piece of knowledge which is contained in such a source of Universal Knowledge. An arbitrary number can be attached to that piece of information which then also exists in the "mind of God." What I understood Colonel Alexander to say was that the United States Military had developed a reliable means of accessing such information. Once viewers were trained to identify known targets, such as a Ferris wheel, by just being given the Ferris wheel's identifying number, they could then be trusted to provide information about unknown targets, such as information having to do with a terrorist attack.

Fewer than one hundred people in the world are known to be able to do Controlled Remote Viewing.

The recent Hollywood movie *Men Who Stare at Goats* details the history of the first seven men who undertook to learn to remote view.

Pauline and I were fortunate to have learned how to remote view from Paul Smith, the man who developed the protocol for the military. He taught us that the key word is "controlled." The two of us, working as a team, learned the once classified military protocol which allows the viewers to access information about people and places throughout the world by "nonordinary" means. My wife describes this as "learning to listen to the mind of God and hear what God is saying to us."

We have proved for ourselves that almost anyone can learn to listen to God. Our colleagues in the Kari Beem Research Foundation have published scientific studies proving that Controlled Remote Viewing is a real human ability. Such studies have been done by others as well and have been published in the most prestigious scientific journals for over thirty years. Controlled Remote Viewing is the proof that I needed to realize that what happens during the near-death experience is completely true and real.

If Pauline and I can simply be given a number that someone else has linked to a Ferris wheel in London and we can then describe and draw that Ferris wheel, this is proof for me that the God Spot accesses information from a real God. A dead child's life is information; an angel telling us something important we need to know is information, and instinct is the process of using information to make decisions. Seeing an angel or a vision of heaven through "nonordinary senses" is no different than describing a Ferris wheel through nonordinary senses, except that the Ferris wheel can be proven to be real. Accessing information about a person's genetic structure as it should be, and using that information to heal a genetic disease or cancer should be possible given what we know about Controlled Remote Viewing.

THE TRANSFORMATION:
LESSONS OF LOVE FROM CHILDREN

The children taught me that when we die, we are still alive. The first child I ever studied who had a near-death experience died from drowning in a community swimming pool. She was documented as having no heart beat for twenty minutes. By any scientific and medical standards, she was dead when we attempted to resuscitate her. Miraculously, with her parents praying at the bedside, after being in a coma for three days, she made a full recovery.

She told me that she had been in heaven. I did not believe her. I thought she was hallucinating, and it must have shown on my face, because she patted my hand and said "You'll see; Dr. Morse, heaven is fun!" "Besides", she said, "I wasn't dead; I wasn't dead at all. I was still alive! Some part of me, a spirit or a soul, something in me was still alive and never died."

Another child who was also clinically dead told me years later that "I was never so alive as the time that I was dead."

The children also claimed that they met "God" and learned lessons of love. Beautiful lessons that we all need to learn, such as the importance of living a loving spiritual life. "Wherever I go, I see pieces of the Light," one girl told me. Another boy told me that the Light is all the love in the universe. We are here on earth to learn about that love, but we should not be afraid to die, as "we don't go into darkness but die into the Light." One of my favorite patients, a young girl of six, told me shyly that she was no longer afraid to die as "I know a little more about it now." I felt completely humbled when she said this as I assume that death is scary and I am afraid of it precisely because I know nothing about it.

My research team published our findings in the American Medical Association's *Pediatric Journal* that near-death experiences are real, meaning that they are not caused by drugs or a lack of oxygen to the brain, and that they are a natural part of the dying process. They are not simply invented by the mind after the fact to explain the scary experience of nearly dying. We published numerous papers on them in the world's most prestigious medical journals, such as *The Lancet,* and our findings are now generally accepted by the scientific and medical mainstream. Other research teams around the world did studies which supported our research, and recently, the United Nations is sponsoring a twenty-five medical center study on NDEs.

We then moved on to try to understand how it would be possible that a dying brain could somehow have a real experience of seeing and being in another world, a "heaven." I trained at Johns Hopkins Medical School, and I assure you that my professors would have failed me instead of giving me awards and honors if they knew that is what I would end up trying to prove. It seems completely unscientific. The "Gods" that I worshipped at the time wrote books that said things like "coma wipes clean the slate of consciousness," and "when you are dead, you are dead and consciousness ends."

These children lived their lives far differently after nearly dying. They became little mini-mystics, transformed by that Light they briefly touched in death. They did not want to die although they were unafraid of death. Instead, they wanted to live life completely.

"Life is for living, and the Light is for later," one of them said to me.

And live they do. I studied them fifteen years after their initial near-death experiences. I also studied adults in their sixties, seventies, and eighties who had near-death experiences as children. In all of them, I found evidence of a "post-traumatic bliss syndrome." This seemed to consist of seeing themselves as an important part of the universe, interconnected with everything on earth in a positive way.

One young lady told me that she was meant to do something very important. I asked her what she thought it might be. She said, "Oh, I don't know. Maybe I will never know what it is. Maybe I will be late for work some day or be in a minor traffic accident, and then that will cause something else to happen, and then something else will happen to save someone's life."

Think about that the next time you run out of gas or are late for work. Maybe you are saving someone's life! Many of the adults, who had NDEs as children, told me of such experiences. One man said that he was driving with his family to go to the zoo. Suddenly he just knew he had to pull over. He waited for several minutes while his wife was looking at him in a puzzled way and the kids were fighting in the back of the car. Then he knew it was okay to continue on. Several miles up the road he discovered that a tractor trailer had just jackknifed across the road. His car would have been demolished if he hadn't stopped and waited those few minutes.

We studied this transformation and discovered an astonishing fact. If patients nearly died but didn't get close enough to death to have a near-death experience, then they developed post-traumatic stress syndrome. This is a difficult-to-treat medical condition in which the patients have headaches, stomach aches, difficulty coping with life, nightmares, and flashbacks of the traumatic event. However, if they came to the point of death and had a near-death experience, then they were transformed in a positive way that apparently lasts for the rest of their lives.

This positive transformation associated with nearly dying seems to be another powerful piece of evidence that they are touched by a "real" God and receive knowledge about living from a source outside their body that they never forget.

YOU DON'T HAVE TO DIE TO HAVE
A NEAR-DEATH EXPERIENCE!

In the late 1800s a researcher studied mountain climbers who fell from great heights and then were saved by falling into a snow bank or some other reason. While they were falling, they frequently had the same experience that the children described. They described stepping out of their physical bodies and often actually saw or heard the impact of their bodies hitting the earth.

I studied children who also fell from great heights and lived. One, a seven-year-old boy, was pushed out of a tree accidentally by one of his friends. Time suddenly stopped for him, and he saw a woman floating in the air next to him. She told him "hold your head just like this" and showed him how to turn his head a certain way. "You will be all right," he was told. Then time speeded up, and he hit the ground fifteen feet below. He was completely unharmed.

In the medical literature, I found a description of coal miners who had been trapped in a mine for several weeks. They described guardian angels telling them where to go and how to survive. New tunnels they had never seen before opened up, lit with a brilliant light and seeming to lead to other realms. Again, just like the children I studied, there was no dreamlike quality to any of this; all of it seemed completely real. In fact, they were accompanied by another miner whom they had never met before and who seemed completely real to them. They had assumed he was just from some other area of the mine or was from a different crew. This miner seemed so real to them that when they were rescued, they were distraught because he suddenly disappeared. They repeatedly insisted that their rescuers go back to find this miner, yet personnel records documented that he did not, in fact, exist. He was so real that one of the rescued miners had to be physically restrained as he attempted to return to the mine to find this "man" who had been so important in their eventual rescue. "He saved our lives," the man shouted. "We can't leave him to die."

Other near-death researchers, such as Diane Komp at Yale and Erlander Haraldsson of the University of Iceland, had documented that near-death experiences occurred in completely healthy children and adults who were near death. Dr. Komp showed that children, who were dying of cancer, would suddenly have intensely real spiritual experiences right before they died and yet were not on drugs and were completely alert and conscious without brain damage. I remember such a patient of mine. With his family and nurse gathered around his bedside, he dramatically said, "Don't you see it . . . that white horse with the man on it? Look, look, he is coming for me! He will take me to heaven, Mother. Don't cry, Mother, I will be safe with him." He then suddenly and unexpectedly died.

I asked my medical students at the University of Washington to ransack the literature to explain how it was possible that a dying or dead brain could have any experience at all, much less a complex experience such as learning new information. I told them that an important clue was that whatever the mechanism is, it must work both for healthy functional brains as well as dying damaged brains.

We discovered that, in fact, buried deep in the medical literature was evidence of a God Spot, an area of the brain that permitted us to have spiritual experiences. It is on the right side of our brains within the right temporal lobe. This is just above your right ear, almost at the center of your brain.

Patients, who have had this area of the brain stimulated by seizures, become extremely religious and often speak of God and spirits. This is similar to patients who have seizures in the motor areas of the brain and move their arms and legs over and over again during the seizure. No one doubts that they have real arms and legs just because the movement in them is triggered by a seizure. Instead, that is one way we learn about the brain areas that trigger arm and leg movements.

Patients, who had this area of the brain damaged by trauma or removed by surgery, were described as "soulless automatons who could not feel joy or sadness or understand meaning in their lives."

The father of modern neurosurgery, Dr. Wilder Penfield, actually stimulated this area of the brain in awake and conscious research subjects who consented to these studies. They would say things like: "Oh God, I am leaving my body" and "I am half in and half out."

Modern day researchers such Mario Beauregard at the University of Montreal and Andrew Newberg at the University of Pennsylvania have added to our understanding of the God Spot. Using sophisticated brain imaging studies, these researchers have been able to describe the complete brain pathways of religious and spiritual experiences.

There is a specific area in the back of our brain in our parietal lobes that allows us to create our sense of self and being in the body. It takes all the input from our five senses and helps to create the world we think of ourselves as existing in. During meditation, this area of the brain is turned off so that this sense of self disappears, and subjects think they are out of their bodies. Then other specific areas in the brain start to function, first in the front part of our brains and then in our right temporal lobes, our "God Spot." We then have the conscious experience of becoming one with a greater universe or interacting with a Source of all love and knowledge.

It is a "God" for some and "quantum nonlocality" for others. It is a highly personal experience. The information obtained through the experience typically has meaning only for the individual. This makes sense to me. I know from my studies of dying children that they frequently have a helper during the experience. If my wife dies before me, I am sure she will be my helper. I doubt, however, that anyone else will have the experience of my wife coming to him at the point of death to assist him in that transition.

In Dr. Beauregard's outstanding book *The Spiritual Brain*, he emphatically states that there is no "God Spot." I was very puzzled by this as he bravely describes his own near-death experience in the book and clearly does not share the "everything is just brain waves" mentality of many neuroscientists. I have read his book several times and have written to him about this. I learned that he shares my opinion that this God Spot could be our link to the divine.

His objections to the term God Spot are twofold:

1) In 1997 neuroscientists at the University of California at San Diego published a paper stating that humans have a "God Module" in our right temporal lobe. They stated that humans are "hardwired" to perceive heaven. This paper was widely interpreted as meaning that spiritual perceptions are "just" in the brain and that we are hardwired to have hallucinations about God and heaven as an evolutionary response to the anxiety and fear of dying. Dr. Beauregard is disputing this sort of God Spot.

2) My description and discussion of the God Spot is extremely simplistic. As a neuroscientist, Dr. Beauregard knows this. His book argues that we have a spiritually oriented brain. It is not just one little spot that is a "link" to the divine but rather an extensive network involving multiple areas of the brain. Dr. Peter Fenwick in England has also made this point. His research with functional MRI studies of the brain indicates that our entire brain seems to be wired to communicate with the divine.

I am a pediatrician, and I am trying to explain this science for non-medical readers. I can defend myself only by sharing with you that both of these brilliant men have told me that my simplistic God Spot concept "is a good first approximation" (Dr. Fenwick's words).

IT TAKES COURAGE AND FAITH
TO USE YOUR RIGHT TEMPORAL LOBE

My wife points out that there is a certain type of information that we receive through our God Spot. It usually has meaning just for us. It can't be obtained any other way. It often leads to surprising and unanticipated results in our lives. Seemingly unsolvable problems, anger and misunderstandings between people we love along with depression and despair are only a few of the situations which call for solutions from the God Spot. When people say to give up a problem to God, they often mean turn off the anxious, analytic, overthinking brain, the noise-making machine and start to listen to the God Spot.

Spiritual insights are immediate. They involve a sense of "aha" or a knowing. Often the solution is one that has always been known but overlooked for no particular reason. So often when I use God Spot information to solve problems in my life, others will typically say, "Oh, I knew that all along." That is a good thing; it means their God Spot reached the same conclusion.

Spiritual insights are odd, nonlogical, and often very funny. They involve seeing around the corner, so logical analysis doesn't apply. They typically complement logical analysis.

I know a friend who was driving down a freeway when a voice suddenly told him to "turn right now or you will die." He did so and was astonished that his car went right through a solid concrete wall, and he ended up on the other side of the highway. At the same moment a truck going the wrong way roared down the side of the road he had previously been on. He would have been killed had he not listened to the voice.

The voice represents a nice example of God Spot knowledge, yet his passing through the concrete wall is hardly a miracle. In fact it is a physics problem. Every physics graduate student knows there is a one in a couple of trillion chances that a car, if all its atoms are aligned exactly right, can pass through a solid wall. This is not a miracle at all, but a nice example of the blending of spiritual knowledge (i.e. the "when" of when to turn the car) with logical analysis of the nature of matter and reality.

Science can take us only so far in understanding our God Spots. We can look to science to learn that we have a large portion of our brain dedicated to interacting with a "God," a loving and universal Source of all knowledge. We can read scientific studies documenting that this area of the brain seems to work perfectly even in dying dead brains. This would indicate that the source of energy to permit the God Spot to work right comes from outside the brain at death. We can learn to do Controlled Remote Viewing ourselves. As less than a hundred people can do it in a replicable way, perhaps most would prefer to read scientific studies that verify that it is a real human ability.

However, my personal experience is that when we use our own God Spots and learn something important about our own lives, there seem to be perverse and odd forces at work that actually prevent the experience from being objectively validated by others. In my opinion, this is so we are constantly tested by faith. One property of the God Spot is that it seems to demand courage and tests our faith in order to interact with the Divine.

Science can tell us that we have a God Spot and that it appears to permit communication with a "real" God, for lack of a better word. And everyone seems to argue endlessly over what that real God is, so I will just stick with what the children who were touched by this God tell me. They say that this "God" is "very nice." One boy told me that he knew It cared about him because It gave him a "piece of bread." Another three-year-old boy said, "It was a happy face for me" and spread His arms wide and grinned and grinned.

To understand the God Spot and what it is saying to us seems to defy the scientific method at this time.

Here is an example of what I mean by this: An elderly lady lived in my neighborhood and knew of my studies on near-death experiences. She also knew I was a member of the National Institute of Discovery Science and was part of the investigation of many odd spiritual and unusual events involving consciousness.

She brought me a tape cassette, and after she played it for me, she asked me what it meant. She could no longer write, so she was in the habit of dictating letters to her friends and then mailing them the cassettes. She was dictating a letter when her tea kettle whistled, so she made herself a cup of tea and returned to the tape recorder. She rewound it to remind herself of her train of thought.

Instead of her voice, she heard a very high pitched squeaky noise that meant nothing to her. Her son was a local television newscaster, and he took the tape to the audio technicians at the television station. They slowed the tape down and said it had been recorded at 7/3s the normal speed for that tape player. They said it could not have been recorded by the cassette recorder that the elderly woman had, but that otherwise it seemed to be a normal recording.

The recording, when slowed down, seemed to be a man's voice saying "Bunny, I have always loved you. I treasured the brief moments we had together. I will never forget you."

The woman thought that the man's voice was her first husband, to whom she had been married only briefly before he was killed in an airplane crash. However, he never called her "Bunny." The only person who ever called her "Bunny" was a young girl who was the child of an acquaintance who had called her "Bunny" for no particular reason. She hardly knew this girl.

I told the woman that I could not solve this mystery for her; it was a spiritual mystery. I asked her to go to sleep at night asking the meaning of the recording and to write down the first thing she thought of in the morning.

She did so. When she woke up, she immediately knew it was the voice of her first husband. Later she wrote to relatives in England where she was from and learned that the young girl was, in fact, related to her first husband and that the two of them called her "Bunny" unbeknownst to her.

This is a typical example of a spiritual experience. It is odd or funny in a way. It is not rational. No skeptic reading it will be convinced of some sort of spiritual reality. The technicians at the television station stated that they could replicate the recording easily; it was recorded at a standard speed for a different sort of recording device. Yet, the skeptic would then have to explain why an elderly woman would go through the trouble of such a hoax and for what gain?

Of course, we know that people have perpetuated such hoaxes and often do it just to have fun with researchers. Yet, I don't find that a compelling solution to this particular mystery.

The woman gained by having her spiritual intuitions validated by the process of unraveling the mystery. She had been having a number of visitations from her first husband. She had a second husband as well, but he was abusive and their marriage an unhappy one. He died many years prior to this. The phone calls back to England to uncover the source of the word "Bunny" led to her learning that the young girl was related to her first husband and shared that nickname for her with him. In turn this validated all of the spiritual premonitions and visitations she had had from him. She died within six months of sharing this tape recording with me.

AN ELUSIVE BLOB OF HEADACHE-CAUSING TAR

I have had similar experiences with my right temporal lobe which have defied objective validation and yet were very real and meaningful for me. I was in France with my French publisher Pierre Jovanovic. I had received a prize for my theories on the God Spot from the European Book Sellers Association for the best science nonfiction book of the year, *Where God Lives*. At the reception I met a French physician, who told me that she did most of her healing by directly placing her hands on the patients and using "energy" to heal them.

I thought that she was probably just kidding herself, that she was in fact doing some sort of massage therapy, and that the patients simply wanted to get well to please her. Perhaps they got better from just being touched and massaged with the muscle relaxation that went with it.

She insisted that I was wrong and that these were specific procedures which unlocked lines and patterns of energy within the body. In turn this triggered specific healing physical reactions. These experiences work best with trauma and muscle memories. Memories can build up toxins and cause blockages in these energy lines.

I listened politely and gave it no more thought.

That night my wife had a terrible headache, an unusual type of migraine headache she was prone to have. We could not speak French and had left all her medicines at home. We had nothing to treat the headaches with. The man at the desk at the hotel did not speak English, and we were unable to get even an aspirin.

My wife suggested that I try the French physicians scalp massage techniques. I laughed and said, "Why not? If it works for her patients, I am sure I can do it, and it will work for you."

I did exactly what the French physician had told me and held my hands exactly as she had described. After about fifteen minutes, something wet and sticky suddenly formed on my hand. I started screaming, "What is this?!" . . . thinking it was coming out of me. I jumped up and started flinging my arms around asking my wife to get a towel and get whatever it was off of me.

She got some towels, but as she wiped my hands, she saw something going up my arms. I forcefully vomited numerous times. We both fell asleep and did not wake up for several hours.

When we awoke, the black sticky stuff was all over the towels. My wife's headache was gone and has never returned. We tried to take a picture of the black stuff, but our camera batteries died. We went across the street and bought new batteries, and they immediately shorted out the camera and it wouldn't work. We decided to at least write down what happened. As we wrote in our journal, the pen ran out of ink. We got another pen, and it wouldn't write.

All we have of the experience is a notation in our journal that fades out as we start to describe the black tar and an angry maid who demanded an extra tip for "all that mess you made." Since we couldn't speak French, we couldn't get her to describe what that mess was.

Again, there is nothing in this story that cannot be explained by a series of coincidences and an overreaction to an odd situation by my wife and me. This story is proof of nothing.

Maybe the black sticky stuff was some odd reaction between something I had on my fingers and shampoo residue in my wife's hair. Maybe she dyes her hair and doesn't tell me, and the hair dye got on my fingers. There are dozens of such lame, implausible explanations.

However, my wife and I "know" with information from our God Spot that this black residue has to do with old trauma in her life that was causing headaches. We know this as powerfully and as certainly as we knew that the target number that the National Public Radio (NPR) reporter gave us was the information that allowed us to draw and describe the Ferris wheel.

USE YOUR OWN GOD SPOT AND DECIDE FOR YOURSELF IF IT CONNECTS YOU TO A REAL GOD

My wife and I now teach the protocol for Controlled Remote Viewing to anyone who is interested. We do this for free as we consider this to be sacred information. As a physician, I have the luxury of donating my time in this manner.

Or you can learn CRV from Paul Smith, as I did, or from Lynn Buchanan, the two remaining sources of the original protocol that has been scientifically validated.

My training with Paul Smith left me with no doubts as to the reality of the God Spot. It was a bizarre disorienting experience that altered all of my previous assumptions about reality. Imagine learning to listen to the knowledge of God, not from some guru in an ashram or a priest but from a jackbooted, former military paratrooper who speaks with clipped military precision of the "signal line" and "objectifying all data." For a field trip, we went to see a military base and admired various tanks and other military equipment. My fellow students were extremely buff, sunglass-wearing young men with names like "Pete Smith" and "Mike Brown." In our spare time, they talked about television programs having to do with cars and chase scenes.

I suddenly realized that these are the modern day shamans. At a time when our society is awash with New Age psychobabble, these men and woman still practiced the spiritual arts that shamans have known about for thousands of years. They are actually using this information in the same way that shamans have always used spiritual knowledge, in secret against the enemies of a given tribe or community. My unease at the highly structured and disciplined approach they took to communicating with "God" only reflected my own unease with the dark side of spirituality.

Author's Note: A shaman is a practitioner of shamanism—communication with the spirit world. They believe they can obtain information and even treat various illnesses by entering the spirit realms.

I realized that they were no longer content with the "wow" of spiritual knowledge. They were aggressively pursuing the "how" of using this knowledge and blending it with other military and intelligence information.

I have attended too many other alternative medicine conferences where spontaneous healings of cancer patients were described and the benefits of prayer documented. Yet no one was talking about how physicians and health care professionals could actually use prayer in a practical way to heal a patient. One reason, I realized at CRV boot camp, was that on some fundamental level no one was really taking prayer and spiritual healing seriously as a real part of our medical regimen in treating patients.

At the end of my final day at CRV boot camp, I was given a total of four unknown targets and was expected to describe and draw them in such detail that the most rigorous skeptic could not claim that coincidence or luck would explain the results. I nailed all four targets. I was so proud of myself. You have no idea how hard it is to be given a series of eight numbers and under the menacing eye of a twenty-year army intelligence operative, who had successfully predicted the terrorist acts on the USS Stark, be able to accurately draw and describe the training targets.

Yet when I was done, he smirked and said, "Son, I guess you think you are pretty hot stuff. Now look at this." He showed me two pictures of almost identical-looking cathedrals. "I bet you would be pretty happy if you drew either one of them as your attempt to draw a target that turned out to be a cathedral, wouldn't you?" I acknowledged that that was true. He laughed and said, "That's why you aren't on our operative teams. Because one of these is in England and one is in France. And before we send a combat team out to the target site, our viewers have to know the difference."

The Kari Beem Research Foundation was born the day he made that comment to me. It both humbled and inspired me. Our foundation is actively using CRV and other mental technologies to investigate genetic and viral diseases. Our studies will have practical applications for the treatment of AIDS, hepatitis C, and degenerative genetic diseases such as tuberous sclerosis.

We are no longer content with the "wow" and have aggressively moved to understanding the "how" of mind–body healing.

I am extremely proud that we have been able to contribute to the training of future generations of remote viewers. Paul Smith and his team are now using techniques that we helped pioneer to revolutionize Controlled Remote Viewing as a science.

AN ANGEL GOT ME IN TROUBLE AT MY HOSPITAL

My obligation and scientific passion is to advance the understanding of the spiritual experiences that occur to dying patients and those who grieve. The scientific advances in medicine that I foresee happening advance this goal only in that the concept of communicating with "God" as a scientific concept will eventually become commonplace. No longer will grieving parents have to say, "You will think I am crazy but. . . ." And then tell you some incredible spiritual event that happened to them.

You don't have to wait until science validates spiritual truths as "real." You can use your own God Spot and find the proof of a "God" in your ordinary life.

I did, and I assure you that I am the least spiritual man I know. My teenage children routinely refer to me by a very nasty name. My ex-wife has been suing me for various wrongs for over seven years. This is not some sort of false modesty, I assure you. I want you to know directly that there is nothing particularly spiritual about me, and yet I learned to use my God Spot in a way that cannot be denied . . . at least by me.

My friend and French publisher Pierre Jovanovic wrote a book about angels. He concluded that they are very real, powerful, and funny. He states that they are ever present in our lives; however we never look for them so we don't see them.

He told me, "Melvin, spend thirty days carefully watching everything that happens around you. You will see an angel, I promise you."

Several weeks later I was called to resuscitate a baby at the hospital. The mother's placenta had separated at home, which is a medical emergency. The baby is losing its lifeline—the mother—and can easily die.

The medics rushed the mother to the hospital, and the baby was delivered by an emergency Caesarian section. It was blue and not breathing.

I tried to thread a tube into the baby's lungs to help it to breathe, but I was unsuccessful. Three times I tried. The baby was dying before my eyes.

Often the anesthesiologist will help out when this happens, but he was desperately trying to save the life of the mother. I had no idea what to do.

Suddenly, I heard a calm voice say, "Can I help you, Doc?" I looked over, and there was one of the medics, leaning against the delivery room wall. I motioned to allow him to try to get the tube in the baby's lungs, and he easily did so. The baby turned pink and survived.

One month later, I was summoned to the Quality Assurance Review Board and asked why I had permitted an unlicensed medic who was not affiliated with the hospital to perform a medical procedure on a patient. I could not explain why, other than the fact that he saved the baby's life. That wasn't good enough, I was told. The hospital's malpractice did not cover medics working on patients.

Then a strange thing occurred. The medic could not be found. No one knew his name. The two medics in the ambulance denied that a third medic was with them. They were aware of hospital policies and would never have even come into a delivery room at the hospital.

The matter was dropped as the medic could not be found. No notes were written by him, and no notes were written about his actions. Only the nurses, the two physicians, and I could testify as to his existence.

One year later the mother wrote me a thank-you letter about her healthy one-year-old boy. In it she said, "Say thanks to that angel in the delivery room."

Once again, this story proves nothing. It is perfectly plausible to think that a third medic was, in fact, with the other two. That actually is commonplace for a third medic to ride along informally. The two medics could simply have denied his existence to cover their own violation of protocol. The medic might have simply not charted his actions in the delivery room. The nurses could have simply made an oversight when they wrote "patient intubated on fourth attempt" but did not identify who did it. Perhaps they thought they were covering for my first three unsuccessful attempts.

Yet, I know, just as I knew that the target number was a Ferris wheel, that he was an angel. On the last day of private practice in Seattle, when I retired to Delaware to pursue my consciousness research full time, many of my patients stopped by to say goodbye. And guess who else? A familiar face also stopped by and shook my hand and said "Hey Doc, thanks for letting me have some practice intubating that infant last year." I was distracted by someone else saying "goodbye," and then he was gone.

Why wait until you die to use your God Spot? Use your God Spot to learn your lessons of love before you die. You never know what can happen. And if you look around enough, you might even meet an angel.

. . . .
About Melvin L. Morse, MD, FAAP

Dr. Melvin Morse, voted one of America's top pediatricians, has researched near-death experiences (NDEs) in children and adults since 1980. According to Dr. Morse, by studying the neuroscience of the NDE, we learn that human beings have an underused area of the brain which is responsible for spiritual intuitions, paranormal abilities such as telepathy and remote viewing, and the power to heal not only the soul, but also the body.

His interest in NDE research evolved from his experiences working in critical care medicine at Seattle Children's Hospital. He published the first description of a child's near-death experience in the medical literature and was funded by the National Cancer Institute to complete the first case-control prospective study in near-death experiences. He is the author of such ground-breaking books as *Where God Lives*, *Closer to the Light*, and *Transformed by the Light*. For more information, please visit his Web site at www.melvinmorse.com or www.spiritualscientific.com.

The author with Melvin Morse

Science and God

Peter Russell, MA, DCS, FSP
<u>www.peterrussell.com</u>

Peter Russell, a thinker and writer with a particular interest in the nature of consciousness, is the author of many books, his most recent being *From Science to God*. Enriched by his background in mathematics and physics, his exploration of consciousness has led him to believe that science may soon come to accept that consciousness is as primary as Eastern philosophers have been teaching for centuries. Russell, who had the privilege of being a student of the renowned Stephen Hawking at the University of Cambridge, says although we experience the world around us as composed of solid matter, it is actually composed of what he calls "mind stuff." Everything, he says, is structured in consciousness.

If everything we know is a form taken on by consciousness, what then is reality? To help answer this and many other questions, I had the privilege of interviewing Peter. Peter says we each ascribe to our world the meaning it has for us. Because of this, we also have the freedom to change our perception. Because of the challenges facing humanity today, now more than ever, he believes that we need to bridge science and spirit.

1. **You say the bridge between science and spirit is light. You also say that time, space, and matter are relatively real; only light is absolutely real. What do you mean by this? What then is this light, and what is its connection to the Light seen in many NDE accounts?**

By chance, I decided to study experimental psychology in addition to theoretical physics. As I studied theoretical physics, I came closer and closer to the ultimate truths of the physical world. Psychology provided the first step in discovering the inner world of consciousness. As I delved into these two fields of study, I realized that light provided the link between these two worlds.

Both the theory of relativity and quantum physics grew out of perceived inconsistencies in the conduct of light. Each of these two great theories of modern physics led to a drastic change in the way scientists studied and understood light. The deeper scientists dig into the nature of light, the more it seems that light plays an important part in the universe. In fact, in many ways, light has been found to be more essential than space, time, or matter.

Having said this, yes, I do think the light that physics is talking about and the Light seen in many near-death experiences are one and the same. But let's go back and explore the first part of the question.

In physics, the speed of light appears to be an absolute. Nothing can go faster than the speed of light. And the speed of light itself is always constantly relative to you. In other words, no matter how fast or how slow you are moving, the speed of light will always measure to be 186,282 miles per second. This is the essence of Einstein's theory of relativity. What comes out of this is that our experience of space and time depends upon our relative motion. So somebody moving by us very fast, close to the speed of light, will experience a different amount of space and time. Their clocks would actually run slower. If you were to actually travel at the speed of light, you would find that time would stop completely and space would contract to nothing.

So if you look at the universe from a light's point of view, there doesn't even seem to be space and time; there is just instantaneous connection. But from our point of view, in material bodies, we do experience space and time. In noting this, one can see from the point of view of physics that light is somehow more fundamental than space and time. Space and time can change according to our perception, our frame of reference. But light itself, the speed of light, remains constant. It never changes. Light, which has no mass, seems to be beyond space, time, and matter. Whatever light is—and I don't think we fully understand what it is—is somehow more fundamental than space, time, and matter. So this is what I mean when I say time, space, and matter are only relatively real; light, which is constant, is absolutely real.

It then becomes interesting to note that in our own subjective experience in meditation and other instances such as near-death experiences, light seems to play a fundamental role. When people are deep in meditation, they often see white light or golden light. In many spiritual teachings this light is considered the most fundamental level of consciousness.

So light seems to be a fundamental quality of consciousness—the most fundamental level of experience, present before we get into the experience of forms, thinking, emotions, and so forth. So although the material or physical world and the mental or nonphysical world seem very different, at the most fundamental levels they are both related to light.

Therefore, the ultimate absolute, if you want to call it

God or whatever, that lies behind both matter and the mind, is light. In both physics and psychology light appears as the first and most fundamental manifestation.

I think what occurs in the near–death experience is that, at that moment of passing over from having a body to whatever lies beyond, consciousness is released from a lot of the constraints that were upon it while it was acting through both a body and a nervous system. This is why many people become aware of an all–pervading Light. In the near–death experience they are touching into that fundamental, universal level of consciousness that shows up as light. Again, this is what we also touch into during meditation and other experiences.

During a near–death experience the mind is free to enter into a direct acquaintance with that fundamental level of consciousness, that universal level. So it's not surprising that qualities such as a sense of complete peace and ease as well as the experience of feeling universal, unconditional love come into the near–death experience. When we're busy functioning in our bodies, doing things, worrying about things, planning, etc., we lose touch with the fundamental qualities of consciousness—light, deep peace, and unconditional love. Only when we are freed from the constraints of our bodies, do we get back in touch with these fundamental qualities.

2. What is reality?

We perceive reality in two different ways, and we need to be careful how we distinguish them. The common way of thinking about reality is the physical reality, the world out there—the world we see and touch and interact with. That is one reality. The other reality is the reality of our experience—what we are actually thinking, feeling, seeing. The two are clearly related. Right now, I am seeing the reality of the world around me: the room, my desk, my chair, etc. All we ever actually know is this reality that is appearing in our experience at any particular time. We never actually know the external reality directly. All we ever know is the inner reality that appears in our mind. We assume, and I think with good reason, that there is an external physical reality out there. We also assume that everyone else is experiencing the same physical reality. But the fact is the actual experience of that reality can change from one person to another. So we each experience our own interpretation or our own particular perception of the external reality. We don't realize that this is actually an interpretation of the reality out there.

So when we ask about the true nature of reality, we have to ask that question from both sides. When we ask, "What is reality?" in terms of our experience, it is actually what we know. It's full of color and sound. It is as it is. We cannot question our experience. If I'm feeling moody or down or blissful or whatever, that is my reality. The other side of the question is, "What is the reality out there, the physical reality?" And the answer to that is one that nobody really knows. Science strives to understand what it's like, but it continually does so by basing its understandings on what we know in the mind. What we know in the mind is that there is color, sound, and other qualities. But when we investigate physical reality closely, we don't find those qualities. We don't find color, for example; we find light of a certain frequency. But it isn't green light or blue light. No color actually exists "out there." The color we see is a quality created in consciousness. It is a subjective experience in the mind. I think that I am experiencing the world and everything else around me, but the only thing that I really know is the colors, shapes, and sounds taking place in my mind. Everything is constructed in consciousness. So as far as what the physical reality is, I think all we can say from a scientific point of view is that it is nothing

like we think it is. This is why modern science is so confusing, yet fascinating.

3. You also say that consciousness is primary. Can you explain this further?

To understand this, we have to step back a bit. The only
thing I can say for sure about you is that you are a conscious being and that you are not a robot or a zombie or
whatever. I make the assumption that I am talking to
somebody who has an inner world of experience of her
own, probably similar to mine. But I don't actually know
directly what is going on in your mind. You can tell me,
and I can judge and make inferences, but all I can say for
sure about you is that you are a conscious being. And
that is true for all people.

I would extend this to other animals. If I am with a
dog, I assume it is having its own experience of the
world; it also is a conscious being. But I still have no idea
what goes on inside the mind of a dog, though I can take
a guess. I'm not talking about self-consciousness here; I
am just talking about the ability to experience the world.
I think a dog is experiencing the world. I think a fish is
experiencing the world. It probably doesn't have emotions or thoughts, but it is seeing, sensing its world. And
I think this ability of consciousness to be aware goes all
the way down. Everything has some degree of awareness. In a much simpler form it is very faint and dim
compared to human awareness, but there is always that
faint glimmer. I don't think there is anywhere you can
draw a line and say that this creature is experiencing the
world and this creature isn't. So I believe the only thing
we can say for sure about the world out there is that it is
conscious in some way or another.

Now, as I said earlier, there are no physical qualities of
color, sound, and such like in the world "out there." They

exist only in our minds as our perception of the world. We don't know what the external world is really like, but one thing we can say about it is that there is the capacity for experience. So that's what I mean by "consciousness is fundamental." It is the one thing we can say for sure about reality.

It's also the one thing we can say for sure about ourselves. We are conscious beings. Many spiritual paths focus on just becoming aware of that inner nature—that we are conscious, that we are aware. Simple meditation upon awareness itself is a well-recognized and noble spiritual path.

4. If time is an illusion, then what is time, and why do we perceive it as real?

First of all, I wouldn't say time is an "illusion." I think time is real, but even physicists don't really know what time is. We just know we have this experience of time, and that the universe seems to unfold one thing after another. As I said earlier, physics shows that time can speed up or slow down depending on the motion of the observer. But I also think that time can speed up or slow down according to the psychological state of the observer. Normally, time passes in a fairly uniform rate for us because our bodies interact with the physical world at a certain pace.

But, when we approach death, we are stepping out of our bodies. Our experience of time is no longer constrained by the pace of the physical world. And so we can experience very different rates of the passing of time. One of the common things in the NDE is people say their whole life flashed before them in seconds. It sounds strange, yet time and time again we have this corroborated. I think this occurs because the mind suddenly works at a very different speed, which causes time to pass at a very different rate. There is still a sense of time, but it's all happening much, much faster.

So time is not an illusion. It is real. But the rate of passing of time can change dramatically once we are free from the bondage of our bodies.

5. Do you think science and physics serve to prove or disprove the existence of God?

Well, it depends what you mean by "God." I am not interested in the idea of a God as some Supreme Being out there looking over us, judging us, that sort of thing. I don't believe God is a sort of "person." I tend to lean towards the mystical notion of God, which is really the "essence of everything," and thus is also the essence of our own consciousness. What most of the great spiritual teachers are pointing to is that we don't normally notice this essence. This is what I was referring to when I mentioned the quality of ease and light and the love which is always there at the base of our consciousness. When we experience deep meditation, an NDE, or some other mystical experience, the mind is free to get in touch with those fundamental qualities. We touch the divine in ourselves. We speak about the light of God, the peace of God, the love of God, for instance. We say God is omnipresent, eternal, never changing. These are all descriptions of this fundamental, core level of consciousness.

I think it's this experience of our own essential nature to which many give the name "God." With mystical experiences, people talk about connecting with a universal quality of consciousness that is in everything and is within all of us. It is this universal quality of consciousness that I am referring to when I talk about God. It is not a separate being. It is our own essential nature. I don't think this is something science can either prove or disprove. When people talk about science proving God, they're usually talking about science proving the God that religion speaks of. But this whole debate is misconceived. The mystical traditions, upon which most of our great religions were founded, talk about a deep personal connection with their innermost essence. For example, when Meister Eckhart, the great fourteenth-century priest, said, "God and I are One," he was forced to recant all his teachings. But in saying that he was one with God, he wasn't talking about himself an individual person. What he meant was that by knowing his true nature, he came to know God.

So getting back to your question, I don't think physics will ever prove the existence or nonexistence of that sense of deep ease, peace, and light that we experience in those moments of connection. The question: "Is physics proving or disproving the existence of God?" is a red herring. The real proof of God comes in one's own experience. That's why during an NDE, people who have no religious background can sometimes have those surprising, deep senses of connection with what a Divine Presence is. It's our experience that proves the existence of God, not physics.

6. What then are your thoughts on the anthropic principle?

I find it fascinating. The anthropic principle comes from the finding that we live in a universe in which all the physical constants are just right for our existence. Change any one, even by a minute amount, and we would not be here. There are two basic interpretations of this. One says it is just coincidence, that the universe is just the way it is. We couldn't possibly experience a universe that wasn't one in which we could exist. The other says that this proves there is some design to the universe. But that design doesn't necessarily need the existence of a God. It could be something that's evolved over many, many creations of the universe. Gradually the universe discovers the right parameters to make the universe work. I find the anthropic principle absolutely fascinating in terms of the coincidences. But I'm not sure what to make of it.

7. **What do you think? Do you believe it's as a result of some Supreme Presence or do you think it's just from the universe creating itself over time and suddenly everything became perfect?**

I suspect more the second option. I don't know that there's a Supreme Being in that sense, so I don't feel it's the design of a Supreme Being. But who knows? I would probably lean toward the universe as an evolving system. And it's evolving into producing more and more life and more and more consciousness. If the universe is in essence consciousness, then I see the purpose of consciousness is to know itself and to continually know itself more fully. Therefore, if there is a Supreme Being, it is the "Being" of the whole universe. It is this "Being" wanting to know itself more fully. That's what consciousness does. It's a "knowing." It wants to know. It's working on manifesting the most conscious beings so that through them the cosmos can know itself.

. . . .
About Peter Russell, MA, DCS, FSP
Peter studied mathematics, theoretical physics, and experimental psychology at the University of Cambridge in England and earned a postgraduate degree in computer science. He then studied Eastern philosophy and meditation in India. Upon his return, he took up the first research post ever offered in Britain on the psychology of meditation.

He speaks, conducts workshops and seminars, and delivers keynote addresses around the world. For more information, please visit www.peterrussell.com.

Spiritual Awakenings

---••◦⟨∞⟩◦••---

Barbara Harris Whitfield
Georgia
www.barbarawhitfield.com

The near-death phenomenon affects the experiencer in many ways. But in addition to the many psychological and physiological aftereffects noted earlier in this book, the NDE also appears to stimulate areas of the brain and unleash energy in the body known as Kundalini. Literally translated as "the curl of the lock of love of the beloved," this refers to the flow of consciousness or energy, present in all of us, that allows us to merge with our Universal Self. Kundalini, which has been practiced as part of the Hindu religion since around the 5th century BC, is believed to lie inactive at the base of our spine until it is aroused and called to travel up through the spine causing a state of complete elation.

Barbara Harris Whitfield, an experiencer herself, has been researching the near-death experience and its aftereffects for many years. Below she describes her work with well-known NDE researchers Kenneth Ring, PhD and Bruce Greyson, MD.

Kenneth Ring, Bruce Greyson, and I have demonstrated in several research projects that near–death experiencers have almost twice as many signs and manifestations of what we call the "Physio–Kundalini Syndrome" as do our control groups.

Whether this opening or arousal which happens during our original experience becomes a subsequent trigger for a later experience of Kundalini, is not known. Experiencers often tell of signs and manifestations of Kundalini arousal without having a dramatic Kundalini experience at all. Anyone who desires to awaken spiritually can invite this energy into their lives to guide them through the journey of spiritual awakening. The more we read and learn, the more powerfully this energy may appear to us as signs and manifestations. At the same time, coincidence beyond the average and possibly even psychic abilities will appear.

A full–blown experience contains a sense of energy surging up the spine, sometimes fanning out over the upper back and shoulders. Possibly there's a roaring noise in the ears or isolated pockets of heat somewhere in the body. A sense of bliss, joy, and peace fill the mind. A feeling of sweet nectar can seem to flow over the face, and then energy moves through the throat, heart, or navel. This is possibly described as a piercing sensation, but also pleasant. After that, or intermixed, can be incredible colors, lights, aromas, and/or sounds.

KUNDALINI ENERGY AND HOW IT WORKS

What changes us in a spiritual awakening? One thing to consider is that we may have had a powerful energy force activated within us. One name that has been given to that energy is Kundalini. Scientists from the Kundalini Research Network (KRN) have begun to define Kundalini as "the evolutionary energy/consciousness force. . . . [Its] awakening affects a transformative process in the psycho–physiological and spiritual realms and results, ultimately, in the realization of the Oneness of the individual and universal consciousness."

Transpersonal psychotherapist Bonnie Greenwell, physicist Paul Pond, and others of KRN[1] hypothesize that Kundalini is associated with

---

[1]Including physicians Evon Kason, Bruce Greyson, Robert Turner, and Lee Sannella

and may be the cause of mystical experiences, psychic ability, creativity, and genius. Some observers note that Kundalini may be linked to some forms of mental illness. One of KRN's goals is to make Kundalini known to the Western world, especially the scientific and medical communities, therapists, health care workers, and those who have had Kundalini experiences but may not realize it.

Phenomena associated with the rising or arousal of Kundalini energy are occurring with increasing frequency to Westerners who have never heard of it and have done nothing consciously to arouse it. The term "rising" is often used in this way to describe the arousal of the Kundalini energy to an undetermined level that may or may not complete itself as a sustained evolution of consciousness. Felt as vast rushes of energy through the body, Kundalini-rising can create profound changes in the structure of people's physical, mental, emotional, and spiritual lives.

WESTERN RESEARCH

Bonnie Greenwell addressed some of the problems and joys of Kundalini-rising in her doctoral dissertation, which she has published as *Energies of Transformation: A Guide to the Kundalini Process.* This book summarizes her six years of research and experience working with individuals who have awakened Kundalini.

After centuries of hiding in nearly every culture on the globe under the guise of a secret esoteric truth, the Kundalini experience is reported more and more frequently among modern spiritual seekers, and it appears to be occurring even among people who are not pursuing disciplined or esoteric spiritual practices. When this happens to those who have no understanding of the profound correlations between the physical and mystical experiences, it can leave them bewildered and frightened, even psychologically fragmented. When they turn to traditional physicians, psychotherapists, or church advisors, their anxiety is compounded by the general lack of understanding in Western culture regarding the potentiality in the human psyche for profound spiritual emergence and its relationship to energy.[2]

---

[2]From *Energies of Transformation: A Guide to the Kundalini Process.*

How Kundalini manifests itself in experiencers is called the Physio–Kundalini Syndrome.[3] Researcher Bruce Greyson did a scientific study of the physio–Kundalini hypothesis. He reported those results at the 1992 KRN conference:

> "As a group, near-death experiencers reported experiencing almost twice as many physio-Kundalini items as did people who had close brushes with death but no NDE, and people who had never come close to death. As a check on whether the physio-Kundalini questionnaire might be measuring non-specific strange experiences, I threw into the analysis the responses of a group of hospitalized psychiatric patients. They reported the same number of physio-Kundalini items as did the non-NDE control group. There were two unexpected and ambiguous 'control' groups in my studies: people who claimed to have had NDEs but described experiences with virtually no typical NDE features, and people who denied having had NDEs but then went on to describe prototypical near-death experiences. In their responses to the physio-Kundalini questionnaire, the group that made unsupported claims of NDEs was comparable to the non-NDE control group, while the group that denied having NDEs (but according to their responses on the NDE scale, did) was comparable to the group of NDErs. In regard to awakening Kundalini, then, having an experience mattered, but thinking you had one didn't."

MANIFESTATIONS

Because Western medicine does not acknowledge the East's physio–Kundalini model, symptoms of Kundalini arousal are often diagnosed as physical and/or psychological problems that fit within the Western allopathic diagnostic categories. For example, the shaking, twisting, and vibrating so well known to experiencers could be diagnosed as a neurological disorder. It is also hard to recognize the energy presence be-

---

[3]Bentov, Sannella, and Greyson 1992.

cause it manifests itself in so many different patterns. Because its symptoms mimic so many disorders of the mind and body, even people
familiar with the Kundalini concept are unsure whether they are wit-
nessing rising Kundalini energy or distresses of the mind and body. The
danger is in accepting prescriptions for drugs that Western physicians
give to alleviate symptoms and possibly stopping the continuation of
this natural healing mechanism. Any symptoms that can be alleviated
by using the Kundalini model should not be treated and suppressed
with drugs.

In studying the manifestations that Kundalini arousal may take,
Greyson compiled a questionnaire entitled *The Physio-Kundalini Syndrome
Index*, containing 19 manifestations in three categories:

MOTOR MANIFESTATIONS

- Spontaneous body movements
- Strange posturing
- Breath changes
- Body locking in certain positions

SENSORY MANIFESTATIONS

- Spontaneous tingling or vibrations
- Orgasmic sensations
- Progression of physical sensations up the legs and back and over
  the head
- Extreme heat or cold (in isolated areas of the body)
- Pain that comes and goes abruptly
- Internal lights or colors that light up the body (or are seen
  internally)
- Internal voices (and internal whistling, hissing, or roaring noises)

PSYCHOLOGICAL MANIFESTATIONS

- Sudden bliss or ecstasy for no reason
- Sudden anxiety or depression for no reason

- Speeding or slowing of thoughts
- Expanding beyond the body
- Watching the body from a distance

Kenneth Ring and Christopher Rosing reported almost identical results as Greyson's in their latest research, The Omega Project: "Near-death experiencers reported experiencing almost twice as many physio-Kundalini items as did people who had close brushes with death but no NDE, and people who had never come close to death."[4]

THE CONCEPT OF ENERGY

Kundalini is a natural phenomenon with intense psychological and physical effects that can catapult a person into a higher state of consciousness. This analysis is based on the reality that we are extensive fields of consciousness as well as biological beings. As fields of consciousness, we have a spirit–body made of various energy systems. Various experiences can manifest in the energy or spirit body. These can be highly emotional and are usually connected to activities in the autonomic nervous system and the hormonal and muscular systems of the physical body. These experiences can be repressed in our memories but are manifested as stress in our energy/spirit/biological body. Felt as "blocks in our energy," they can be released emotionally and physically.[5] Thus, Kundalini is fueled by emotion and helps us to release a lifetime of buried stress, resulting in a physically, emotionally, mentally, and spiritually more healthy person.

Whether this energy is called Chi, Ki, prana, Kundalini, bioenergy, Ruach ha Kadosh, Holy Spirit, vital force, or simply energy, the assumptions about it are similar. Several healing aids use a concept of releasing this stored energy: Shiatsu, polarity, acupuncture, acupressure, Reikian body work, bioenergy integration, holotropic integration, T'ai Chi and

---

[4]Ring and Rosing. "The Omega Project," *The Journal of Near-Death Studies*, 1990.
[5]Working with Kundalini energy and specifically by balancing the chakra system, alternative therapies suggested in this book can do more to alleviate these unwanted sensations than Western allopathic medicine has shown.

some forms of massage. In discussing an energy model, there is a common limitation set up by the tendency to concretize the energy, to make it tangible, to view it as physical stuff with physical properties. The concept of energy in the human body, and any form of life, is best understood as dynamic, a verb not a noun. There is no such thing as energy in physical form. Rather, there is activity described in energetic terms.

So when we speak of life energy, we characterize activity, not a measurable physical entity. According to the Chinese explanation, energy is like the wind, invisible but with visible effects such as waves on a pond stirred by a breeze. The concept of energy is a useful way of describing the deeper hidden patterns and processes that underlie the more visible effects. The results of the energy, the visible waves on the pond, can be seen in the lives that we lead, the love that we share, and the selfless service that we extend. Or as the Bible puts it, "By their fruits you shall know them." (Matthew 7:20.)

This invisible energy appears to be a deep, hidden pattern or process of integration that unifies all of our dimensions, physical, mental, emotional, and spiritual. We could also call it the creative intelligence that is working to make us whole.[6]

My first encounters with Kundalini energy were intense. Over the years they have tapered off to gentle, subtle, and infrequent. Here's an example of a joyful experience:

I'd take my daily four-mile walk in the hot Florida sunshine. Often, I came back feeling euphoric and swam or showered and then meditated. Sometimes I perceived tingling sensations moving up my back and feel myself surrounded in Light. I became acutely aware of the love that connects and is all living things. Sometimes, I felt sweet currents like honey flowing downward in my head, behind my face. I felt my hands expand and then my very being went out into It. I chuckled inside over my feeling of bliss, and I heard the chuckle echo and rebound through the universe. On the days that happened, I perceived the energy fields around everything.

---

[6]This information comes from an editorial I wrote for *The Journal of Near-Death Studies* (13:2, Winter 94) entitled "Kundalini and Healing in the West."

CHAKRAS—ENERGY CENTERS OF TRANSFORMATION

Chakra is Sanskrit for wheel and describes energy centers or trans-ducers that convey energy from one dimension into another. In this case the energy is conveyed from our environment to our energy body to our physical body, or in reverse–from our inner life to our awareness (if we are awake or conscious of our inner life) and then out to our environment. There are seven major chakras, and many more minor ones, contained in our subtle energy body that interact with our physical body. Each can be visualized as a center where many of the streams of energy–nadis or meridians—come together through the human body. *Each chakra mediates a different level of consciousness with the outer environment.*

This system works for our growth and healing potential. Chakras modulate discrete frequencies that represent every variety of human experience on the mental, emotional, physical, and spiritual levels. A pain in our hearts, a bright idea, a gut feeling, a tingling up our spines are all feelings originating in the vortex of a chakra energy center. So are experiences of Oneness, sexual desire, self–pity, a beautiful singing voice, and even addictions.[7] A lump in our throat, butterflies in our stomach, pressure in our heads—all originate from a chakra picking up our inner life or perceiving the outer environment, then broadcasting it to us through our physical system until we feel it and can focus on it.

After a spiritual awakening, many of us want to stay in the higher chakras, the higher spiritual levels, and not deal with the lower three. However, we need the balance of all seven.

Beginning at the bottom, the first chakra is located at the base of the spine and opens down toward the ground. It keeps us alive in the body and draws sustenance from the soul or True Self. It is our sense of grounding, our work of survival on the planet. When working properly it is our sense of security. An imbalance brings on fear.

When we talk about getting grounded, we mean staying with issues of this reality, coming back to practical issues and common sense. Experiencers and spiritual seekers in general have a tendency to intel-

---

[7]From a workshop and unpublished book by Gloria St. John, *A Journey Throughout the Chakras.*

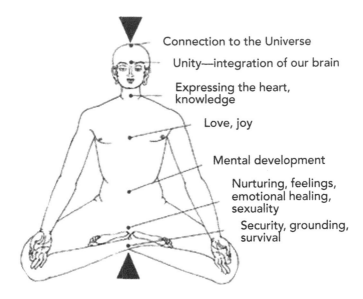

Connection to the Universe

Unity—integration of our brain

Expressing the heart, knowledge

Love, joy

Mental development

Nurturing, feelings, emotional healing, sexuality

Security, grounding, survival

lectualize and fantasize, or go into their heads and indulge in wishful or magical thinking. A great many New Age concerns can turn into escapist delusions. This danger can be averted by solid grounding–getting down to basics, or first chakra issues.

The problem of staying grounded comes up over and over again at support group meetings and research conferences. If you need grounding, it's advisable to stop reading books on Kundalini for a while.[8] Put yourself with safe friends who are grounded, take a barefoot walk outdoors—if possible, hug a tree or lie down on the earth. Adjust your diet to foods that are grounding, like meats, root vegetables such as potatoes and carrots—and the favorite standard among researchers and experiencers, fast-food french fries! The salt and grease will bring you down immediately. We also agree that during these periods you should meditate and practice yoga less.

---

[8] I caution against reading Kundalini literature during emotional turbulence because it can promote more energy flow, or awareness of energy flow into your body. Your false self and True Self struggle for control, and focusing on Kundalini energy or using it to distract can lead to ego inflation. Stay grounded. The waters are rough enough without making them rougher for yourself.

Grounding requires the willingness, honesty, and courage to face ourselves as we are and our world as it is—no distance, no exclusions, no avoidances, and no anesthesia. When we are solidly grounded, our heart chakra can function openly because our first chakra is balancing it.

The second chakra is approximately two inches below the navel. If it is healthy and well-balanced, the second chakra is responsible for fluid actions and nurturing, being able to accept our own feelings, and tolerating others. We feel at home in the world. If damage was done to this chakra in childhood or if it is out of balance now for some other reason, there is a sense of separation, abandonment, rejection, anger, rage, fear of loss, etc. Many teachers believe that this is the chakra of emotional healing, going back to very early childhood development. The second chakra is also the seat of our sexuality.

The third chakra is called the solar plexus and is at the level of the diaphragm. It includes the realms of social interaction, education, mental development, and career. It equips us to interact effectively with the fundamentals of the external world. The virtues of justice, fairness, and equality and the institutions of law, politics, and education develop from the third chakra. Feeling hungry or empty is also a third chakra expression.[9]

As I said above, avoiding these first three chakras is another way of attempting spiritual bypass or high-level denial. Since we need to live in the physical world, we will achieve harmony and balance only by embracing these three levels of consciousness defined by chakra one, two, and three. Not to embrace them invites disease, disharmony, and imbalance.

During a spiritual awakening, our partially dormant and often totally shut down upper four chakras may be aroused or opened. Anyone pursuing psycho-spiritual growth will open these chakras over time. If we are aware of this and encourage these openings by doing our emotional work-dealing with our unfinished business-we will know when our consciousness level is shifting from one chakra to another.

The fourth chakra is located at heart level and relates to our capacity to love, to open up our hearts, and to give. When this chakra is blocked,

[9]From Gloria St. John's workshop.

a person may appear to be cold or inhibited, or may exhibit passivity in his or her life. This chakra governs joyfulness and is the master control center for regulating the emotions. Many, if not most, NDErs that Bruce Greyson, Ken Ring, and I interviewed appeared to have had a heart chakra opening. You can tell by a vivid description of love—what we thought it was before and especially what we know it is now. In the classic *A Christmas Carol*, Scrooge's transformation at the end of the story is an excellent example of a heart chakra opening.

We have heard of a few cases where relatives have taken experiencers to court because of the aftereffects of a sudden heart chakra opening. Like Scrooge, these new experiencers want to give away their posses-sions. I don't mean to be a wet blanket on expressions of the heart; expressing my heart and extending myself on the heart level are my reasons for living. It is the way I live, but I need to caution that heart openings without healthy grounding can backfire, and we can hurt ourselves, our families, and unsuspecting others.

The fifth chakra is located in the throat and is a synthesis of head and heart energy. Those who have opened this center are able to *express* their heart experience of being alive. We are standing in the Light of our own soul. We are truly in a relationship with ourselves and the Universe.

The sixth chakra is between our eyebrows and often is called the third eye. Its opening is a direct result of spiritual practice. Meditation, selfless service, and compassion are its prerequisite. From this opening there is a realization of unity, a marriage of opposites, the blending of male and female, mind and emotion, resistance and flow. In our inner life we discover our soul flame's identity and fall madly in love with our self.[10] It used to be that the closer we got to God, the more paradox there was in our lives. Now we move closer to God, and at the same time confusion and paradox dissolves. In more grounded terms, this means a synthesis between both sides of our brain which then births a higher wisdom and creativity.

The seventh chakra at the top of the head funnels unlimited spiritual

---

[10]By "Soul flame's identity" I mean that we find contained inside our core that perfect mate we've been looking for. That's when we fall madly in love with our self. This is experiential and emerges as our false self dissipates.

energy in and draws energy up from the lower centers in the process we know as enlightenment. We do not pray; we are prayer. We are no longer doing, just being. We have become our Higher Self.[11]

A WORD OF CAUTION

This map of consciousness mediated through our energy body has been studied in great depth by ancient scholars and scientists in the East. There have been no easy translations yet to give Westerners a clear grasp of how Kundalini energy and the chakra system can work in our lives when we are so embedded in Western culture. Our best guide to all of this is our personal inner voice. As we travel our individual journeys, our inner life will become clearer and that subtle voice stronger. Read and learn from all available teachers and guides, but keep only the knowledge and information that rings true for you. Throw away the rest.

EGO INFLATION

The experiencers with Kundalini symptoms who contacted Bruce Greyson and me were often scared, concerned, and wanted to know more. Some wanted to help with the research and occasionally claimed to be authorities. Some claimed that their Kundalini arousal had transformed them into gurus.

Probably the biggest problem at this early stage of understanding is ego inflation. Many who have read the Eastern literature identify strongly with the gurus. Eventually we pass through this stage, realizing that we are Westerners and that it's hard to translate these Eastern metaphors when our cultural roots are so completely different. Our reward for getting through ego inflation is humility, which is the solid foundation of a truly spiritual, healthy, and whole human being. Some don't experience ego inflation and others get stuck in it.

Humility is the willingness to continue learning our whole lives. Being humble is that state of being open to experiencing and learning

---

[11]St. John, *op. cit.*

about self, others, and God.[12] In this openness we are free to avoid the pitfalls of ego inflation and to connect with God again here in this reality. In this state of humility and second innocence, we can experience whatever comes.

SPIRITUAL BYPASS

If we try to ignore our pain and achieve the higher levels of our consciousness, something, usually our false self/negative ego or shadow self, will hold us back until we work through our particular unfinished business. Trying to bypass the work that needs to be done on our negative ego/shadow backfires. This is called spiritual bypass, premature transcendence, or high-level denial.[13] Spiritual bypass can be seen in any number of situations, from being born again in the fundamentalist sense, to focusing only on the Light, to becoming attached to a guru or technique. The consequences often are denial of the richness and healthy spontaneity of our inner life: trying to control oneself or others; all-or-none thinking and behaving; feelings of fear, shame and confusion; high tolerance for inappropriate behavior; frustration, addictions, and compulsions; and unnecessary pain and suffering.[14]

Recently I heard two glaring examples of spiritual bypass. First, a prison counselor complained of inmates who carried Bibles everywhere and refused rehabilitation because they had been so-called "born again." They are classic examples of high-level denial. Second, a family therapist had been treating a severely dysfunctional family in which the father was an alcoholic and sexual offender. He had molested all of his daughters and, as soon as that was revealed, claimed instant healing in a spiritual experience. He joined a fundamentalist church whose minister did the family a terrible disservice by supporting the "spiritual awakening" of this charming and persuasive talker, claiming the father no longer needed to feel guilt or remorse.

While at first glance these seem to be extreme examples, many of us

---

[12]Whitfield, *Spirituality and Recovery*, 1985.
[13]Whitfield, *Co-Dependence*, 1991. Small, *Awakening in Time*, 1991.
[14]This is a compilation of C. Whitfield's ideas.

know someone who has never done any inner work and is making everyone around him crazy with constant Bible quoting or by extolling some definitive path. When I see someone pushing an exclusive, restrictive system, I become cautious. Spiritual awakenings are universal, include everyone, and exclude no one. They include all beliefs, are anti-nothing, require no allegiance, and embrace all.

This chapter above comes from Barbara Whitfield's book *Spiritual Awakenings: Insights of the Near-death Experience and Other Doorways to Our Soul* (Deerfield Beach, FL.: Health Communications, Inc., 1995).

. . . .

About Barbara Harris Whitfield

Barbara was research assistant to Bruce Greyson, MD, director of research for the International Association for Near-Death Studies at the University of Connecticut School of Medicine. Having had two near-death experiences a week apart from each other while suspended in a Stryker frame circle bed in 1975, she was one of the key subjects in Kenneth Ring's groundbreaking book on the near-death experience, *Heading Toward Omega: In Search of the Meaning of the Near-death Experience*. Ring writes about her again in his latest book *Lessons from the Light*. She has taught many courses on the aftereffects of spiritual awakenings and has written several books including *Full Circle: The Near-Death Experience and Beyond*, *Spiritual Awakenings: Insights of the Near-Death Experience and Other Doorways to Our Soul*, *The Natural Soul* and co-authored *The Power of Humility* with her husband, author and physician Charles Whitfield, MD. Look for Barbara's new book *Victim to Survivor and Thriver: Carole's Story* coming out in January of 2011.

She has appeared on *Oprah, Donahue, Larry King Live, CNN Medical News,* and more, including several documentaries both nationally and internationally. She is in private practice in Atlanta, Georgia with her husband Charles L. Whitfield, MD, helping adults who were repeatedly traumatized as children. For more information, please visit www.barbarawhitfield.com.

Investigating Ghosts and the Paranormal

---◆❀❀◆◆---

Loyd Auerbach, Dave Tango, Josie Varga

While some are true believers, others are completely skeptical about the existence of ghosts, arguing that these paranormal entities do not exist and are just a result of our imagination. After all, they reason, if ghosts are real, why haven't most of us experienced such a phenomenon?

I can't say why some experience paranormal activity and others don't, but I can say that ghosts are positively and absolutely real because I had the "privilege" of a ghostly encounter in my own home. The following passage comes from the chapter entitled "A Ghost Named Andrea" found in my previous book *Visits from Heaven*.

> When my six-year-old daughter Lia kept complaining about seeing a ghost in her room, I didn't think much of it. I thought it was just her imagination. But after her complaints to both me and her father persisted for more than a month, I began to wonder if there was something more going on.
>
> One day while I was on the phone with my friend, a me-

dium named Anthony Quinata, he nonchalantly asked me
why I had not told him that I had a ghost in my house. I was
stunned beyond words as he continued to tell me that he
sensed Lia had been complaining about seeing a woman in
her room. He then told me to hang on and about a minute
later came back on the phone and asked, "Do you want to
know her name?" I was totally speechless and wondered nervously, "What does he mean by her name?"

Anthony quickly interrupted my thoughts and told me that
I indeed had a ghost in my home, and her name was Amanda
or, he explained, a name that sounds like Amanda. I stood
there in my living room with the phone pressed to my ear. I
couldn't believe what I was hearing and wasn't sure I wanted
to hear more. But Anthony continued, "She lived in your house
a long time ago. She used to sleep in Erica's (my oldest
daughter's) room. She says that she is very fond of Lia and
often visits her in her room just to watch over her."

I wanted to let out a scream, but my mind was too busy
scanning the house for any signs of Amanda. "Who has the
pink room?" he asked. Lia's room was pink. "Who has the
purple room? He went on. Erica's room was purple. "Is there a
linen closet in the hallway outside of Lia's room?" Yes, there
is. "Do you have a big yard with a white fence around it?" Yes.

At this point, I couldn't hold it in any longer and yelled,
"Anthony, STOP! How do you know that?" Anthony lives in
Colorado, and I live in New Jersey. He had never been to my
house before nor had I ever described my house to him. Yet,
he was accurately describing my house.

I can't say that I was relieved when Anthony replied, "She
is showing me your house. Do you have a clock stuck between
8:45-10:45?" I was almost frantic at this point. "No, I don't know
what you're talking about. I don't have a clock stuck on that
time!" Anthony insisted that I did; Amanda was telling him so.

"Does Lia cough a lot at night?" Again, I couldn't believe
what I was hearing. My daughter suffers from frequent sinus
infections and often coughs at night. "Yes," I replied almost

telepathically. "Why do you want to know?"

"Amanda is telling me that she watches over Lia. She said she is not ready to let her go. She does not mean to scare Lia."

"What? What does she mean she's not ready to let her go?" At this point, my motherly instincts set in. Maybe Amanda did not mean to scare my daughter, but she was. I yelled into the phone telling Anthony to tell Amanda to leave Lia alone to which he replied, "You just did. She's standing right next to you."

I felt like I was going to faint. "Anthony, you're scaring me!" I shouted.

His feelings were somewhat hurt, but I didn't mean it the way it sounded. After all, I am a believer and have no doubt whatsoever in the afterlife.

Anthony tried to calm me by assuring me that this spirit was earthbound and that he would guide her to the Light. Knowing that I am Roman Catholic, he then asked me if I happened to have holy water in the house which I did. I was then instructed to get the holy water and sprinkle the water throughout Lia and Erica's rooms as we both prayed. He then told me to picture Amanda in a bell jar in my backyard. This made no sense to me, but I wasn't about to argue; I wanted this spirit out of my home.

My heart was racing the entire time but after about ten minutes, Anthony said, "Josie, she is no longer in your house. She's in your backyard. I will now help to guide her to the Light."

This was all very hard for me to believe. So there was a ghost in my house named Amanda who was very fond of my daughter. And my friend, an amazing medium, was able to ask her to leave and guide her to the Light, all while speaking over the phone?

Of course, the true test would come later when my daughter went to bed. Would she complain about things moving in her room as she had done for over a month? Would she continue to refuse to sleep claiming that a ghost was in her room?

Astonishingly, Lia stopped complaining completely from that day forward. She has not complained about sleeping in her room since. She has stopped running into my room crying and asking to sleep with me and my husband. She stopped, just like that. Was this just a coincidence? No, I don't believe it was.

Remember the clock that Anthony said was stuck between 8:45-10:45? Initially, my husband and I could not find this now infamous clock. Truthfully, I did not want to find it.

But one week later, I was reaching for something in the back of a cabinet in my living room. In the back corner my eyes caught sight of an old clock that belonged to my parents. My heart began to race once again. I stared in utter disbelief. There, before my eyes, was the clock that Anthony (through Amanda) told me about, and it was indeed stuck between 8:45-10:45.

Shortly after, I ran into my neighbor and asked her if she knew if a woman named Amanda ever lived in my house. She has lived in my neighborhood her whole life so if anyone would know, it would be she. No, there had been no Amanda at my house, but she said, "There was an Andrea, though, who lived in your house back when it was first built." So Amanda was actually a kind-spirited (no pun intended) ghost named Andrea.

AN INTERVIEW WITH
PARANORMAL EXPERT
LOYD AUERBACH

Since my experience, I've often wondered why Andrea did not cross over. Why did she remain in my home? Why was my daughter the only one who could see her? What exactly are ghosts? To help answer my questions, I had the privilege of interviewing Loyd Auerbach, the Director of the Office of Paranormal Investigations and the author of several books dealing with the paranormal including, for example, *A Paranormal Casebook: Ghost Hunting in the New Millennium* (Atriad Press, 2005).

1. **What are ghosts? Are all ghosts earthbound or as some say "stuck" here?**

The term "ghost" has covered a variety of experiences in many cultures. In general most people use the term "ghost" to mean a spirit or some form of a person after he has died. However, the word is also sometimes applied to any figure of a person or animal experienced in any location where the person or animal is not really there, and especially when the ghost represents someone or some animal that has died. In effect, there's often no distinction made as to whether the "ghost" is a conscious being or just some kind of recording of past people, animals, or events.

Parapsychologists do make the distinction and often use the term "apparition" to refer to the concept of human personality or consciousness (or that of an animal) appearing in some form after death. There are other categories for similar—but different—experiences.

Parapsychology and its predecessor psychical research essentially created three main categories of what have often been considered "ghostly" happenings. The three are different conceptually, but events around each can appear similar and can even indicate unique combinations of phenomena. Investigators of these phenomena should know the parapsychological perspective of these three categories, since within the field there is much more agreement about them than you'd ever find amongst psychics—who often have their own personal perspectives—and the amateur ghost-hunters.

What I call my "big three" are apparitions, hauntings, and poltergeists. In shortened form, they are spirits, recordings, and living-agent psychokinesis.

An apparition is our personality (or spirit, soul, consciousness, mind or whatever you want to call it) surviving the death of the body, and capable of interaction with the living (and presumably other apparitions). It is pure consciousness. Apparitions are seen, heard, felt, or smelled (thankfully, not tasted!) by people through the process of telepathic communication.

The model of an apparition is that it is consciousness without form. As the apparition has no form and no sensory organs or normal ability to communicate, he or she essentially connects to the minds of living people. The apparition essentially broadcasts sensory information (what he or she looks, sounds, feels, and smells like) to the minds of us living folk. Our brains/minds process the signals and add them to what our normal senses are picking up. Some people do better with visual input, while others with auditory or different kinds of information. Some can process combinations.

But because they have no physical form, they are not seen with the eye or heard with the ears and such. It's why in a crowded room with lots of living people and a ghost, some see the ghost; some hear him; some feel his presence; some smell his cologne, and some get different combinations of those perceptions. And of course, lots of people in the room may get nothing at all. This is also why ghosts can't be photographed—they don't reflect light.

As for the "earthbound" thing, one might say that we living folk are earthbound (unless you count the folks in the various space programs). Apparitions are present here and now with us—they are people, just people without bodies.

As far as being "stuck," they, like us living folks, keep themselves "stuck" in various situations. Ghosts are here for various reasons: unfinished business, being afraid of what's next (a big one), being in denial that they're dead, and similar psychological/emotional reasons. But clearly as soon as they let go of the emotionality of what their issues are, they seem to "go" to whatever is next.

2. What are the differences among ghosts, apparitions, poltergeists, and spirits?

As mentioned above, for us a ghost is a spirit, an apparition, or a disembodied consciousness.

The term "poltergeist" can be traced back hundreds of years but has come to represent something very different from the literal translation of the German word for "noisy ghost." In poltergeist cases the physical effects are the central themes including movements and levitations, appearances/disappearances of objects, unusual behavior of electrical appliances, unexplained knockings and other sounds to temperature changes as well as a combination of all elements. Rarely are ghostly figures or voices seen or heard (though these are not out of the question, as some very few cases demonstrate a telepathic projection usually of a nonhuman archetypal form by the poltergeist agent).

The model we work from is called recurrent spontaneous psychokinesis or RSPK. It is PK that happens without conscious control and happens over and over. It doesn't come from an apparition or ghost but from someone living or working in the environment where the poltergeist outbreak is happening.

3.   How do ghosts move objects?

The same way living people do; it's mind over matter, which is called psychokinesis or PK.

Author's Note: The word psychokinesis is derived from the Greek words *psyche* meaning life or soul and *kinein* mean to move. PK occurrences have been recorded since ancient times and include, for example, object movement and bending of metals.

4. Can you tell me a little about your background and how you first became involved in paranormal investigation?

Contrary to what most people expect, it was not any psychic experience that got me into parapsychology—I use that term instead of "paranormal investigation" as the in-the-field research is part of what interested me in parapsychology.

In actuality, I used to watch TV shows from a very early age that influenced me such as *Topper, The Twilight Zone,* and *One Step Beyond.* Looking back, *Topper* probably gave me my first "taste" of ghosts. Early on, I also read many books on mythology, science fiction, and especially superhero comics. I was also a bit of a science geek as a kid. Combine all of that, throw in a dash of *Star Trek* and *Dark Shadows,* and I think I almost had to discover the books in the library on parapsychology. I believed then, as I believe now, that psychic abilities are probably normal and untapped. This never seemed a strange conclusion to me.

In the early '70s, the short-lived TV show *The Sixth Sense* coupled with my being able to meet and talk with some NY area parapsychologists (through a neighbor who was the yoga teacher for one of them) pushed me over the cliff, and I just had to learn more.

I read extensively in the field before college—and by the way I read the academic books by Rhine and others as well as more popular books by Susy Smith, Hans Holzer, and many others. On my reading list were even more "occult" books including many on vampires and werewolves. I had been advised by parapsychologists to study some field of science, and after a very brief stint in astrophysics, I found myself engrossed in cultural anthropology and gained an undergraduate degree from Northwestern University in that subject.

In my studies at Northwestern, I was able to focus the topics of many of my papers towards supernatural folklore, divinatory practices, psychic belief systems, and the like, thanks to the guidance of some great professors. During my senior year, I took a multipart seminar offered by John Bisaha and Brenda Dunne at Mundelein College in Chicago. It was there I learned about John F. Kennedy University's fledgling graduate parapsychology program (from guest lecturer K. Ramakrishna Rao) in California.

In 1979 I entered the program at JFK University, graduating with an MS in parapsychology in 1981. It was due to coursework in the graduate program that I began doing field investigations; my first project happened in my first quarter consisting of a complex poltergeist case with a telepathic projection of a "black knight."

After grad school, I moved back to New York where I worked as a public information and media consultant to the American Society for Psychical Research in New York City from 1982 to mid-1983. While there, I helped a little with some of the lab research being conducted by Dr.

Karlis Osis and Donna McCormick and did a number of field investigations (essentially being "mentored" at this by the late Dr. Karlis Osis and the phenomenal psychic Alex Tanous). In addition, through my position I worked with a number of other researchers in the tristate area.

Late 1983 I came back to the Bay area as the media consultant to the graduate parapsychology program at JFK University as well as teaching a number of classes in the program. Once back, I put lots of time and energy into conducting further field investigations of cases dealing with apparitions, hauntings, and poltergeists, essentially making that my "specialty." Over the years I've worked with a number of parapsychologists whose interests have run the gamut from lab research to field investigations. [Note: the parapsychology program ended at JFKU in the late 1980s.]

With the disappearance of the graduate parapsychology program, I started the Office of Paranormal Investigations in 1989 to take up the cases the university was getting.

5. Why are some ghosts residual energy while some are considered intelligent and interactive?

As mentioned above, since "ghost" typically refers to people after death, this is not the right question. The right question might be "why are some figures seen and thought to be ghosts' residual impressions while some are considered intelligent and interactive?"

That's the same as asking why some TV programs are live and some are taped, or wondering "Is it live or is it Memorex?"

Place memory is a term parapsychologists and psychics use to denote the imprinting of historical information—events in the past—on a location (house, piece of land, etc.); the place has memory of its past that we

can perceive. In other words, it's another term for residual impressions. But the most common term is
"haunting."

Like the poltergeist, the haunting relies on the living.
Unlike a poltergeist case where the phenomena are
caused by the agent, a haunting is received by people.
Hauntings actually show that we are all psychic receiv-
ers (clairvoyant) to some degree.

Ever walk into a house and get a feel for the "vibes"
(the house feels "good" or "bad")? Of course, that feeling
could be because of normal perceptions such as the
décor is nice or "off," but you may also be psychically
perceiving emotions and events embedded in the environment.

One ability proffered by many psychics over the ages
is psychometry: the ability to "read" the history of an
object by holding or touching it. Objects, we're told,
"record" their entire history, and some people can deci-
pher that with psi. But what is a house if not a big
object?

(**Author's Note:** According to *Wikipedia*, "psi" is a term
that denotes anomalous processes of information or energy transfer, processes such as telepathy or other forms
of extrasensory perception that are currently unexplained
in terms of known physical or biological mechanisms.)

In haunting cases, people report seeing (or hearing or
feeling or even smelling) a presence (or several) typically
engaged in some sort of activity. It could be a man's figure walking up and down the hallway, or footsteps heard
from the attic, or a man and woman physically fighting
until one is dead, or even the sounds of two people making love coming from an adjoining room.

The events and figures witnessed in hauntings tend to
be repetitive both in what's experienced and when they

occur (at approximately the same time). Speaking with the "ghosts" tends to do no good, because they just continue to go about their business as though you're not even there. In other words, they're essentially holograms instead of conscious beings capable of interacting.

Hauntings seem to be some kind of environmental recording of events and people. The house or building or land somehow records its history with the more emotion-laden events and experiences coming through "louder" and "stronger." That people report mostly negative events and emotions (around suicide, murder or other violent crimes, or emotional fights) is likely due to an issue with the way people report any unusual or emotional events in their lives.

You might think of a haunting as a loop of video or audio tape playing itself over and over for you to watch. Trying to interact with it would be akin to trying to interact with a show on your television—you can turn it off or change the channel, but I wouldn't expect the actors to suddenly stop and talk to you directly.

The number of apparition experiences that are reported are much more than haunting experiences, but the number of apparition cases—where the apparition appears more than once and sticks around for a while—is far surpassed by the number of haunting cases.

The sheer majority of apparitions are seen once by a relative or friend or loved one typically within 48–72 hours of that person's death (though sometimes as long as a week or two after) as if the person is coming to say goodbye.

In other words, most people don't stick around as a ghost for more than a day or two. Longer-term apparitions tend to have a psychological/emotional need or strong desire to stay here. Such needs or desires include denial of death, fear of "what's next," a strong desire to stay with one's loved ones, or even anger at a life cut short.

Not everyone with such strong desires or needs sticks around as an apparition, and there are likely some environmental factors that allow such people to remain when the conditions and the psychology coincide. These factors, I personally suspect, include both geomagnetic conditions and other as yet unidentified factors in the physical environment.

6.   What do you believe happens when we die?

Near-death experiences suggest that we move into another existence. Apparition cases suggest that some of us can exist in the here and now in a disembodied form and still interact.

But what do I believe? I believe I'll find out when it happens, and I'm in no hurry. I hope to stick around as a ghost—I have many places to see around the world (no need to buy a plane ticket) and many people to "haunt."

7.   What was the most amazing paranormal experience you've ever encountered?

That's tough to say as I've witnessed so many extraordinary things over the years.

From a personal perspective, it would be experiencing the ghost at the Moss Beach Distillery walking through me repeatedly for over two minutes and then having three psychics witness it as they came into the room.

8.   Do you have anything else that you'd like to add?

Yes, and it relates to what I think is the most important advice for anyone wanting to really understand ghosts, hauntings, and poltergeists:

Learn more about psychic abilities and experiences.

We connect with apparitions via telepathy. Apparitions communicate with us telepathically. We perceive imprints in the environment apparently through a form of clairvoyance. If apparitions can sense their environment, they are doing so directly without the use of their senses—in other words, clairvoyantly. Both telepathy and clairvoyance are forms of ESP. Don't ignore what parapsychologists have done and learned about ESP through research in the lab and in the real world.

We move things via psychokinesis. Ghosts move things via psychokinesis. So learn about psychokinesis, both in the real world and in the laboratory.

. . . .

About Loyd Auerbach, MS, Parapsychologist

Loyd has been a consultant to various television producers and writers in the United States, Japan, and Great Britain, providing scientific, creative, and promotional input. His wide media exposure includes many prominent appearances on paranormal-related programs for the Travel Channel, the History Channel, A&E, the Syfy Channel, and more. He has also appeared on ABC's *The View*, *Larry King Live*, the *Today Show*, *Unsolved Mysteries*, and many others.

He is the creator and principal instructor of the certificate program in parapsychological studies at HCH Institute in Lafayette, CA, and has been an adjunct professor in Integral Studies at JFK University since 1983. A popular speaker, Loyd served as president of the Psychic Entertainers Association (PEA) for several years.

For over three decades, he has been investigating cases of reported paranormal phenomena to help people understand what may (or may not) be going on in their lives. In 1989 he founded the Office of Paranormal Investigations (OPI), an outgrowth of the JFK University graduate program, which is a group for people to call when they believe they have a psychic or paranormal disturbance and a resource center for the mass media, businesspeople, scientists, law enforcement agencies, and attorneys. For more information, please visit his Web site at www.mindreader.com.

AN INTERVIEW WITH
GHOST HUNTERS'
DAVE TANGO

Poltergeists, as Loyd Auerbach noted above, may cause many physical disturbances by moving objects, creating unexplained sounds, flipping light switches, and affecting electricity. Typically these spirits are depicted by orbs in photographs, apparitions, energy, shadows, and vortexes. Some believe that the vortex (often depicted by a long column of light in photographs) is the gateway used by spirits or ghosts to travel from one dimension to the next.

The popular weekly *Ghost Hunters* reality television show has earned the highest ratings of any other Syfy program. The show, based on The Atlantic Paranormal Society (TAPS), is founded and produced by Jason Hawes and Grant Wilson. Using various devices, Hawes and Wilson along with other team members investigate various locations for poltergeists, ghosts, or other paranormal activity. The team, which includes Investigator and Evidence Analyst Dave Tango, spends several hours taking temperature and electromagnetic field readings along with audio and video recordings searching for any sign of paranormal activity. They use high tech equipment including digital thermometers, EMF (electromagnetic field) scanners, night vision cameras, computers, etc.

Tango has worked with TAPS for the past five years but has always been interested in the paranormal and enjoys being able to investigate the unknown. Despite his success, he is well grounded and says, "My heroes are the kind of people who do things for the less fortunate, who are always giving without wanting anything in return."

Although *Ghost Hunters* draws millions of viewers each week, Tango says success isn't judged by the ratings but by helping others who are frightened by their ghostly experiences. He is also well known for his efforts to raise awareness for Tourette's syndrome, a lifelong disease he himself is battling. The inherited neurological disorder causes both motor and phonic tics (sudden, repetitive movements).

Dave took time out of his busy schedule to answer some questions about ghosts and the paranormal in general.

1. **How did you first become involved with ghost hunt-ing and the show *Ghost Hunters?***

   My father got me interested in ghost hunting. When I was growing up, we always loved to read or watch TV shows that had to do with ghosts or the paranormal. I started ghost hunting at the age of seventeen. A friend and I would go to local places that were said to be haunted and check them out. We came across this house in Roselle Park, New Jersey that had some pretty strange things happening. *Ghost Hunters* was in the beginning of its second season when I gave them a call for some help. Lo and behold, they came and did an episode at the location. We were thrilled that they asked us to join them. The episode went really well, and I learned a great deal from the experience. When it was over, we said our goodbyes, and I thought that was it. Two weeks later while sitting in a movie theater, my phone started to vibrate. I went to the lobby to answer it. They said that they liked me and asked me if I wanted to join the group. The rest is history.

   (Author's Note: Dave's father Bruce Tango has joined the show as a guest investigator on several episodes. Bruce is a former Elizabeth, New Jersey police officer.)

2. **What are your thoughts on ghosts and the afterlife? Have you always believed in the afterlife? Do you believe that consciousness survives death? If so, do you believe *Ghost Hunters* provides proof?**

   I do believe in ghosts because I have seen many unex-plained things. Some of the evidence we have caught proves that consciousness can survive death such as electronic voice phenomenon (EVP). We have caught EVP's that answer our questions or state a name of a person who is related to the deceased or even the deceased themselves.

(Author's Note: EVP's are a form of afterlife communication in which voices are captured on recording devices such as digital recorders and telephone answering machines. For more information about this phenomenon, visit www.aaevp.com.)

3. **You have investigated many cases of reported ghost sightings via *Ghost Hunters*. Which case stands out in your mind the most and why?**

The case that stands out the most is the Leap Castle in Ireland. The locations in Europe had such a rich history, and I felt differently just being there. Also, many of the people there accept their hauntings as normal activity. While investigating a part of the Leap Castle called "The Bloody Chapel," my friend Dustin Pari was knocked off his feet by an unseen entity. Both Dustin and I were very shaken by the incident. I had never witnessed such intense activity. I got angry at whatever did that to my friend and told it to come after me. Unfortunately it didn't, but I'd love to get back there again sometime.

4. **Ghosts are believed to be entities that are stuck between this plane and the next. What are some of the reasons that you've found would keep a ghost earthbound or stuck?**

There are many different theories out there. Some ghosts are thought to be just residual energy like a tape on repeat. Others are considered to be intelligent, and these are the ghosts that are thought to be able to communicate with us. Some people think that dying a tragic or untimely death can lead you to be stuck or also having a strong attachment to a person or item. All ghost hunters are looking to find answers, and hopefully someday we will discover them.

5. Do you have any advice for anyone who believes that he may have a ghost or unwanted entities around him?

First and foremost, people should investigate their homes. For example, they should try to determine what could be making these noises. We do a lot of disproving while investigating. This shows people how many noises and such can be accredited to old pipes, uneven floors, and the like. If people can't find an explanation this way, then I would suggest they do a little ghost hunting themselves or find a reputable ghost hunting group to investigate their home. Ghost hunting equipment doesn't have to be expensive. A twenty dollar digital recorder can catch electronic voice phenomenon.

6. What is the message that *Ghost Hunters* attempts to share with viewers? How did the show originate?

I believe the program originated because the Syfy channel was looking for a reality show about a ghost-hunting group. The Atlantic Paranormal Society (TAPS) happened to be in the news about a case and was chosen as the paranormal research group to follow it. *Ghost Hunters* attempts to find hard evidence that there is something else after we pass away. We also try to show people that not everything is paranormal and that many things can be logically explained. *Ghost Hunters* leaves it up to the viewers to decide whether or not they believe in the paranormal.

**7. Studies have shown that more and more people con-
sider themselves to be spiritual and not religious.
Why do you think this is so?**

I think that some people may consider being religious as
going to their specific religion's location (church, temple,
etc.) every week. Spirituality is more of having a belief in
something higher than us. Everyone who is religious has
spirituality, but not everyone who is spiritual goes to
church on a weekly basis.

. . . .
About Dave Tango

Prior to *Ghost Hunters*, Tango worked as a trained illusionist in his
home state of New Jersey. In addition to this show, he has a leading
role on another cable show, *Ghost Hunters Academy* in which he
and fellow investigator Steve Gonsalves travel with five academy
recruits to locations presumed to be haunted. The show's purpose
is to find the next ghost hunter. For more information, please visit
www.the-atlantic-paranormal-society.com and www.syfy.com/
ghosthunters.

Author with Dave Tango

$\eta D \mathcal{E}_{\delta}$: The Evidence

Mark Pitstick, MA, DC
www.soulproof.com

The following chapter is based on excerpts taken with permission from Mark Pitstick's book *Soul Proof: Compelling Evidence We Are Immortal Spiritual Beings—And What That Means for Your Life?*

When I was nine-years-old, my Uncle Cliff's car collided with a semi. He nearly died from severe multiple injuries and was in the hospital for a long time. When he finally came home, he was pale, thin, missing teeth, and couldn't walk. From his hospital bed in their living room, he spoke through a wired jaw about what he experienced when he almost died. He described walking in a meadow of lush green grass, hearing beautiful music, and seeing Jesus. He felt an accelerated awareness with everything being more brilliant and colorful than usual. He also no longer feared death. Apart from missing his family, he felt so peaceful that he didn't care to come back.

Since then, many near-death experiences, such as the ones described in this book, have provided impressive evidence for the continuation of consciousness beyond the grave. That many of these cases have been validated by respected scientists further points to the authenticity of nonphysical realities.

Tens of thousands of NDE cases, many of them documented by doctors and scientists, have demonstrated the persistence of awareness after "death." Typical stages during an NDE include: a feeling of being outside of the body, hearing a buzzing or ringing sound, going through a tunnel, seeing radiant light, meeting departed loved ones and spiritual beings, sensing beautiful scenes and colors, hearing angelic music, feeling peaceful and at home, learning lessons, being told it's not one's time to stay on the Other Side, and a rapid journey back into the successfully resuscitated body.

Although NDEs were first described thousands of years ago, they are much more common now because of advances in medical resuscitative capabilities. Many more people are now successfully brought back from the brink of biological or irreversible death. These NDErs were temporarily clinically dead, that is, had cessation of their heart, lung, and/or brain functions. During that time a significant percentage of them had fascinating and life-changing experiences.

Clinical reports of near-death experiences first came to my attention in the 1970s when I was working as a respiratory therapist and attending theology school. While the topic of NDEs was sometimes met with skepticism by health care professionals, my earlier experience with Uncle Cliff helped me keep an open mind. I interviewed a number of patients who were successfully resuscitated and asked them, "Do you remember anything during your time while unconscious?" Several excitedly told me about beatific experiences with classic NDE traits.

Millions of adults in the United States have had an NDE or out-of-body experience (OBE). This high incidence and the immense amount of validated research on NDEs constitute the most impressive evidence indicating life after death. Taken together with the other categories, NDEs provide irrefutable proof that our real selves do not die.

I have categorized NDE information into the following sections: historical continuity, verifiable cases, pediatric validation cases, life previews, out-of-body experiences, empathetic NDEs, blind persons and NDEs, and transformative aspects.

HISTORICAL CONTINUITY

NDEs have been reported independently across time in various cultures, a fact that further increases the credibility of this phenomenon. They were first reported thousands of years ago as described in *The Tibetan Book of the Dead*, *The Egyptian Book of the Dead*, and *The Aztec Song of the Dead*. These descriptions were lost or little known for centuries yet score remarkably high on modern NDE measures such as the "Near–Death Experience Validity Scale" by Ken Ring, PhD. Their reports of what souls encounter after death also mirror those of other cultures and transcendent experiences via consciousness altering substances.

In *The Light Beyond*, Dr. Raymond Moody states that there have been cases of NDEs far back in history, dating to references by the Greek philosopher Plato in 347 BC. Pope Gregory the Great's sixth–century *Dialogues* are a set of deathbed visions, ghost stories, and near–death accounts providing evidence of the soul's immortality. Dr. Carol Zaleski, author of *Otherworld Journeys*, says the literature of the Middle Ages is filled with such accounts.[1]

A massive amount of NDE literature exists thanks to Raymond Moody, Ken Ring, Bruce Greyson, Melvin Morse, P.M.H. Atwater, Michael Sabom, and others. Current studies of diverse age groups in other cultures show the same patterns or universality of reports. Research findings lead to many questions such as: What is the nature of this consciousness? How can accurate awareness be explained when people are nearly dead, blind, or unconscious? And since this consciousness exists during at least part of the dying process, does it exist after actual bodily death?

VERIFIABLE CASES

NDE evidence with verifiable aspects strongly point to the existence

---

[1]Raymond Moody, *The Light Beyond* (New York: Bantam, 1988), 104–5.

of awareness surviving physical death. In *Lessons from the Light*, Ken Ring, PhD, says that many people " . . . tell of leaving their bodies for a moment and having a panoramic and detailed perception of the environment around their body. Suppose, then, these descriptions could be checked independently and verified. If one could show that these patients could not possibly have seen what they did naturally or acquired this information by other means, we would have some fairly impressive evidence to support the objectivity of NDEs."

Much research has been done and the evidence is clear. As Ring concludes, "We now have good evidence, and from multiple sources, that the NDE is indeed an experience that has its own objective character and is, in a phrase, 'on the level.' (After considering evidentiary cases) I hope you will be reassured that the doubts about the validity of the NDE can be safely dispatched on purely scientific grounds."[2]

In *Messages from the Masters*, Brian Weiss, MD, describes a number of NDEs with verifiable aspects. One woman suffered massive head trauma from a severe auto accident and was very near death. As the doctor spoke with the family about the inevitably fatal outcome, the patient floated out of her body. She found her family even though the conference was far from where the medical team was working on her. Upon overhearing the conversation, she tried to communicate that she wasn't dead. After her recovery, she accurately repeated the conversation between the surgeon and her family.

Another patient awoke in a very agitated state after major surgery. During the procedure, she floated above her body when her blood pressure and heart rhythm became abnormal. From this vantage point, she could see the surgeons and read the anesthesiologist's notes in her chart. Upon awakening in the recovery room, she was still panicked because of these complications. She correctly told Dr. Weiss what had been written on her chart even though she had been unconscious. Because of the positioning of her body to the doctor, she couldn't have seen the notes even if she had been awake.

Dr. Weiss concludes, "I have heard these and other stories of clinical

---

[2]Ken Ring, *Lessons from the Light* (Portsmouth, NH: Moment Press, 1998), 56–58.

accounts of patients with near–death and out-of-body experiences from so many physicians that I cannot explain them away on medical or physiological grounds."[3]

There are so many validated NDE cases that they are collectively known as "tennis shoe stories." In *Closer to the Light*, Melvin Morse, MD, and Paul Perry describe the story of psychologist Kim Clark who was counseling a patient named Maria after she had a cardiac arrest. They state, "The woman wasn't interested in what Clark had to say. Instead, she wanted to talk about how she had floated around the hospital while doctors struggled to start her heart. To prove that she had left her body, the woman insisted that there was a shoe on the ledge outside Clark's window. Clark opened the window, but could see no shoe. 'It's out there,' the woman insisted. Clark leaned out, but still could not see the shoe. 'It's around the corner,' said the woman. Courageously, Clark crawled onto the ledge of her fifth–floor window and around the corner. There sat a shoe, just as Maria had described."[4]

The NDE literature is also full of accounts of survivors who, while clinically dead, encountered departed relatives who were unknown to the subject during life. Later, positive identification was confirmed by photographic or anecdotal evidence. In addition, many patients develop extrasensory abilities during and after the NDE.

Another verifying aspect involves so-called "surprise" meetings on the Other Side with people the survivor didn't know had died. For example, one woman was very ill at the same time that her sister was near death on a different floor of the same hospital. During her NDE, the woman watched from above the resuscitative efforts on her body. To her surprise, she met her sister and they enjoyed a great conversation until the sister began moving away from her.

The woman states, "I tried to go with her, but she kept telling me to stay where I was. 'It's not your time,' she said . . . Then she just began to recede off into the distance through a tunnel while I was left there alone. When I awoke, I told the doctor that my sister had died. He

---

[3]Brian Weiss, *Messages from the Masters* (New York: Warner Books, 2000), 168–171.
[4]Melvin Morse and Paul Perry, *Closer to the Light* (New York: Ballantine, 1990), 20.

denied it, but at my insistence, he had a nurse check on it. She had in fact died, just as I knew she did."[5]

In *Transformed by the Light*, Morse and Perry relate a similar case of a woman who was bleeding profusely after delivering a baby. As medical personnel worked on her, she could see them from a vantage point above, and her intense pain suddenly disappeared. She went through a tunnel toward bright light, but before she reached the end, "A gentle voice told me I had to go back. Then I met a dear friend, a neighbor from a town that we had left. He also told me to go back. I hit the hospital bed with an electrifying jerk, and the pain was back. I was being rushed into an operating theater for surgery to stop the bleeding. It was three weeks later that my husband decided I was well enough to be told that my dear friend in that other town had died in an accident on the day my daughter was born."[6]

PEDIATRIC VALIDATION CASES

Young children, who describe the sequence of events during NDEs just as adults do, provide an especially impressive category of evidence. The literature is rich with verifiable accounts of pediatric NDEs that include many complex details about resuscitative procedures that are incomprehensible to young children. Children have not been exposed to religious or cultural views about what happens after death. They tend to view death as a vacation and something the departed will return from.

Two examples of pediatric NDE cases are described in *Closer to the Light* by Morse and Perry. The first involved an eight-year-old boy who fell from a bridge and hit his head on a rock in the water. After floating face down for at least five minutes, he was pulled from the water by a policeman. The boy had stopped breathing and didn't have a pulse; after performing CPR for thirty minutes, the policeman declared him dead. Even so, a helicopter emergency team started resuscitation and

---

[5]Raymond Moody, *The Light Beyond* (New York: Bantam, 1988), 173.
[6]Melvin Morse and Paul Perry, *Transformed By the Light* (New York: Ivy Books, 1992), 123.

rushed him to the hospital. The boy didn't regain consciousness until two days later when he accurately described his rescue and resuscitation in great detail. He knew all of this, he said, because he had been watching the whole time from outside his body.

The second case involved a NDE at age nine months; Mark told his parents about this experience at age three. His parents had never told him about his cardiac arrest, and most children don't remember events at that age. "Then, following a Christmas pageant, he said that God didn't look like the man in the play they had just seen. When his father asked him what he meant, Mark told him what had happened during that frantic night two years earlier: 'I saw nurses and doctors standing over me trying to wake me up. I flew out of the room and (went to the waiting room, where I) saw Grandpa and Grandma crying and holding each other. I think they thought I was going to die.' He then reported seeing a long, dark tunnel and crawled up it.

"The bright light at the end of the tunnel kept him going and he found 'a bright place' where he ran through the fields with God. He was very animated when he described this run with God. He said that one 'can double jump in Heaven' . . . God then asked if he wanted to go 'back home.' Mark said 'no,' but God told him he would come back again some other day." Mark vividly remembered his experience until age five and at the time Morse wrote the book, was a well-adjusted teenager.[7]

LIFE PREVIEWS

NDEs occasionally provide glimpses into the future as well. These so-called life preview experiences provide another validation aspect since, in a number of cases, the events foreseen did come true.

Dr. Moody describes a personal encounter with a woman who had a life preview during her NDE in 1971. In 1975 several months before the publication of *Life after Life*, Moody's children were trick-or-treating at Halloween. A friendly couple asked the children's names; when the old-

---

[7]Melvin Morse and Paul Perry, *Closer to the Light* (New York: Ballantine, 1990), 121, 4, 40–42.

est said, "Raymond Avery Moody," the woman looked startled and said to Mrs. Moody, "I must talk to your husband."

Moody states: "When I spoke to this woman later on, she told me about her NDE in 1971. She'd had heart failure and lung collapse during surgery and had been clinically dead for a long time. During this experience, she met a guide who took her through a life review and gave her information about the future. Toward the end of the experience, she was shown a picture of me, given my full name, and told that 'when the time was right,' she would tell me her story. I found this encounter remarkable."[8]

Bruce Greyson, MD, states that about one-third of those recalling a life review during an NDE had visions of personal future events. Dr. Ring reports several life preview cases in his books *Heading Toward Omega* and *Lessons from the Light*, including the following one.

> One NDE survivor Nel found herself looking at a giant television screen during her life review. She made a conscious decision to return to her physical body but just then a second TV screen showed her glimpses of what was to come: a prolonged period of pain, family members who would suffer physical pain, a sister-in-law who would die prematurely. Dr. Ring, who has known Nel for more than fifteen years, is convinced that the events she foresaw during her NDE did indeed take place, just as she was shown.[9]

OUT-OF-BODY EXPERIENCES

The term out-of-body experience (OBE) usually refers to a person's awareness leaving the body without being clinically dead. OBEs sometimes happen spontaneously during meditative states; the phenomenon of "astral travel" is one such example of an OBE. Intense experiences, for example, childbirth or being in imminent danger, can also trigger OBEs. In the past, people often kept such occurrences to themselves for fear of

---

[8]Raymond Moody, *The Light Beyond* (New York: Bantam, 1988), 28–29.
[9]Ken Ring, *Lessons from the Light* (Portsmouth, NH: Moment Press, 1998), 151.

being considered crazy. As such, the frequency of OBEs is likely much greater than has been reported.

A ten-year-old girl who attended one of my workshops with her mother described an OBE she had at age two. Her mom left her with a baby-sitter for the first time ever and gave clear instructions to attend to the baby if she cried. The baby-sitter, however, had his own ideas about child rearing and ignored the infant when she cried. Receiving no comfort from her mother for the first time, the little one cried and cried until she experienced a strange event.

Even though she couldn't see out the window from her crib, she could see another version of herself on the sidewalk below. This "other self" reassured her and told her it would be okay. The infant's OBE continued as her awareness floated out into the living room and saw the baby-sitter there. She remembers the clothing she had on and the appearance of the sitter. Her mother verified the facts as told by this youngster who seems wise beyond her years.

An OBE verified by physical evidence occurred with Robert Monroe who wrote *Journeys Out of the Body*. Monroe discovered his ability to travel out of his physical body and wanted to nonphysically visit a co-worker who was vacationing in New Jersey. As told by attorney Sidney Freeman in *Life After Death*:

> He wanted her to remember the 'visit' so he said he was going to pinch her. 'Oh, you don't need to do that, I'll remember' she replied mentally. Nevertheless, he pinched her — in the side, just above the hips. He tried to do it gently. She screamed, 'Ow.' That Tuesday they were both back at work. Did she remember the 'visit,' he asked. No, she said.
>
> Did she remember the pinch? 'Was that you?' she replied. 'I was sitting there, talking to the girls when all of a sudden I felt this terrible pinch. I must have jumped a foot. I thought my brother-in-law had come back and sneaked up behind me. I turned around but there was no one there. I never had any idea it was you!' They went into his private office. She lifted her sweater slightly above her skirt. There were two brown and blue marks at exactly the spot where he had pinched her.

He apologized for hurting her. He thought he had done it gently and said he wouldn't do it again. This remarkable incident
showed a physical effect from an out-of-body visit.[10]

In 1974 I experienced a profound OBE during meditation while lying
on the grass on a warm spring day. After about twenty minutes, I felt as
if my body was becoming part of the earth. I couldn't feel my arms or
legs and felt like my consciousness was several miles up in the sky. At
that moment, my fear of death and change decreased dramatically. I felt
totally assured that there is a spiritual reality that renders physical
change relatively meaningless. Thirty-five years later, the memory of
that experience is still clear and inspiring.

EMPATHETIC NEAR-DEATH EXPERIENCES

Another type of near-death experience is the empathetic or shared
NDE. In these cases, loved ones or health care providers of a dying
person have other-worldly experiences around the time of death.

Joan Borysenko, PhD, relates a beautiful empathetic NDE that occurred at the moment of her mother's passing. Her mother had long
been cynical about and critical of Joan's spiritual work. Joan and her
son Justin were present as her mom passed over. At that moment, the
room was filled with light and both realized what Justin verbalized: "I
feel like Grandma is holding the door to eternity open to give us a
glimpse. Can you feel it? You must be so grateful to your mother. You
know, she was a very great soul. And she embodied to take a role that
was much smaller than the wisdom in her soul and she did it as a gift
for you so that you'd have something to resist against."[11]

Why are such reports surfacing more now? There is a greater societal
openness to these topics, especially among baby-boomers whose parents are aging and dying. Hospital visitation policies have changed, and
more family members are present during the death of loved ones. As

---

[10]Sidney Freeman, *Life after Death* (Commack, NY: Kroshka Books, 1998), 79–80.
[11]Personal communication with Joan Borysenko; story also told in *Fire in the Soul* (New
York: Warner Books, 1993), 147.

such, they can potentially experience empathetic NDEs. Finally, improvements in pain management now allow dying persons to enjoy more clarity.

"Sue" recently had a psycho-spiritual session with me and while in a deep hypnotic state, experienced a healing trip to spirit side. She e-mailed me the next day with the following message:

> After I left our session Saturday, I felt wonderfully different; there are no words I can use to sufficiently describe it. My mother called me at midnight and told me my grandmother was not doing very well. Grandma and I have always been very close, and I've often thought we were soul mates. We stayed with her through the night and called the emergency squad around 4:30 a.m.
>
> At the hospital, I was with her praying, holding her hand, and encouraging her to follow the Light. At 2 p.m. Sunday, the most beautiful flash of indescribable love and light encompassed and overwhelmed me totally. I literally cried out, 'Grandma, it is so beautiful!' She took her last breath immediately after that. It was absolutely amazing. I remember having that feeling during our session, only it wasn't as intense.

In *The Last Laugh*, Dr. Moody discusses reports of empathetic NDEs: "Dozens upon dozens of first-rate individuals have related to me that, as a loved one died, they themselves lifted out of their own bodies and accompanied their dying loved ones upward toward a beautiful and loving light. Others have said that, as they sat with their dying loved ones, they perceived deceased relatives coming to greet the one who was passing away. Lots of doctors and nurses have described how they perceived patients' spirits leaving their bodies at the point of death."[12]

I experienced this phenomenon firsthand many years ago while working in hospitals. I was usually assigned to the emergency room

---

[12]Raymond Moody, *The Last Laugh* (Charlottesville, VA: Hampton Roads Publishing Company, 1999), 4–5.

and intensive care units where I assisted during much resuscitation. In those days, dying patients seldom received conscious attention to their emotional and spiritual needs. So while working with critically ill patients, I spoke directly into their ears, reassured them that everything possible was being done, and encouraged them to trust God. On several occasions, I saw a faint white light emanate from the patient's chest region just before the time of death was announced. Looking back, it seems that my empathy for those in transition may have enabled these sixth sense experiences that I revere to this day.

A fascinating variation of an empathetic NDE was relayed to me by several people in England. An older woman passed on, and after her funeral, the family was gathered for dinner with fifteen close family members. The widower's head slumped down during dinner, and the family assumed he had fallen asleep after several long and difficult days. After several minutes, someone became concerned and checked on him but found no sign of breathing or heartbeat. They called their neighbor who was a doctor, and she came right over. The doctor verified the absence of vital signs, now eight or nine minutes since the widower had slumped over.

She asked the family if they would like her to try and "bring him back," at which time a distraught female family member let out a loud wail of despair. At that, the old man immediately jolted back to life. He said that he just had to go make sure his wife had made it over okay because she was no good at finding her way anywhere on her own. He would not be staying "there," he commented, because he still had too much to do "here." He was taken to the hospital by ambulance where no sign of any health problem could be detected. Since then, he seems to have a new lease on life and has been energetic and healthy.

BLIND PERSONS AND NDES

NDEs reported by those who are blind constitute particularly impressive evidence for the survival of consciousness beyond physical death. In *Books of the Dead*, Stan Grof, MD, discusses, " . . . reported cases where individuals, who were blind because of medically confirmed organic damage to their optical system, could at the time of clinical death see the environment . . . Occurrences of this kind, unlike most of the other aspects of near-death phenomena, can be subjected to objective verification. They thus represent the most convincing proof that what happens in near-death experiences is more than the hallucinatory phantasmagoria of physiologically impaired brains."[13]

As amazing as verifiable NDEs are, they are even more astonishing when the subjects are blind. In the foreword of *Mindsight* by Ken Ring, PhD, and Sharon Cooper, PhD, researcher Charles T. Tart, PhD, states, "The authors of this book have practiced essential science, real science. They have looked at the facts about NDEs, particularly NDEs among the blind, and provided us with extremely stimulating and thought-provoking material that we must take into account in coming to terms with reality . . . these facts argue strongly that there is some very real sense in which we are 'spiritual' beings, not just material beings."[14]

Ring and Cooper provide an example of a validation NDE in a blind person. Irreversibly blinded earlier in the day after a surgical accident, Nancy later went into respiratory arrest and was unconscious. As the hospital staff wheeled her down the hall, her gurney hit the elevator. At that moment, Nancy describes stepping out of herself and watching the events around her. She looked down the hall about twenty feet and saw two men standing there, her son's father and her boyfriend. Then she looked down at her body still lying on the gurney.

She saw the IV, black ambu bag covering her face, the surgical head cover on her, white sheets, and three staff people on her left and right. At that point, Nancy says, "And then the classic white light, bright, the most beautiful light, soothing, comforting just washing over (me)."

Afterwards, interviews with her boyfriend and ex-husband corroborated the details outside the elevator. The positions of the ambu bag and staff members would have blocked her from seeing the two men and other details. Of this, Ring and Cooper state, "Thus, we conclude that in all probability there was no possibility for Nancy to see what she

---

[13]Stanislav Grof, *Books of the Dead* (London: Thames & Hudson, 1994), 31.
[14]Ken Ring and Sharon Cooper, *Mindsight: Near-Death and Out-of-Body Experiences in the Blind* (Palo Alto, CA: Wm. James Center for Consciousness Studies, 1999), xv.

did with her physical eyes . . . Yet, she did see, and, as the corroborative testimony we have provided shows, she apparently saw truly . . . There is no question that NDEs in the blind do occur and, furthermore, that they take the same general form and are comprised of the very same elements that define the NDEs of sighted individuals."[15]

In my radio interview with Dr. Ring, he added that a panel of vision specialists was not able to come up with alternative medical explanations that could explain these findings. This research, he stated, makes a very strong supportive argument for the religious and spiritual beliefs of many people about the existence of afterlife.

TRANSFORMATIVE ASPECTS

A common and enduring aspect of NDEs is the accompanying transformative effect. NDErs have such a strong belief in afterlife that any fear of death is nearly or completely extinguished. Survivors of NDEs typically reorder their life priorities and often change to more meaningful jobs involving service to others. They also view their bodies as vehicles for their souls and take better care of themselves.

My good friend Ed Sarno, PhD, had a NDE after open heart surgery. At bedtime on his first day home from the hospital, his dimly lit room filled with bright light and he felt more energetic, joyful, and peaceful than he ever had in his life. He was given the choice to cross over or remain on earth. He decided to stay. As soon as he made this choice, the light subsided and he was back in a painful postoperative state. But his life is now radically different. He knows—without a doubt—that he can't lose: if he lives to one hundred years of age, that's great; if he dies today, he gets to resume the wonderful journey he glimpsed.

A deep faith and internalized belief about God and afterlife are common after NDEs. These dramatic lessons impart a lasting hope and assurance of things not seen but nevertheless vitally real. Says Nancy Bush, past-president of the International Association for Near-Death Studies, "Most near-death survivors say they don't think there is a God. They know."

---

[15]Ibid., 109–122.

A *U.S. News & World Report* article stated that, "no matter what the nature of the (near-death) experience, it alters some lives. Alcoholics find themselves unable to imbibe. Hardened criminals opt for a life of helping others. Atheists embrace the existence of a deity, while dogmatic members of a particular religion report feeling welcome in any church or temple or mosque." Further, those who had undergone NDEs became more altruistic, less materialistic, and more loving. Having stared eternity in the face, people returning from NDEs often lose their taste for ego-boosting achievement.[16]

Such positive transformations also occur in children. Studies that track pediatric NDErs show that they are happier, have less drug use, enjoy better relationships, and in general are more hopeful than those around them. Their glimpse of the Light and life beyond apparently affects them for the better throughout their lives.

Interestingly, even when there is orthodox religious training to the contrary, NDErs do not describe death as an entrance into either a fiery hell or golden streets. Instead, they commonly describe dying as a transition, an entry into a higher state of consciousness. Other comparisons are to a reunion, homecoming, awakening, graduating, or escaping from jail. They don't view God as a punishing, judgmental despot but, rather, as a totally fair and loving Presence that works with each soul no matter how sinful or awful their deeds while on earth. As many NDErs put it, you are one with the One.

Changes in spiritual views happen to nonbelievers in God and the hereafter just as frequently as to believers. After an NDE, most everyone becomes more spiritually oriented. They have learned that an emphasis on loving compassion—not doctrines and denominations—is most important and that the Light is all-encompassing.

NDEs usually engender more enlightened theological views. Having glimpsed the Light, these near-death survivors know firsthand that the Creator completely and always forgives and understands. They have experienced an almost unbearable degree of love and acceptance and know that the Infinite is not vengeful and judgmental. Most NDErs no longer fear eternal punishment in hell nor believe any such place exists.

---

[16]*U.S. News & World Report*; March 31, 1997.

Moody states, "One NDEr I spoke to had been a minister of the fire and brimstone variety. It wasn't infrequent, he said, for him to tell his congregation that if they didn't believe the Bible in a certain way, they would be condemned to burn eternally. When he went through his NDE, he said the Being of Light told him not to speak to his congregation like this anymore. But it was done in a nondemanding way. The being just implied that what he was doing was making the lives of his congregation miserable. When this preacher returned to the pulpit, he did so with a message of love, not fear."[17]

NDErs are usually affirmative on the question of universal salvation, that is, a never-ending opportunity for a heavenly afterlife for all. Some people question whether Source Energy embraces everyone, especially those committing morally reprehensible acts like rape, murder, and molestation. Dr. Ring states that the answer by NDErs is unqualified: everyone gets to enter the Light. This runs counter to some teachings and some question, "Even Hitler?"

Of this, Ring states, "I remember an answer that was given to this query by an NDEr friend of mine who, as a child, had suffered severe sexual and physical abuse from her father. When she found herself in the Light, she asked it telepathically, 'Does everyone come here?' She was told 'Yes.' Then, she herself asked the very question that represents the limit for most people: 'Even Hitler?' 'Yes.' And, then, pushing the Light even further, she found herself asking, 'Even my father?' Again, 'Yes.'"[18]

There is no doubt in my mind: we are timeless souls, eternal spirit beings, continuous manifestations of energy. This immortal aspect of ourselves is part and parcel of God and is indestructible. Our real selves can't and don't "die." Many cultures celebrate the transition from formed to formless dimensions and rightly so. Those who pass on have graduated from this physical experience. Their souls evidently fulfilled required lessons and moved on to the next set of growth opportunities.

I know with every fiber of my being that a heavenly eternal life is always an open-ended possibility for each one of us, no strings attached. Creator is love, life, and eternal energy and so is Her creation.

---

[17]Raymond Moody, *The Light Beyond* (New York: Bantam, 1988), 39–40.
[18]Ken Ring, *Lessons from the Light* (Portsmouth, NH: Moment Press, 1998), 163.

We each have the potential to reflect our high natures, to be bright and veritable torches of light. My strong, internalized knowing carries me through life's tough times. "Death" and aging are just transitory stages in life—just as important and necessary as birth and youth.

My inner assurance that we all can enjoy a sublime life after death makes it easier for me to accept life's changes. "Losing" loved ones, whether they pass on or when relationships change, is easier because I know that I can see them again and love is one of the few constants in life.

I hope this information helps your faith and knowledge and lightens your journey on earth.

. . . .

About Mark Pitstick, MA, DC

Dr. Pitstick has over thirty-five years experience and training in hospitals, mental health centers, pastoral counseling settings, and holistic private practice. His training includes a premedical degree, graduate theology/pastoral counseling studies, a masters in clinical psychology, and a doctorate in chiropractic health care. He was certified in past life regression therapy by Brian Weiss, MD and the after-death contact technique by Raymond Moody, MD.

Dr. Pitstick is the author of *Soul Proof: Compelling Evidence You Are an Infinite Spiritual Being*. He also wrote *Radiant Wellness: A Holistic Guide for Optimal Body, Mind & Spirit*. His books have been endorsed by Drs. Wayne Dyer, Elisabeth Kübler-Ross, Deepak Chopra, Bernie Siegel, Ken Ring, Alan Cohen, and others.

A frequent radio and TV talk show guest, Mark hosted "Soul-utions," a nationally syndicated radio show about soul issues and practical spirituality. He also was the executive producer for the *Soul Proof* documentary film.

He leads nationwide workshops on spiritual awareness and holistic wellness. Dr. Pitstick has been a review editor and contributor to many magazines and ezines. Mark founded the *Radiant Wellness Centers* that utilize advanced health care approaches. For more information, please check the Web site www.soulproof.com.

The Medicine of Metaphysics

Steven E. Hodes, MD
www.meta-md.com

The following chapter is based on excerpts taken with permission from Steven E. Hodes' book *Meta-Physician on Call for Better Health . . . Metaphysics and Medicine for Mind, Body And Spirit.*

The near–death experience leaves the involved individual with a sense that his experience was totally real, more so than ordinary waking consciousness. Despite arguments that they are the result of hypoxia (lack of oxygen to the brain), the clarity and sharp memory of the experience which does not fade over time is a powerful argument against the hallucinatory nature of the experience.

I can remember a time when I completely doubted the validity of a spiritual universe. My feeling was that science supplied all the truth that anyone needed to know about the natural world. Religion was a human invention, a necessary sanctuary against the unexplained, unwelcome chaos of existence. This made perfect sense to me. In the absence of any evidence to the contrary, I had no choice but to doubt the existence of God, the soul, or any notion of life after death. Until my encounters with individuals who had had personal "unexplained" experiences, I was on the edge of atheism and agnosticism. I had no reason to believe that spiritual belief was anything more than a delusion. It was the credibility of these individuals who crossed my path and shared their stories with me that convinced me otherwise. These were people who had nothing to gain, nothing to sell, and much more to lose by appearing strange and offbeat.

Their experiences had a profound and life-altering effect upon my consciousness and contributed greatly to a profound change in my attitudes and beliefs regarding the nature of reality. There was something so compelling in those personal anecdotes that I could not ignore their metaphysical implications. I classified these mystical stories into near-death experiences, after-death communications, reincarnation memories, and medium and psychic experiences.

In one such NDE example, I was approached by Sue, a nurse for at least twenty years. After discovering my interest in the paranormal, she sought me out to tell me of an experience that she had shared with few others. It began when she came on duty one morning at 7 a.m. There was a "Code Blue" cardiac arrest in progress, and the full team of doctors and nurses were working on an elderly man. He was unconscious, and they were prescribing drugs and applying paddles to his chest. They had run out of meds and someone asked Sue to run up to the critical care unit (CCU) and bring some back. She ran up the back stairs, obtained the drugs, and returned. She did not really participate in this "code" any further. The patient survived, went to the CCU, and a week or so later returned to the same floor. She had not even realized that it was the same patient, but when he saw her he noted, "You were there when they did my cardiac arrest. They didn't have enough medication, and you had to run up the back stairs and get some." She was a bit taken aback and immediately thought he was considering some type of lawsuit. "How did you know?" she asked nervously. The patient laughed and replied, "I was with you when you ran up the stairs!"

Sally, a lovely young woman who is happily married with several children, sought me out to tell me about her after-death communication experience or what Josie Varga refers to as a "visit from heaven." She had a lover when she was quite young several years before her marriage. Apparently her former beloved was older, and her family was not in favor of their relationship. But they were deeply in love, and they shared a truly profound and meaningful bond, despite her family's objections. His adoration was evident in a personal expression of endearment that he always used to say to her: "I'd like to wrap you up like a doll and carry you with me."

Several months into the relationship, he developed cancer. His case was advanced and she watched him deteriorate rapidly. It was disheartening to watch his condition worsen, but Sally was with him constantly. Knowing that death was near, he told her that she would someday meet and marry someone else. He promised that when the time was right, he would provide her a sign to let her know it was okay. She protested that she could never love again. He soon died. Although heartbroken, after a year or so she eventually began to date again. She was out on a dinner date one night with a man who really liked her. She liked him too, but she was still just going through all the emotions—still numb from the death of the man she loved, still feeling pain and sadness. Suddenly, her date turned to her and said, "I'd like to wrap you up like a doll and carry you with me." Sally dropped her fork, turned white, and asked, in a quivering voice, "How could you possibly say that?" Confused, the young man said that he didn't know where that came from. It just popped into his head. Clearly, Sally got her "visit from heaven" as it was promised to her. Subsequently, she married the man, and they began a family together.

If traits of the mind such as personality, memories, and love transcend death, can we then conclude that the mind is separate and distinct from the physical brain? We tend to think of the brain as something that resides within the confines of our head. In everyday life it would seem to be home for our thoughts and feelings as well as the internal stage upon which the events of our daily lives play themselves out. We seem to jump from event to event, thought to thought, and feeling to feeling often without any sense of coherence or direction.

It might seem that we tend to cling to familiar thoughts and images. And the mind seems to direct us to habitual ways of living, eating, and thinking.

Is the mind one and the same as the brain? Is it the powerful synthesizer of reality or merely an illusion, the "emergent" product of the electrochemical transmissions of the brain? Neurophysiologists and mystics might agree to disagree. Emergent is used to describe how something as incredible as the mind, or consciousness, can form as a result of neural and electrochemical processes. Essentially it is a descriptive term that doesn't explain how this actually happens. To say that the mind emerges is to say we really have no clue how we are conscious beings with thoughts. But at least we have a word that describes the mystery of the mind.

Here's some food for thought: What if the brain doesn't produce the mind at all? What if the individual mind—yours and mine—reflect, or is, an inherent property of the universe? What if the brain is simply a transmitter of the mind or consciousness, in the way a radio tunes into signals that would otherwise be undetected and unknown? Philosopher David Chalmers believes the mind is a fundamental force in the universe, like gravity, which is not derived from anything else. It just is.

In our usual state of consciousness, we humans believe ourselves to actually be our thoughts and emotions. We find it difficult, if not absurd, to comprehend any other state of awareness. Meditation may be the solution to the contemporary disease of the chaotic mind. As old as human consciousness, it is a haven of peace in a sea of trouble. Although there are many forms of meditation, it seems to me that mindfulness is a practical and useful approach toward healing the "monkey chatter" of our minds. In this meditative exercise, we observe our thoughts and feelings. We are the witness—we do not try to ignore or suppress them. We observe them as one would a series of floating clouds. The metaphysical implications are profound.

This method centers on an awareness and focuses on the in-and-out flow of the breath. Ideas and feelings that are the residue of the restless mind are allowed to float into consciousness and then to leave the same way. When we become aware that we have been entertaining a thought or emotion, we can then redirect our awareness to the breath. All this is done with a sense of peace and calm. When we slip back into the flow of thoughts, we can catch ourselves and, with infinite patience, calmly redirect our attention back to the breath. Practice improves the performance and the state of calm that ensues.

If we are not our thoughts or emotions—then who are we? Buddhists would insist that our Higher Self—our higher consciousness—is what we are.

Is the mind the same as the soul? There is great controversy over this point as well. The mind may be the soul's manifestation in the physical form. The mind may be that aspect of the soul which creates and reacts in any one lifetime. No matter. In effect, it is our "home."

If we truly are higher consciousness, this leads me to ask: What is death? Death is not necessarily the tragedy it seems to be. This notion may be too much to fathom when you are in the throes of grieving for a loved one who has died. We are mortal beings. Our emotions and feelings are the result of the love we shared with another, and we have every right to experience them fully when they occur. However, when you understand the true nature of death, it is possible to begin to see the death of a loved one as more than just an enormous tragedy, more than the source of enormous personal pain and suffering.

If we can truly come to terms with this expanded notion of life, one independent of the physical body, it will be a tremendous source of healing from our grief.

For those experiencing the deterioration of their physical bodies, death can be regarded as a release and an unburdening of suffering. For those left behind, the process of mourning and moving on in life is a lesson for us as well.

We all suffer from the loss of those we love and who loved us. There will never be a way to avoid this inevitability. But we should also cultivate the awareness that our own suffering can be a selfish response to their leaving us behind. If we can see past our personal grief, we can be at peace with our loved one's liberation from a body that was ready to be discarded.

Our attachment to seeing and experiencing death as a tragic loss is the source of much of our fear and suffering. What if we came to believe that the essence of who we are is eternal? What if our most precious human feeling—love—did not dissolve into the universe when we or our loved ones died? What if we knew that our struggles in this lifetime were challenges our soul undertook prior to this incarnation?

There is no question that we would look at our own lives from a totally different perspective. We would never again see ourselves as victims of the cruel winds of fate. We would find our losses and defeats more acceptable and be able to recover from them with less debilitating consequences.

By fearing death less, we could embrace life more. We could be more joyous and less depressed, and our energies could be applied to making this lifetime more meaningful.

We would finally understand that in order to be healthy and whole, we're required to have the awareness that we are body, mind, and spirit. We would know that loved ones never leave us and we never leave them, because love survives the end of the body. It lives in our hearts and remains with the soul that goes on.

. . . .
About Steven E. Hodes, MD

Dr. Hodes is a board certified gastroenterologist with over thirty years private practice based in New Jersey. He received his medical degree from The Albert Einstein College of Medicine and also has a degree in religious studies from Franklin and Marshall College.

Embracing his role as a metaphysician, he says he began to see himself as a "meta-physician" . . . a doctor transformed (meta) by awareness of the mind, body, and spirit connection. Dr. Hodes has devoted himself to speaking and writing about metaphysics and healing. He is the author of *Meta-Physician on Call for Better Health: Metaphysics and Medicine for Mind, Body and Spirit*. For more information, please visit his Web site at www.meta-md.com.

The Reincarnation Case

Carol Bowman MS, Paul Von Ward, Josie Varga

Buddhists believe when their spiritual leader passes, his soul is reincarnated. And this newborn life becomes the heir apparent to the Buddhist "throne." So when the thirteenth Dalai Lama passed in 1935, the Tibetan government was faced with the task of finding the child in whom the next ruler of Tibet would incarnate. That same year, the Regent of Tibet, a senior lama named Kewtsang Rinpoche, went to observe visions in Lake Lhamo Lhatso which is considered sacred by the Tibetans. For centuries the lake was believed to offer visions of the future. As the Regent stared at the lake, he saw various visions that led him to the home of a two-year-old boy named Lhamo Dhondrub.

As the story goes, the little boy recognized Rinpoche by saying, "You are a lama of Sera." He spoke to him in a dialect proper to central Tibet but unknown in his region. The boy then passed several tests including picking out items that once belonged to the thirteenth Dalai Lama and possessing many of the same distinctive bodily marks that once belonged to his predecessor.

With the satisfactory completion of these tests, they were convinced that they had found the reincarnation they had been searching for. Later when the young Lhamo Dhondrub was brought to his predecessor's chambers, he is said to have pointed at a small box and exclaimed, "My teeth are in there." His servants were stunned to find that the box did indeed contain dentures that belonged to the former Dalai Lama.

In 1940 the then four-year-old Lhamo Dhondrub or Tenzin Gyatso as he is now known became the fourteenth Dalai Lama and to this day remains the spiritual leader of Tibet.

Another example of reincarnation and one of the most studied past life cases is the story of Shanti Devi. At the age of four, Shanti repeatedly spoke about her husband and child. She told her parents that her husband owned a cloth shop in Mathura (India) and they had a son. At first her parents attributed these outbursts to fantasy, but when the references to a previous life persisted, they became concerned. She continued to give explicit details about her former life including the house she lived in and clothes she once wore. She even gave the name of her husband, Pandit Kedarnath Chaube.

When Shanti was about nine-years-old, a meeting was arranged between her and her former husband. In attempt to trick the young girl, she was told that the man was her former husband's brother. To this Shanti blushed and replied, "No, he is not my husband's brother. He is my husband himself." She gave Chaube detailed information that only his former wife could have known.

There have been references to reincarnation since the beginning of time including many in the Bible. For example, Jesus said, "Before Abraham was born, I am."

"You are not yet fifty-years-old," the Jews said to him, "and you have seen Abraham!"

"I tell you the truth," Jesus answered, "before Abraham was born, I am!" (John 8:57-58)

Strong cases for reincarnation continue to surface today. For example, through the study of xenoglossy (a phenomenon in which people can write and speak a language that they never learned) researchers are realizing that there must be some truth to the idea of preexistence. Spontaneous past life recall as in the case of Shanti Devi is a further indication of reincarnation.

Past life recall need not be spontaneous, however. Hypnotic regression is a form of therapy in which people are intentionally regressed to a previous life. Many notable physicians including Dr. Brian Weiss and Dr. Michael Norton have been using past life regression as a form of therapy. By helping patients understand what took place in a past life, they are able to help them deal better with their current problems and situations.

What I find particularly interesting is the use of birthmarks in an attempt to confirm previous lives. It has been said that birthmarks or even mortal wound marks obtained in an earlier life may persist as prominent birthmarks in the next incarnation of that life. I have a very prominent birthmark on my right hand (about two inches in length and an inch in width in the shape of a crescent moon) and have often wondered if this is an indication of my own past life.

One of the most incredible cases in support of reincarnation is the case of Jeffrey Keene, a fire chief from Westport, Connecticut. Through a series of events, Keene discovered or should I say came to believe that he is the reincarnation of a Civil War general named John B. Gordon. In 1991 while on vacation in Sharpsburg, Maryland, he stopped to see where the Civil War battle of Antietam was fought. While walking through the field, Keene was overcome with grief and anger for no apparent reason. Tears streamed down his cheeks as he struggled to breathe.

A bit shaken by what had taken place, he left the field making a quick stop at a gift shop. There he purchased a copy of a magazine on the Battle of Antietam. He put the magazine away and did not look at it again until over a year later when he opened the magazine to see a picture of General Gordon. He was stunned by the resemblance and felt

a strong connection to the stranger in the photograph. He proceeded to read the magazine and learned that Gordon had nearly died from several gunshot wounds during a battle on Sunken Road (the same field in which he experienced the anger and grief).

From that day forward, Keene began

to uncover several similarities between himself and the Civil War hero. In addition to many spontaneous memories, he noticed that he shared many similar physical features with General Gordon. Some of these features include: eye color, height, writing style, habits, and birthmarks.

Keene's book *Someone Else's Yesterday* chronicles his journey into his past life. His story was also profiled in the A&E documentary "Beyond Death." For more information, please visit his Web site at www.confederateyankee.net.

Can cases as those noted above be proof for reincarnation? To answer this along with other questions, I enlisted the help two reincarnation experts Carol Bowman and Paul Von Ward. We begin with Carol Bowman, a renowned past life therapist, author, and researcher. According to Carol, reincarnation is a natural phenomenon. Understanding the connection between our past lives and present one, she says, leads to profound personal benefits.

1. **How did you first become involved with reincarnation/life after death research and past life regression therapy?**

I first became interested in reincarnation in the late 1960s as a college student in Boston. During a moment of heightened awareness while sitting on a beach listening to the surf, I had a profound realization that a part of me exists beyond time and space. I knew without a doubt that the innermost part of me would survive physical death. After that epiphany, I began reading books about Buddhism and Hinduism that confirmed my personal experience.

Beginning in my early twenties, I started developing lung problems: two bouts of pneumonia, pleurisy, chronic bronchitis, and asthma. By my midthirties I was getting worse. During the height of one of my illnesses, I saw a vision of myself as a man in the nineteenth century lying in bed dying of consumption. It was a powerful waking vision that left me confused and scared. I wondered if it could be a past life memory. And if it was, did it portend an early death for me in this life?

As fate would have it, shortly after that vision a friend told me about someone who was passing through our area that did past life regression therapy. I really didn't know what past life regression was, but I thought perhaps it could help me understand my frightening vision if it had something to do with a previous life.

During that two-hour session, I saw two lives and deaths: one was of the nineteenth century man who died of consumption, and the other was of a young mother who died in the gas chambers of a concentration camp during World War II. Neither life was a big surprise to me, especially the second one because I had had dreams about World War II since childhood. But the results were tangible: I started getting better. My lungs began to heal from the trauma of those two deaths.

After that session, I decided that I wanted to learn all that I could about past lives and learn to become a past life therapist. I sought out experts in the field, and I went to graduate school to earn a degree in counseling.

2. What is the argument for reincarnation?

The concept of reincarnation has been part of most cultures throughout the world for at least as long as there has been recorded history. I imagine that ancient people observed the seasons of birth, death, and rebirth in nature and felt the stirrings of the same life cycles within themselves.

Reincarnation and rebirth have been a part of written and oral religious teachings for thousands of years. It is an integral part of Hinduism and Buddhism, and of the Jewish mystical tradition, the Kabbalah, which searches for the meaning of existence and the nature of the universe. There is evidence that it was a belief that was current during the time of Jesus. One of the fathers of the Christian Church, Origen, wrote: "Every soul comes into this world strengthened by the victories and weakened by the defeats of its previous life." There are passages in the Bible that could be interpreted as meaning that the soul dies and is reborn in another body. The fact that this belief was explicitly deemed heretical in the fourth century and that the Church found it necessary to stamp out the belief through persecution is evidence that it was a belief popular enough to threaten the power of the early Christian Church. This persecution, I believe, left a mark on the collective psyche in Judeo–Christian cultures and forced the belief underground.

There are also a vast number of people who have had their own spontaneous memories, either as children or as adults. Ordinary people have been profoundly affected by these glimpses into their immortality. Because of their religious beliefs, though, many who have the experience are reluctant to talk about it openly. But that is changing.

3. What is the single most compelling piece of evidence for reincarnation?

There are many cases of very young children mostly under the age of five worldwide who have spontaneous and vivid memories of previous lives. Some of these children remember enough specific details of their previous lives that their former identities can be established. If they died recently, it is possible to verify their memories through relatives or friends who knew them in the past or through historical records. In these remarkable cases, when the past life identity is known, there is usually a strong correspondence in behavior, skills, attitudes, and physical characteristics between the previous personality and the present one. Some of the similarities are uncanny and defy any other explanation than reincarnation.

I've been investigating these cases for over twenty years and have collected hundreds of them. The most compelling is of a young boy named James Leininger, who at age two, started having frequent, terrifying nightmares of his plane crashing. These nightmares went on for months. As the nightmares diminished in frequency, James began to tell his parents that he was a pilot; he was also obsessed with toy airplanes and anything to do with real planes. Even as a two- and three-year-old, James knew much more than he could have about WWII fighter planes.

Over the next few years, he spontaneously revealed many more details about his life as a pilot, including the type of plane he flew (a Corsair, which was used in WWII), the name of the boat from which his plane took off, and the first and last name of one of his friends on the boat. His father, who had been a hard-core skeptic because he simply didn't believe in reincarnation, kept coming up with more evidence that what his three-year-old was telling him was factual—things that could be checked against existing naval records. Eventually from James' statements, his father was able to pinpoint the identity of a pilot whose description matched what James was telling him. The pilot was James Huston, Jr., who was shot down over the Pacific in 1945. He was only twenty-one when he died. And he flew a Corsair.

Amazingly, James Huston has a surviving sister in her late eighties in California. When the Leininger family approached her about their son's memories, she was stunned that a little boy in another part of the country knew intimate details about her family's personal life—things she had never before shared with anyone. Even more startling was the fact that when James Huston's sister shared photos of her deceased brother, the facial resemblance was striking.

4. Based on your research, what do you believe happens when we die? What are your thoughts on the survival of consciousness?

It seems that after we die, our consciousness, soul, or that eternal essence within us sheds the physical body and continues in some form. Consciousness, along with specific information about previous lives, remains viable in some energetic form. That information serves as an energetic template that informs a new body and a new personality. Some specific characteristics from previous lives' memories, behaviors, attitudes, emotions, and some physical characteristics (usually the physical imprint of fatal injuries) are re-expressed in a future life.

So, as I see it, consciousness is a continuum from death through rebirth. Not everything carries over, but enough specific aspects of personality do, so that we can see the continuity from one life to another.

5. Dr. Ian Stevenson had researched the connection between birthmarks and reincarnation. What are your thoughts on this?

The late Dr. Ian Stevenson of the University of Virginia began researching children's spontaneous past life memories in the early 1960s. His forty-something years of research provide almost 3,000 well-documented cases of this phenomenon from around the world. In almost 1,000 of these cases, the child's former identity could be verified because of the child's recollection of his former name and where he lived. Dr. Stevenson went to great lengths to investigate these cases for fraud, error, wishful thinking, or some other explanation. Many of them defy an explanation other than rebirth or reincarnation.

I have seen the same with the hundreds of cases I've collected. There are patterns to these cases: the young age at which these memories surface, the facts about the deceased's life that the child couldn't possibly have known, and the uncanny resemblance in personality and even physicality between the two lives.

The sheer number and frequency of these cases point to a natural phenomenon. These cases cannot prove reincarnation, but they can certainly offer strong and compelling evidence for it.

In 1997 Dr. Stevenson published a two-volume tome called *Reincarnation and Biology* which documents around two hundred cases of children who have birthmarks or birth defects that correspond to fatal wounds, disease, or injury to the body suffered in a previous life. For example, one child recalled the life of a school teacher who was shot in the head while riding his bicycle to school. The child remembered his former name, the town where he lived, and many details of his former life. When the grandmother took him to the other town, the three-year-old led his grandmother to a house where he identified his former family. The accuracy of his memories alone was astonishing. Then the family discovered two small, round birthmarks on the child's head that corresponded to entry and exit wounds of the bullet that killed the school teacher. The site of these birthmarks and the correspondence to the fatal wound was verified by medical records Dr. Stevenson examined.

With cases such as these, Dr. Stevenson has provided *physical* evidence linking the body of one lifetime to another. Or more simply, he has provided physical evidence for reincarnation. Skeptics can find alternate explanations for other aspects of children's past life memories to explain away these remarkable coincidences: the uncanny knowledge the child has of someone who died before he was born, or the similarities in personalities. Physical correspondence between the two bodies is much more difficult to explain away.

. . . .
About Carol Bowman, MS

Carol is an internationally known author, lecturer, counselor, past life regression therapist, and pioneer in reincarnation studies. Her first two books *Children's Past Lives* and *Return from Heaven* are now classics in the reincarnation genre; they have been published around the world in sixteen foreign editions.

A frequent radio and TV guest, she is a leading spokesperson for children's past lives. She appeared on *Oprah*, *Good Morning America*, *Unsolved Mysteries*, the *Art Bell Show*, *ABC Primetime*, A&E, the Discovery Channel, and the BBC in England. She has also lectured around the globe. For more information, please visit www.carolbowman.com.

Paul Von Ward is an interdisciplinary cosmologist, psychologist, author, and lecturer who is well known for his research on the nature of consciousness and reincarnation. Interdisciplinary cosmology, he explains, offers a bigger picture than science's conventional view of reality.

1. How did you first become involved with reincarnation research?

As a sophomore in college I became acquainted with the Hindu idea of transmigration. This notion of a wheel of rebirth did not fit my fundamentalist Christian worldview of a single life and the rest of eternity in heaven or hell. As I read more widely in the 1970s, I developed a general sense of Eastern reincarnation.

Later in 1979 I received a channeled reading suggesting that I had some previous lifetimes relevant to the current one. This intrigued me enough to work with a couple friends who were psychologists to develop our ability to conduct past life regressions. Working with ourselves and others, we accumulated a number of interesting coincidences suggestive of past life connections.

I became aware of the controversy about the Bridey Murphy* case and other studies, including Roger Woolger's work with clients who seemed to slip into a realm of past life memories.

In 1983 I decided to do a series of past life regression sessions with a well-known psychologist colleague in the San Francisco area. He produced bits of information corroborating aspects of my intuitive considerations of possible previous incarnations.

However, what I had experienced left no indication of mundane implications for reincarnation—if it were real—beyond a few memories or possible psychological traumas. The evidence I had encountered could result from many subjective processes. So for the next decade, I continued my work in the "real world."

In 1991 I met Ian Stevenson, MD, and became acquainted with his work on children's memories of apparent previous lives. His evidence went beyond memories that one might access through what Carl Jung had called the collective unconscious. Ian had found similar birthmarks, deformities, and skills in certain cases. It suggested that if reincarnation was real, it had real implications.

A dozen years later after I had finished the research for two other books, my publisher encouraged me to begin an historical overview of the various perspectives on reincarnation. That triggered memories of my talk with Ian, and I began to look more deeply into his cases and those of other researchers.

During a meta-analysis of the cases, an evolving picture of two-life correspondences began to emerge. The best documented cases all contained evidence that pointed to an integral package of physical and personality traits that were apparently passed from life to life. I quickly aborted the historical and philosophical book and started the Reincarnation Experiment. My report of the pilot project is published in *The Soul Genome*.

Author's Note: In 1952 while under hypnotic regression, a woman by the name of Virginia Tighe from Pueblo, Colorado claimed to be the reincarnation of Bridey Murphy, a nineteenth-century Irishwoman. Although many of her claims did add up, some did not. So while some considered the Bridey Murphy study a verifiable case for reincarnation, others considered it hearsay.

2. **What, in your opinion, is the argument for reincarnation? And what is the single most compelling piece of evidence?**

Throughout recorded history humans have expressed beliefs in some form of rebirth. They were based on individual people from families and tribes around the globe whose lives reminded elders of people they knew about from a previous generation. For instance, Plato wrote of a simple soldier who expressed math as if he were a reborn student of Pythagoras.

Physical features, personality traits, or knowledge unique to a person no longer alive but found in a new child suggested to ancient people that the deceased being had been reborn. Since these similarities did not necessarily appear in the same biological family, people suspected it could not all be inherited from the children's physical parents.

As cultures progressed and people began to accrue knowledge about various states of consciousness, they grew more aware of the independence of the mind from the body. It became conceivable that the mind or spirit could survive death and somehow become embedded in a new physical incarnation.

As early supernatural religions developed, different concepts of reincarnation evolved in different cultures. Their ideas varied depending on the different types of evidence and the spiritual leaders' own subjective worldviews. In a self-fulfilling cycle, they interpreted the evidence to fit their already existing beliefs.

In today's discussions of reincarnation, one finds the same conflicting ideas based on unverifiable information. Dreams, hypnotic regressions, psychic readings, emotional intuition, and alleged memories or knowledge all offer clues used to support subjective beliefs about reincarnation and individual cases.

While many of the clues derived from the above-mentioned subjective sources may be valid, we cannot assume them to be true until we have corroborating evidence from objective sources that an observer can verify for himself or herself. Fortunately, science is evolving a model of reality that can finally test the validity of the reincarnation hypothesis. Its concept of a psychoplasm* that may be involved in human reproduction is already producing some compelling evidence of a soul genome with a past life legacy.

*Author's Note: The term *psychoplasm* implies an energetic biofield that contains the genetic patterns and information bytes that carry forward the individual soul genome's stage of evolution at the point the immediate previous lifetime ended. It challenges the assertion that newborns are "blank slates" except for traits that can be completely accounted for by the parental genomes.

This compelling new evidence for the reincarnation hypothesis is a multifaceted psychophysical inheritance drawn from a series of past lives from which each new human develops.

3. Tell me about the Reincarnation Experiment?

This project is the first-ever effort to integrate all the areas of empirical evidence that suggest humans begin life with a well-developed set of predispositions derived from the lives of unrelated prior generations. It treats reincarnation as a natural phenomenon that can and must be subject to scientific analysis.

To test the reality of reincarnation, science needs a theoretical process or mechanism capable of accounting for all areas of evidence. From a meta-analysis of its cases the Reincarnation Experiment hypothesized a psychoplasm-like mechanism that facilitates scientific evaluation of alleged past life matches.

This model contains what is called the "five-plus-2" factors. The five psychophysical factors are (1) basic genotype features, (2) mental level and orientation, (3) emotional type, (4) interpersonal style, and (5) areas of creative focus. The plus-2 areas of evidence are preserved memories and "unacquired" knowledge and skills. The Experiment compares evidence from both lifetimes in all of these areas. When most of them match to a degree that cannot be attributed to chance, we assign a high level of confidence in attributing the case to the process known as reincarnation.

4. Based on your research what do you believe happens when we die? Do you believe that life after death can be scientifically proven?

Based on the evidence analyzed so far, it appears that the individual's personal field of consciousness and its epigenome survives death in a holographic energy field that exists outside humanity's fourth dimension reality. It is analogous to the proton that blinks out of existence but does not lose its energetic integrity.

Based on validated communications (after near–death
or out–of–body experiences and ones from the deceased),
I believe we can conclude that a self–aware consciousness (in a holographic form) survives and communicates
between dimensions.

At this point, science does not have the tools to prove
what happens in the other dimensions of our universe.
However, it can document the inputs and outputs (as in
past lives and present lives) and develop a theory to account for what appears to happen in that other dimension.

Until our model can reliably predict its expected outcomes in advance, science can only assert that something like the idea of reincarnation accounts for the
evidence. If the Reincarnation Experiment continues its
work over several generations, we may be able to demonstrate reincarnation does affect our world.

Reincarnation research is at the point in a scientific
process similar to the "black–hole" theory seventy years
ago. Scientists back then could see activity (inputs and
outputs) around an impenetrable point in space but
could not prove what happened inside. That is the current situation in reincarnation research. At this point we
are all guessing on the basis of a wide variety of clues.

5. **In the past, it was believed that science disproved
   the metaphysical. Nowadays, however, scientists are
   realizing just how much the two are related. Do various theories (dark matter, string theory, Big Bang,
   dark energy, quantum physics, etc.) bridge the gap
   between science and the metaphysical? If so, in what
   way?**

Science cannot disprove the metaphysical and neither
can the metaphysical trump science. Each discipline has
methodologies for seeking new knowledge that offer a

limited view of our complex universe.

Nothing has been proven until both epistemologies (ways of knowing) have come to agreement about the nature of reality. At that point we have metascience where both believers and skeptics are looking at the same evidence. They may still disagree about its ultimate meaning, but they do so with an understanding that they are both looking at the same data.

Clues from intuitive and other dimensional sources have given us much insight into things like multiple dimensions, other centers of consciousness, nonhuman perspectives, and the place of humans in the web of life. This inner knowing has driven scientific speculation about string theory, an energetic genome, and a quantum plenum of zero–point energy or the conscious ground of being from which everything manifests.

As science has grown so has metaphysical speculation. As techniques or paths to knowing, they are not in conflict; they complement each other. Only when they become congruent about particular issues can intellectually and emotionally mature humans say, "This we know." Until then we still "see though a glass darkly."

6. What are your thoughts on the survival of consciousness?

From the perspective of the universe, "survival" is not an issue: consciousness in some form or the other is always there. It is like energy, which cannot be destroyed but is conserved in various forms. Consciousness does not simply dissipate; it shifts from one dimension to another and back again.

Consciousness, as the root source of all quantum activity, both causes and records each action and what's learned from it throughout the universe. Reincarnation is the mechanism by which all self-evolving species preserve what they learn to contribute to the evolution of our self-learning cosmos. Soul genomes are integral to the continuing process of self-creation.

7. Is there anything else that you would like to add?

We must keep in mind that human knowledge, from whatever source, is still evolving. The tools used in science are still quite limited. The voices humans hear from more advanced beings (ABs)—from this and other dimensions—also represent limited knowledge. Thus, we have only a partial understanding of the universe's various dimensions, how consciousness fits into it, and what the role of *Homo sapiens* is in the bigger picture.

People who claim to have the truth—and develop a fixed faith about the nature of planetary reality and life beyond—are afraid to live with the uncertainty of a still-evolving universe. In my view, as conscious beings, we are also players in the game of daily choice and chance that will determine how this universe ends and reincarnates. We are integral parts of its self-learning.

. . . .

About Paul Von Ward, MPA, MSc

An interdisciplinary cosmologist and psychologist, Paul is known internationally for his concept of "natural spirituality" based in an evolving, self-learning universe; research on the apparent intervention of advanced beings (ABs) in human development, and evidence of the survival of the individuated soul genome. His books on these topics are *Our Solarian Legacy*; *Gods, Genes & Consciousness*; and *The Soul Genome*. Paul's academic background includes degrees from Florida State, Harvard, and other institutions while his career included roles as a military officer, a US diplomat, a nonprofit executive, and a Protestant minister. He is now a prominent researcher in emerging science and the boundaries of human experience.

In addition to books, he writes articles and has produced television programs, educational videos and audio tapes on topics related to his areas of research. He has travelled professionally to more than one hundred countries, speaks Spanish and French, reads several languages, and lectures widely at conferences and on radio and television. For more information, please see www.vonward.com.

--------•-◦⟨∞⟩◦-•--------

The Opposing View

Many are reluctant to accept the case for reincarnation and karma simply because doing so means that they must then accept full responsibility for their actions in their present life, knowing how they live now can impact the quality of any future lives. Admittedly, I am no exception. I was born and raised to believe that we go to heaven and that's that. So the idea that I will live again with all the results of my karma is a hard one for me to swallow. But the fact is I can't ignore the vast body of anecdotal and empirical evidence, such as in the past life cases stated above, either.

However, let's examine briefly the case against reincarnation. Critics argue that some are intentionally bending the truth to reinforce reincarnation. Others claim that past life therapy feeds the ego of its clients by telling them that they were someone famous in a past life.

Some even claim that people are simply expressing forgotten past memories. And still others contend that reincarnation is just a "mass consciousness belief" we have all created. After all, if reincarnation were true, why don't we all (or at least most of us) clearly remember our past lives?

Many also say that the Bible teaches the very opposite of reincarnation. Was Jesus not resurrected in body and soul after the third day?

James Webster argues this point in his book *The Case against Reincarnation: A Rational Approach*. He writes, "The teaching of the reincarnationists that we must return again and again to earth life to become perfected is equivalent to saying that once one has passed through kindergarten, grade schools, and university, he must return to kindergarten over and over again to study everything that is to be learned pertaining to life."

Webster also mentions an interesting point brought up by William

Howitt, a strong supporter of early Spiritualism in England. He reasoned that if reincarnation were true, some spirits who cross over would have not been able to find their family and friends. Yet, he says, he had never heard one such complaint from any spirit communicating through a medium.

Some believe that the argument against reincarnation is actually stronger than the case for it. However, those who attempt to debunk reincarnation, it seems to me, rarely have a valid alternate explanation for convincing past life accounts such as the Shanti Devi and Jeffrey Keene cases noted earlier. Nor can they explain how a child can suddenly speak a foreign language he or she has never been exposed to before. They tend to summarily dismiss these cases as déjà vu or the act of willful fallacy. Perhaps, they contend, the child just happens to have incredibly advanced linguistic abilities.

Famous Canadian neurologist Wilder Penfield believed that memories are stored in our DNA. Based on his many experiments, he believed hidden in each of us was a complete record of our past. This would certainly help to explain cases of past life memory.

While I will not argue for or against reincarnation, I will say, again, that it is hard to ignore the growing body of anecdotal and empirical evidence. Truthfully, we must draw our own conclusions.

Final Thoughts

For, as has been given, it is not all of life to live, nor yet all of death to die. For life and death are one, and only those who will consider the experience as one may come to understand or comprehend what peace indeed means. 1977-1

Edgar Cayce

Earlier in this book, Charles Thomas Cayce described his thoughts on the afterlife as a "knowing beyond knowing." This appears to be the common thread that flows through all the accounts in this book. All NDErs say that they don't believe there is life after death, they know it. Likewise, they don't believe there is a God or Supreme Source, they know there is. They also know that we are much more than just our physical bodies. We are eternal beings connected in Oneness with a purpose.

Albert Einstein once said, "We are part of the whole which we call the universe, but it is an optical delusion of our mind that we think we are separate. This separateness is like a prison for us. Our job is to widen the circle of compassion so we feel connected to all people and all situations." Can you imagine how different this world would be if we were able to widen this circle of compassion and recognize that we are all connected? There would be no black or white, just twin souls. If we all understood that we are eternal, we would have no reason to fear death. In fact, we would in some ways welcome it. Our lives would be forever changed.

Those of us who have had a near-death experience or other spiritually transformative experience often realize that separateness is just an illusion. The new paradigm of Oneness states that we are all one unified field of consciousness. Think of it this way: if we are all Oneness and separateness is a delusion, then it cannot be that some of us are dead while others are alive. Everything is either alive or dead. And since clearly we are not all dead, it can be said that everything and everyone is alive always.

Yet, many don't realize that we are eternal until they are outside the bounds of our four-dimensional perceived reality (three of space and one of time). In other words, not until we pass on or are in some other meditative or transformative state can we come to know our true reality. The reason for this inability to grasp the true nature of reality is summarized well by Dr. Jeffrey S. Eisen, an enlightenment teacher and therapist. In his book, *Oneness Perceived: A Window into Enlightenment*, he writes about the problem with the direct perception of reality: "The problem with our quest to know reality is us. We want to know reality in the same sense that we know a perception; we want to know what it looks, smells, tastes, sounds, and feels like, but it is not to be! When science investigates reality, it always suffers from the same problems. It asks things of things . . . things like what does it smell like; what color is it; what is its size, shape, and mass; is it energy or matter, wave or particle; how did it begin; what are its smallest components and how can we measure them? It too 'expects' the answers to be qualitative, subjective, in terms of the qualities of sensory perception or their cognitive analogs. This is qualitative knowing, metaphorical knowing. However, a little thought will bring us to the conclusion that real answers cannot be in illusory terms. The only qualitative fact about reality that we can be reasonably certain of is that it is not qualitative."[1]

---

[1]Dr. Jeffrey S. Eisen, *Oneness Perceived: A Window into Enlightenment* (New York: Paragon House, 2003), 11.

Although I've personally never had a near-death experience, I have had a spiritually awakening one. My husband's friend who died during the September 11 attacks on the World Trade Center came to me in a vivid dream or what I call a visit from heaven. The experience is noted in full detail in my book, *Visits from Heaven*. But suffice it to say that it was unlike anything else I have ever experienced before or since. While in a dream state, I had an OBE (out-of-body experience). During the experience, I believe (or more accurately, *know*) that I traveled to another dimension and encountered Rich face-to-face, a man that I had never met while he was on this earth. Yet, I knew beyond a doubt that it was him. I literally felt my spirit self moving.

As I looked at him, he seemed so close that I remember moving back a bit. I also remember that this experience was so real that I often remarked that it was perhaps more real than anything I have experienced on earth. The first time I said this, my husband John looked at me somewhat stunned and remarked, "Really?!" I was actually just as surprised as he was by my own words at the time. I mean how could something that I experienced in my dream state be more real than reality here on earth? Could it be that while traveling to this other dimension, I encountered true reality? Could it be that this is the same reality that we come to know during a near-death experience?

I will say that I, too, felt total calmness and peace. I felt a feeling of connectedness that is difficult to explain. There was no fear, only understanding. I will also say that I no longer fear death. Although I have always been a believer in the afterlife, I often worried about what awaits me on the Other Side. But the gift that I received through Rich's visit taught me that I have no reason to fear death. Fearing death would be like fearing something that has a zero percent chance of happening. It makes no sense.

I also know that those who have gone before us are always with us and are often there to greet us when we, ourselves, make the transition to the Other Side. Very often our loved ones come to greet us before we actually leave this earth. In 2003 my wonderful Uncle Tony died after a two-year battle with glioblastoma, the most common and unfortunately the most aggressive type of primary brain tumor. During one of his final days, he was lying in his bed unable to speak. With him were his

daughter Maria, his wife, and other family members. Suddenly, his eyes moved to an area of the room by the closet as he lifted his pointer finger and motioned everyone in the room to look in that direction. But no one was there. Why was he pointing to the closet?

Without warning, a gentle breeze came through the room as the bifold closet doors flew open, startling everyone in the room. No windows were open, and no one was near the closet. How, then, did the closet door suddenly open? Realizing that her father's gaze was still fixated on that same spot, Maria asked her father to lift his finger again if there was someone in the room with them. To this, he obediently lifted his finger.

What my uncle experienced was a deathbed vision which is actually very common. These visions have been recorded throughout history across all religions and cultures and are considered one of the most compelling proofs of life after death.

Another example of this phenomenon is the story of Bill Davis, a Vietnam War veteran, who passed after suffering from CLL leukemia and hepatitis due to his service in the war. A few years prior to his death, he would often talk to a female spirit who, he said, appeared to him while he slept. He would even see her during his waking hours and his wife would over hear him asking, "What do you want? Why are you here?"

He told his wife that this spirit kept visiting him. In his son Bill Jr.'s words, "My Dad flat out said, 'She stands at the end of my bed and wants to take me with her.' My mom would try to trick him and talk and stand at the end of his bed, but there was no fooling him. He always knew the difference, no matter how sick he was."

Days before Christmas 2008, his father received a procedure that would allow him to leave the hospital and spend the holidays with his family. But he probably knew he wouldn't survive the week. Although he had hoped that the procedure would work, the odds were not in his favor. During his last thirty-six hours, Bill was no longer able to open his eyes but was still able to hear those around him.

That Christmas ended up being a wet one as rain covered the northern California area for most of the day. It was an unusual day of high winds and thunder. Then suddenly during the late afternoon hours, the weather calmed leaving no hint of wind as a ray of sun peeked through the cloud-covered sky. Minutes later, Bill began to choke as his lungs filled with blood and water.

He then unexpectedly opened his eyes making eye contact with everyone one at a time in the room and started to cry, appearing seemingly afraid of what was taking place. According to his son, he held out his arms as if to block something. "At this point, I couldn't control myself and was literally on top of him, hugging and kissing him and holding his face. We told him repeatedly that it was OKAY and to let go. He no longer looked at us then as he focused his attention on my mother. They looked at each other deeply for several seconds and were both crying. Then he closed his eyes and took his last breath. My mother and daughter were at his left and my wife was at the foot of the bed."

At the moment of Bill's death, his loved ones experienced an incredible phenomenon. "Within five seconds after he took his last breath, I felt something go either through me or past me," said Bill Jr. "It's hard to describe. It gave me that dizzy feeling that often accompanies an amusement park or elevator ride, except this was much more powerful. My wife, mother, and daughter all felt the very same sensation. Then it became very cold in the room; there was no mistaking the change in temperature. We all experienced goose bumps and chills. It was as if the heater hadn't run all day; it was like a fifteen or twenty degree drop. At that moment, my dad looked completely at peace. All the stress seemed to have left his face and he looked about twenty-five years younger. He even had a little grin on his face."

In another room at this same time was his daughter's boyfriend Ryan. He had no idea that Bill Sr. had just passed. Ryan was distracted by the television and the trauma of what was happening when the double glass doors in the living room blew open without warning as though pushed by hurricane force winds. However, there was no wind. It was completely calm both inside and outside. Ryan got up to make his way over to the doors in order to close them. It was then that he felt something move through the room. At that point, he sensed someone pass by him and realized that the elder Bill must have just passed. At that moment, he said out loud, "See ya, Buddy," and closed the door.

Months later, Bill's son returned to the house to help his mother move. They were all done with the move and went back into the house to grab the last remaining box of cleaning materials. It was then that Bill Jr. became very emotional realizing that it would be the last time he would see the house; the place held both special and difficult memories for him. It was hard to let go.

"I became very emotional and started crying," he explained. "I was looking up into the sun and closed my eyes. Then out of nowhere, the same double glass doors in the living room flew open again. A small whirlwind started up on the porch kicking leaves in my face and causing me to cover my eyes. It was like a small twister or one of those dust cloud tornados.

"Within fifteen seconds, the wind stopped. It was once again completely calm. I then turned to my mother and said, "I guess he's not staying here either; he's coming with us." His mom wholeheartedly agreed.

As Bill Jr. related this story to me, it was very apparent to me that he shared a very strong bond with his father and that he loved him very much. So I have no doubt that his father will continue to make himself known to his son and the rest of his family.

Nothing, absolutely nothing can break the bonds of love . . . not even death. The fact is we may perceive death as a reality, but it is actually illusory. Love lives on. We live on.

About the Author

This is Josie Varga's fourth title. She is also the author of *Make up Your Mind to be Happy*, *Visits from Heaven*, and *Footprints in the Sand: A Disabled Woman's Inspiring Journey to Happiness*. Besides being a former communications consultant, she has also served as the director of communications and editor for a trade association. As a speaker, Josie helps the bereaved by sharing her message that life never ends and love never dies. She also teaches others to focus on the positive by explaining why happiness is all a matter of how we think.

She also has several other book projects in the works, including *God or Chance?*—an unparalleled book which provides mathematical and scientific statistics (based on the anthropic principle) answering the question: Was the universe the result of chance or was God or some other Supreme Being responsible?

In addition to her book writing, she has completed several treatments for reality television including a television series for her book *Visits from Heaven*. A creative thinker, Josie is the holder of two patents. She lives in Westfield, New Jersey, with her husband and two daughters.

For more information about the author, please visit her Web site: www.josievarga.com. You may also contact Josie through her Web site; she loves to hear from her readers.